LITERACY AND LITER

Literacy and Literacies offers a unique, comprehensive survey of both classical and anthropological literature in the field of literacy studies, ranging from theoretical work to particular cases. It explores questions of power, subjectivity, and historical process as they are raised by and developed in studies of literacy, and draws on the history of literacy, critical education studies, and the anthropology of literacy, to develop a new synthesis. James Collins and Richard K. Blot argue that neither the generalizing, universalist claims of the "consequences of literacy" thesis, nor the contextualizing, situated studies of the "New Literacy" offer satisfactory approaches to the phenomenon of literacy. Through their analysis of two domains – that of literacies and power and that of literacies and subjectivity – Collins and Blot reveal important historical processes associated with literacy practices while also challenging received assumptions about literacy, intellectual development, and social progress.

JAMES COLLINS is Professor of Anthropology and of Reading at the University at Albany, State University of New York. He is the author of *Understanding Tolowa Histories: Western Hegemonies and Native American Responses* (1988), and has contributed to a number of books and journals.

RICHARD BLOT is Assistant Professor at the Graduate Program in Literacy Studies, Lehman College, City University of New York. He has published in a number of journals, including *TESOL Quarterly, Anthropology and Education Quarterly*, and *Latin American Anthropology Review*.

STUDIES IN THE SOCIAL AND CULTURAL FOUNDATIONS
OF LANGUAGE

The aim of this series is to develop theoretical perspectives on the essential social and cultural character of language by methodological and empirical emphasis on the occurrence of language in its communicative and interactional settings, on the socioculturally grounded "meanings" and "functions" of linguistic forms, and on the social scientific study of language use across cultures. It will thus explicate the essentially ethnographic nature of linguistic data, whether spontaneously occurring or experimentally induced, whether normative or variational, whether synchronic or diachronic. Works appearing in the series will make substantive and theoretical contributions to the debate over the sociocultural-function and structural-formal nature of language, and will represent the concerns of scholars in the sociology and anthropology of language, anthropological linguistics, sociolinguistics, and socioculturally informed psycholinguistics.

Editors	*Editorial Advisers*
Judith T. Irvine	Marjorie Goodwin
Bambi Schieffelin	Joel Kuipers
	Don Kulick
	John Lucy
	Elinor Ochs
	Michael Silverstein

A list of books in the series can be found after the index.

LITERACY AND LITERACIES

TEXTS, POWER, AND IDENTITY

JAMES COLLINS
University at Albany/State University of New York

RICHARD BLOT
Lehman College/City University of New York

PUBLISHED BY THE PRESS SYNDICATE OF THE UNIVERSITY OF CAMBRIDGE
The Pitt Building, Trumpington Street, Cambridge CB2 1RP, United Kingdom

CAMBRIDGE UNIVERSITY PRESS
The Edinburgh Building, Cambridge, CB2 2RU, UK
40 West 20th Street, New York, NY 10011-4211, USA
477 Williamstown Road, Port Melbourne, VIC 3207, Australia
Ruiz de Alarcón 13, 28014 Madrid, Spain
Dock House, The Waterfront, Cape Town 8001, South Africa

http://www.cambridge.org

First published 2003

Printed in the United Kingdom at the University Press, Cambridge

Typeface Times 10/12 pt   *System* LaTeX 2$_\varepsilon$ [TB]

A catalogue record for this book is available from the British Library

ISBN 0 521 59356 5 hardback
ISBN 0 521 59661 0 paperback

For
Fiona, Jocebed, and Rosa
and for
Aida, Chenoa, and Denis

"Another damned, thick, square book! Always scribble, scribble, scribble, eh, Mr. Gibbon?" (The Duke of Gloucester, upon hearing of a *second* volume of Edmund Gibbons' *Decline and Fall of the Roman Empire*)

CONTENTS

FIGURES

x

FOREWORD

The title of this path-breaking book is a good clue to its intentions. The first term signals a focus on the importance of literacy in contemporary society: "a key word in our culture [that] has a status in the current era rather like that of 'science' in the nineteenth" (p. 3). The plural "literacies" signals the authors' attention to a key shift in academic approaches to the field, a shift of focus from a single thing called literacy, seen as a set of "autonomous" skills with far-reaching almost determinist consequences, to a recognition that there are multiple literacies; unravelling what practices might be validly and helpfully termed literacies, what should be included, where the boundaries should be drawn, and what it means to develop a theory of multiple literacies is a major focus of the book. The shift to plural approaches in the 1980s came to be called the "New Literacy Studies" (NLS) (Gee, 1991; Street, 1993; Collins, 1995) and since its path-breaking challenge to the dominance of the autonomous model, scholars in this field have provided a rich array of carefully documented accounts of how literacy practices vary from one cultural and historical context to another. Introducing the concepts of literacy events (Heath, 1983) and literacy practices (Street, 1984; 2000; Barton and Hamilton, 1998), NLS provided a lens, a methodology, and a literature based on them that enabled us to "see" behind the surface appearance of reading and writing to the underlying social and cultural meanings.

However, Collins and Blot argue that this field is itself now in need of revision (as Brandt and Clinton [in press] suggest in a recent seminal article, there are "limits to the local"). The provision of more and more ethnographies of literacy, whilst itself necessary and productive at a time when educational institutions are reverting to a narrower, decontextualized, culturally insensitive, and often ethnocentric view of literacy, does not of itself answer that case. Policy makers in the development field, bringing the "light" of literacy to the "darkness" of the "illiterate," and educationalists in countries like the USA and the UK similarly arguing for the economic and social benefits of a narrowly defined and disciplined "literacy" can simply argue that all of those counter-examples of the complexity and meanings of literacy in people's everyday lives are not relevant to their agenda. Local, everyday, home literacies are seen within that frame as failed attempts at the real thing, as inferior versions of the "literacy" demanded by the economy, by educational institutions, by the politics of centralizing and homogenizing tendencies. Critics of NLS, then, accuse it of "relativism" and argue that its attention to the local will exclude children from varying backgrounds from access to the language and literacy of power.

MacCabe (1998), for instance, is happy for researchers in the NLS tradition to adopt an intellectual relativism that allows them to see the variety of literacy practices in their chosen sites of study, an approach which "does indeed fit very well with the imperatives of anthropological fieldwork." But, he argues, "it does not follow in any way that the teacher can take the same attitude . . . the teacher tries to inculcate the values that are the very purpose of a school." From the policy perspective, this argument can be seen to privilege a particular view of the "values of the school" and is thereby inappropriate in a plural and multicultural society. But what is appropriate? On the one hand, the appropriate tends to be defined by dominant interests that privilege their own narrow cultural standards, under the guise of representing universal values. But on the other, as Delpit (1986) points out, there has been a danger that a more liberal position that validates the variety of literacies children bring to school, in practice privileges those children who already have the cultural capital associated with dominant groups in society and continues to exclude the children whose home literacy practices vary from the mainstream. These policy debates, according to NLS scholars, need to be linked to sound theoretical principles: how do we construe literacy; what is the relation between the acquisition of literacy – usually in formal educational settings – and the uses of literacy in everyday life, between literacy "in and out of school" (Schultz and Hull, 2002)? For the theoretical position to be able to speak to such policy issues it is important not simply to concede MacCabe's view of researchers as relativists, as though they were contemporary archaeologists digging up evidence of exotic cultural practices that belong to a different world than that which our children are entering through the school system. This archaeological view of research runs the danger of romanticizing such local practice against that of the dominant culture. It is here, perhaps, that NLS has hit an impasse: how to account for the local whilst recognizing also the general – or the global. It is here that Collins and Blot offer a way forward: it is at this level that the present book provides a shift for literacy studies equivalent perhaps to that evident in the first big shift from the autonomous to the ideological model some twenty years ago.

The clue to the new position being mapped out by Collins and Blot is, again, in the title line: the subtitle "Texts, Power, and Identity" signals the key themes that can lift the account of local literacies towards a more general, theoretically comparative set of terms whilst not losing the specificity that NLS has brought to the field. The first imperative is to track and explain the peculiar persistence of the earlier "autonomous" model of literacy particularly in Western societies in the recent past: why "flawed perspectives have such a hold." In order to answer this question "historical and ethnographic perspectives are necessary but insufficient." The first step, Collins and Blot suggest, is to consider more closely "what is a text?" This question is particularly relevant at the current time as new modes of computerized and digital representation become widespread. At the same time, new theoretical perspectives on modes of representation are also emerging; Kress and van Leeuwen (1986; 2001), for instance, have argued for a shift of emphasis away from language as the major focus of communicative practices towards a range of "modalities" – visual, gestural, and oral as well as written – and they have offered both a theoretical framework for analyzing these practices and the beginnings of practical applications, as in Kress and colleagues' (2001) work on the "rhetorics of the science classroom." "Text" then, should be a major focus of attention and offers a way of moving the New Literacy Studies on from its particularistic impasse.

In order to address the question "what is text?" we are immediately confronted with issues of power – the second term in Collins and Blot's title schema. NLS from its outset addressed issues of power, counterpoising the autonomous model with an "ideological" model of literacy. What this meant, at that time, was that not only were uses of literacy to be seen as a way in which groups in society might exercise power and dominance over other groups, withholding or providing access to literacy for instance to chosen groups, but more subtly that the very assumptions about literacy – the models that people held underpinning their uses of literacy – were also sources of power relations. If agencies and educational institutions could convince others that the only model of literacy was theirs – for instance, that literacy was an autonomous, neutral, and universal set of skills – then the particular cultural values that underpinned this surface neutrality could be sustained whilst not appearing to be so. In this disguised sense the autonomous model was an extreme example of the ideological model, although more explicit models of the "proper" literacy such as religious literacies or Hirsch's notion of "cultural literacy" were also prevalent. It was, then, in this sense that NLS moved towards analysis of literacy in terms of an ideological model. What Collins and Blot add is a further French intellectual tradition, to complement the mainly Anglo perspective of many NLS scholars. They add Derrida, de Certeau, Foucault, and Bourdieu in ways that lift the debates about literacy beyond the Anglophone concern with educational policy, as in the "Reading Wars," and towards broader philosophical and theoretical issues.

Finally, they link the two key terms, text and power, with a third: identity. Again NLS scholars have sometimes addressed issues of identity, notably recently in the work around the literacies of the academy (cf. Ivanič, 1998; Jones et al., 2001), but also in some of the ethnographic accounts of local resistance to colonial literacies (Besnier, 1995). What Collins and Blot bring to these debates is a more integrated account of how text, power, and identity are linked plus a fully rounded-up development of the theoretical roots of such concepts. They return to the debates of the early phases of NLS concerning a "great divide" in the work of Goody, Olson, and others but give it a more thorough working over in the light of these theoretical traditions. They apply these broader perspectives to practical issues in education and schooling, using amongst other sources Collins' own field material amongst the Tolowa people (Collins, 1998) and others in North and South America and the Caribbean defining themselves in the early and mature stages of American history broadly conceived. What they offer, then, is a kind of intellectual map for pursuing some of the insights developed by scholars who have recognized the limitations of the autonomous model of literacy but broadening the horizon and deepening the intellectual roots of such an endeavor. Careful attention to each of the key terms in the title "Literacy, Literacies, Texts, Power, and Identity" can provide us with a framework for addressing key issues that face both researchers and practitioners in our present encounters with literacy. It will itself become a key text in that endeavor.

References

Barton, D. and Hamilton, M. (1998). *Local Literacies: Reading and Writing in one Community*. London: Routledge.

Besnier, N. (1995). *Literacy, Emotion and Authority: Reading and Writing on a Polynesian Atoll*. Cambridge: Cambridge University Press.

Brandt, D. and Clinton, K. (in press). Limits of the Local: Expanding Perspectives on Literacy as a Social Practice. *Journal of Literacy Research*.

Collins, J. (1995). Literacy and Literacies. *Annual Review of Anthropology, 24*, 75–93.

Collins, J. (1998). *Understanding Tolowa Histories: Western Hegemonies and Native American Responses*. New York: Routledge.

Delpit, L. (1986). Skills and Other Dilemmas of a Progressive Black Educator. *Harvard Educational Review, 56*(4), 379–385.

Gee, J. (1991). *Social Linguistics and Literacies: Ideology in Discourses*. Brighton: Falmer Press.

Heath, S. B. (1983). *Ways with Words: Language, Life and Work in Communities and Classrooms*. Cambridge: Cambridge University Press.

Ivanič, R. (1998). *Writing and Identity: the Discoursal Construction of Identity in Academic Writing*. Amsterdam: John Benjamins.

Jones, C., Turner, J. and Street, B. (eds) (1999). *Students Writing in the University: Cultural and Epistemological Issues*. Amsterdam: John Benjamins.

Kress, G., Jewitt, C., Ogborn, J. and Tsatsarelis, C. (2001). *Multimodal Teaching and Learning: the Rhetorics of the Science Classroom*. London: Continuum.

Kress, G. and van Leeuwen, T. (2001). *Multimodal Discourse: the Modes of Contemporary Communication*. London: Arnold.

Kress, G. and van Leeuwen, T. (1996). *Reading Images: the Grammar of Visual Design*. London and New York: Routledge.

MacCabe, C. (1998). A Response to Brian Street. *English in Education, 32*, 26–28.

Schultz, K. and Hull, G. (2002). Locating Literacy Theory in Out-of-School Contexts. In Hull and Schultz (eds.), *School's Out!: Bridging Out-of-School Literacies with Classroom Practice* (pp. 11–31). New York: Teachers College Press.

Street, B. (1984). *Literacy in Theory and Practice*. Cambridge: Cambridge University Press.

Street, B. (ed.) (1993). *Cross-Cultural Approaches to Literacy*. Cambridge: Cambridge University Press.
Street, B. (2000). Literacy Events and Literacy Practices. In M. Martin-Jones and K. Jones (eds.), *Multilingual Literacies: Reading and Writing Different Words. Comparative Perspectives on Research and Practice* (pp. 17–29). Amsterdam: John Benjamins.

PREFACE

There is a useful phrase in Spanish to describe the development of this book, and probably many other significant research and writing projects: *Se hace el camino al andar* "One makes the road by walking." The field of literacy studies is large and heterogeneous, and the debates are longstanding and contentious. When we first conceived this book project, our aim was to achieve a synthesis of the main debates – roughly, a contrast between universalizing and decontextualized views of "the" consequences of literacy and situated, particularizing arguments for a plurality of literacy practices. We intended to organize such a synthesis by attending closely to questions of political economy: how the forms and dynamics of social development identified by Marxian analyses of power, inequality, and subjectivity were implicated in the forms, practices, and evaluations of literacy. In drafting our initial chapters, however, we discovered the value of arguments made by post-structuralists and practice theorists for moving beyond the usual "universalist" versus "relativist" terms of the literacy debate. In particular, we learned from such sources to appreciate the historical depth and conceptual ubiquity of dichotomies such as "oral" and "literate." What follows is, therefore, less a "grand synthesis" than a series of synthesizing moves, in which we explore debates and materials concerning the issues of text, power, and identity via historical and case-oriented arguments and analyses. We think we provide *a* synthesis, though certainly not *the* synthesis of this diverse and fast-changing field. We have found the work of this book demanding, engaging, and ultimately very worthwhile.

Literacy and Literacies is anthropological in conception. For us that means that it provides a broad picture of the human endeavor, in this case, accounts of literacy that range from Ancient Sumer to contemporary information technologies. It also explores how the social and historical and the cultural and cognitive interpenetrate – for example, how practices of nationalism create and are created by literate subjects; how post- or anti-colonial religious movements involve a prophet's inscribed visions. We assume that historical perspective matters greatly for how we understand an object of study, as does ethnographic detail and, more basically, the orientation to ordinary life that ethnography implies. Our book is not, however, organized as a single historical account, nor is it focused solely on how ethnographic situation shapes literacy. Instead we present a series of sustained arguments about texts, power, and identity, demonstrating that these concepts are each and together significant for our understanding of literacy. In developing our argument, we proceed by developing historical perspectives on our topics of analysis while also, across the book, examining a range of case studies of literacy practices.

In the chapters which follow, one line of argument is that literacy practices such as reading and writing are integrally connected with the dynamics of identity, with the construction of selves. That is partly what the much-decried crises of literacy in the United States are about. The last two US presidents have tried to fashion themselves as "education presidents" by promoting their own reading programs. That literacy has become overtly political is in part because education is increasingly central in the creation of a workforce and citizenry, and this, of course, is a globalized phenomenon. From an elite perspective, an important part of the "problem" with the general population is either deficiencies in education (labeled "illiteracy") or transgressions of official literacy (e.g. "pornography").

That literacy practices are integral to senses of self is clearly the case in our personal situations as authors. We are drawn to the field in part because of our own histories. Collins did not read in school-appropriate ways until the age of nine, and because that is very late in US educational scheduling, he was slated for Special Education exclusion at the end of the third grade. Unforeseen family events prevented this from happening, but the experience left him with a lifelong skepticism about education. Blot reads voraciously but writes only with great difficulty and much prodding, for the need to know, through reading, can easily overwhelm the authority to speak, through writing. The "damaged identity" from schooling, the sense of inadequacy before the text-to-be: such things are common enough in the contemporary world. In our case, however, they specifically contribute to senses of the self defined in tension with authorized literacies and hence to an abiding interest in mundane as well as official literacy, in subversive as well as approved literacy practices. Our point, developed at length throughout the various chapters of this book, is that literacies as communicative practices are inseparable from values, senses of self, and forms of regulation and power.

ACKNOWLEDGMENTS

The making of most if not all books involves an endless round of questioning, consulting, claims, and criticism. In our case, a collaboration extending over five years, this is particularly true. We are indebted for a range of modest institutional supports and, more importantly, for generous personal feedback from friends and colleagues. Collins worked on the manuscript while on a faculty sabbatical from the University at Albany/SUNY in 1998; he also received an Individual Development Award for books and some travel monies from his union, United University Professions, in 1999. The Departments of Anthropology and Reading at Albany provided student assistants for compiling some of the bibliography. Blot worked on the manuscript while on sabbatical from Lehman College/CUNY in 1999; his research and writing were supported over two years (in part) by grants #69483-00-29 and #61526-00-30 from the PSC-CUNY Research Awards Program of the City University of New York, and by a George N. Shuster Fellowship Award from Lehman College, CUNY, for Summer 2001. (On a personal note, Ms. Rene Thompson provided a dining room table and a fine Yorkshire view while Collins worked on initial drafts of chapters 2 and 4.)

Both of us are indebted to audiences at the CrossLondon Literacy Seminar in April 1998 and University of California/San Diego (the Center for Research on Excellence and Achievement in Teaching and Education and the Department of Ethnic Studies) in January 2001 for comments on chapters 2 and 4 respectively. Louise Burkhart provided incisive commentary and criticism on chapter 6; as did Andrew Feffer for chapter 4; Louis Flam for chapter 1; Peter Johnston for chapters 1–4; John Lofty for chapters 1–3; Mike Hill for chapter 5; John Pulis for chapter 6; and Stef Slembrouck for chapter 7. Marcia Farr and an anonymous reviewer for Cambridge University Press read the entire manuscript and provided much excellent advice. Bambi Schieffelin, our series editor, read early drafts of several chapters and provided smart, timely advice. She also combined patience and encouragement with what was at times a rocky process of collaborating and writing. From all those above we have benefitted, though probably not always as they intended; all errors of fact, interpretation, and presentation remain our own.

Blot wishes to express thanks to librarians Eugene Laper and Sandrea DeMinco of Lehman College for their invaluable assistance locating materials, and to Diana Almodovar who assisted in gathering them. Thanks are due also to Steven Mullaney, Director, and to the participants in the National Endowment for the Humanities 1992 Summer Seminar: Inventing the New Worlds: Texts, Contexts, Approaches at the University of Michigan for a genuinely interdisciplinary discussion over six weeks which stimulated and complicated Blot's understanding of European encounters with the Americas. A special thanks to Joe and Pat Greene whose Columbia County, New York, home afforded a quiet retreat for thinking and writing at critical junctures over the length of the project. We wish to thank Fiona Thompson for discussing and locating our cover illustration, and David Rose for preparing the index. We also wish to thank our editor at Cambridge University Press, Andrew Winnard, production editor Jackie Warren, and copy-editor Kay McKechnie for keeping us more literate than we would otherwise have been.

Our immediate families – Aida, Fiona, and Rosa – have put up with the work of this book with encouragement, advice, humor, and the right amount of impatience. We thank them all.

Publishers' permissions

The authors wish to thank the following publishers for permission to reproduce text from the works cited in the following chapter epigraphs:

page 34:   The Wesleyan University Press
page 67:   Cornell University Press
page 99:   The University of Pennsylvania Press
page 121: (upper epigraph) Latin American and Iberian Institute, University
           of New Mexico
           (lower epigraph) The University of Arizona Press
page 155: (upper epigraph) The Johns Hopkins University Press
           (lower epigraph) The Free Press

Note

I

INTRODUCTION: TEXTS, POWER, AND IDENTITY

Puzzles and pluralities of literacy

Literacy is a curious thing. It seems to envelope our lives and be central to modern living, yet most of humanity has done without it for most of human existence. As a term, it points to a striking range of possibilities – such that we now speak not only of "school literacy" and "vernacular literacy" but also "cultural literacy," "computer literacy," "moral literacy," and even "emotional literacy" (Steiner, 1997). But the term is also subject to notable recent efforts to define and restrict its essence, for example, through legislating a particular way that reading or writing must be taught in school. As a field of study, literacy entangles some of the most difficult problems in social analysis – among them the question of text, that is, of language, situation, and meaning – yet it is also a very familiar topic, the source of many proclaimed crises and the subject of many slogans and sound-bites about how to live, raise children, and prepare for the rigors and excitements of the new century.

Literacy often seems to pervade our lives. Increasing numbers of people make their living interacting with a computer screen. Many find reading a welcome escape, and they "bury" themselves in a good book, perhaps a romance or a futuristic fantasy or, if young, a tale of the wise doings of the cleverly marketed Harry Potter. Many compose themselves by composing: diaries, letters (now of course often electronic), jotted-down poems, songs, especially in late adolescence, and, for those many adults working with "information," there are ubiquitous notes, memoranda, schedules, and reports. And yet this intensive intertwining of text and life is a fairly recent phenomenon and of limited societal scope.

Human life in its recognizable essentials – involving us big-brained primates with families and social living, full-fledged language, sophisticated art, and complex technology – has existed for more than fifty thousand years. Yet the earliest precursors to writing – tokens used in farm produce and, later, manufactured goods (Schmandt-Besserat, 1992) – appeared no earlier than ten thousand years ago, and systematic record-keeping for political–economic and religious purposes developed only with the rise of ancient city states (e.g. in Mesopotamia) about five thousand years ago. In addition, these early literacies were restricted for the use of tiny elites. Indeed, it was not until the last 150 years, and primarily in the twentieth century, that universal education – that is, literacy for everyone – became a goal of most nations. Many fundamental human achievements predate the rise of city states, let alone the twentieth century. From the early Neolithic through the post-Neolithic, i.e. from about 8000 BCE to 3500 BCE, well before the onset of full-fledged writing, was one of the most creative periods in human history. Agriculture and the domestication of animals occurred, as well as expanding knowledge in technology. Each of these testifies to a careful and cumulative process of intellection: observing, comparing, testing, communicating, reworking, what Lévi-Strauss (1966) famously called "the science of the concrete." As far as can be known from ethnological, historical, philological and archeological investigations, humans have always observed, classified, philosophized, and told stories throughout their existence (Postgate, 1992; Redman, 1978). Like language, kinship, and engagement with nature, myths and stories appear to be part of a pan-human condition and capability, and often the form and content of myths and stories are surprisingly complex. Many educated people know that the Homeric epics such as the *Odyssey* began as oral tales, but fewer know that many comparable "oral literatures" (e.g. the Vedic hymns) were found throughout the world, in societies largely unencumbered with states or literate traditions. Although literacy often seems essential to our lives, many aspects of what make us human – language, intellect, the capacity for social living, technical resourcefulness – do not rely on literate practices or do so only recently and secondarily.

If we turn from the sweep of human history and restrict our attention only to the contemporary period, literacy presents us with other puzzles. On the one hand, the term refers to highly diverse undertakings; on the other hand, we are currently witnessing a steadfast effort to restrict what "really counts" as literacy. Concerning the diversity, in addition to bread-and-butter "reading" and "writing," there have been numerous calls in recent years for other kinds of literacy. One, "cultural literacy," was proposed in the late 1980s as part of the controversy over multicultural education; such literacy referred to a supposed body of shared knowledge, the basis for an envisioned common national culture (Hirsch, 1987). A few years later, a former Secretary of Education and national drug enforcement official called for "moral literacy," which seemed to consist of character traits preached, if not practiced, by US conservatives (prudence, monogamy, self-reliance, etc. [Bennett, 1996]). Throughout the 1990s, educators were exhorted, and exhorted others, to prepare the young for "computer literacy": a reasonable knowledge of and facility with the current state – changing every few years – of personal computer or web-based information technology. A specialized variant along this line is the proposal, from a researcher of how people use digital technology, for us "to develop in our children 'readership skills for a culture of simulation'" (Turkle, 1999, p. 82). This impressive diversity of possible literacies – from moral literacy to simulation reading – suggests that "literacy," as a key word in our culture, has a status in the current era rather like that of "science" in the nineteenth: it refers loosely to any body of systematic useful knowledge. This plurality of senses is, however, countered by a contrary pressure to determine precisely and authoritatively which practices, which ways with text, legitimately fall under the rubric "literacy"; or, more colloquially, to ask what "real literacy" is.

The 1990s in the United States saw a rise of direct political involvement in methods of literacy teaching. What some have called "the Reading Wars" (Lemann, 1997) have pitted those with a broad and generous view of early learning and reading and writing development, the so-called "whole language" camp, against those with a narrow or more prescriptive view of just how reading and writing are to be taught, the so-called "phonics" camp. A conservative coalition of legislators, foundations, fundamentalist Christians, and their allied academics, the "phonics" camp is currently quite influential. It has managed to pass legislation prescribing reading teaching methods in major states, such as California and Texas; to promote a series of regimented intervention programs nationally; and, as well, to change federal research criteria for what would count as acceptable research on literacy (Allington and Woodside-Giron, 1999; Schemo, 2002). What is most notable about this are not the successes of the phonics movement, for those could turn out to be short-lived. Rather, it is that seemingly narrow and mundane aspects of classroom pedagogy – how many minutes per day are to be spent reciting the alphabet or reviewing spelling rules – have become a heated public political issue.

The striking variety of kinds of literacy that people describe or desire and the fundamentalist impulse to control how literacy in school shall be taught illustrate seemingly contrary aspects of the nature of literacy. It seems there is no single literacy, instead a multiplicity of practices and values get the same label. Indeed, the label "literacy" can be and is extended to areas that have no or little connection to text, or at least to processes of decoding entextualized information; "moral literacy" does not in itself require reading. Nonetheless, the control of literacy, its use, and the conditions under which people become literate is an enduring political and religious preoccupation. The various inconsistencies just noted – that literacy seems essential to contemporary lives but of secondary importance in a fuller account of humans and their potentials; that the term refers to highly diverse phenomena, but also that there is a current struggle in the US to decree just what reading or writing really are – are foreshadowed in academic debates about the nature of literacy.

Research in this field has often presumed dichotomies such as literate versus illiterate, written versus spoken, educated versus uneducated, and modern versus traditional. The title of this book itself presents a dichotomy – literacy/literacies – which it initially develops, then complicates and reformulates. At issue will be a distinction between universalist or "autonomous" models (Street, 1984) of *literacy* – which conceive it as a uniform set of techniques and uses of language, with identifiable stages of development and clear, predictable consequences for culture and cognition – and relativist, sociocultural or situated models of *literacies* – which conceive literacies relationally, that is, as intrinsically diverse, historically and culturally variable, practices with texts. The former concern with unitary literacy is associated with the early work of historians on the technology of printing, of anthropologists on the evolutionary consequences of literacy as a "technology of the intellect," and of comparative and historically inclined psychologists on the cognitive divide between literates and nonliterates. The autonomous view assumed that there is a clear, cumulative distinction between literacy and orality, and, in initial and subsequent formulations, it has argued that the literacy of the West is somehow exceptional to all other literacies. Since it sharply divides speaking and writing, and initially placed much emphasis on the alphabet, it roughly lines up with the "phonics camp" in the current reading controversies.

Conversely, the situated study of multiple literacies has focused on the diversity and social shaping of those ways with text we call literacy, emphasizing the *ways* as much as the *texts* (Heath, 1983; Lofty, 1992). It emerged from anthropological and historical criticism of claims made for a unitary or autonomous literacy, questioning literacy's causal role in social or cognitive development. The situated perspective was developed by revisionist historical scholarship, which reframed the debate about literacy and social development in the West (Graff, 1981a). The perspective is perhaps best exemplified in detailed ethnographic studies of inscription and discourse, which undermine the notion of separable domains of orality and literacy. Since it insists on the interrelation of speaking and writing, and questions the priority given to alphabetic coding in social evolution, the situated perspective loosely supports a "whole language" view of literacy (Edelsky, 1996).

As with many complex and consequential debates, there are no easy resolutions. Facts and information, or new research perspectives, do not of themselves carry the argument. Historical perspective does not settle the issue of what literacy is, nor do ethnographic field studies. Detailed field studies of how people actually practice and value reading and writing as part of their wider conduct and communication have demonstrated that social life is not easily divided into spoken and written domains. They have further shown that how speaking or writing are understood and valued has as much to do with politics and economics – that is, with institutions, resources, and struggles to obtain, impose, and resist authority – as with any given technique or technology of inscription. Nonetheless, although situated studies have presented intriguing counter-cases, widening the range of phenomena discussed, situated studies have often operated with the same categories as autonomous studies, making it difficult for them to change the terms of debate.

As we will see, adherents of the autonomous model of literacy have made arguments about the difference and superiority of Western culture and intellect *vis-à-vis* nonliterate or differently literate societies. These claims are untenable and have been systematically criticized; nonetheless, echoes of these claims continue to inform policy and scholarship about literacy. Understanding why flawed perspectives have such a hold on our current thinking has practical value – it will give insight into why the field of literacy pedagogy is so politically polarized, why "whole language" and "phonics" pedagogies are seen as polar opposites. Such understanding also has a more general intellectual value, for it forces us to also explore why historical and ethnographic cases are necessary, but insufficient, for rethinking inherited viewpoints.

It is our argument in this book that although revisionist historical research has deflated and undermined the grander claims about the "consequences of literacy," it still has to account for the abiding significance of ideas about, institutions of, and practices involving literacy in modern Western societies. In addition, although ethnographic scholarship has demonstrated the pluralities of literacies, their context-boundness, it still has also to account for general tendencies that hold across diverse case studies – for example, the frequent historical correlation of female gender and restricted access to literacy and schooling. In what follows, we argue for a way out of the universalist/particularist impasse by attending closely to issues of text, power, and identity. We begin with the question "What is a text?" because it is so self-evidently involved in disputes central to the literacy debate: whether a written document, or other form of inscription, has meaning separable from the contexts in which it is produced and consumed. This apparently simple question about text-and-meaning has generated much discussion and argument in philosophy, literary criticism, and anthropology. What has been most significant in these debates, for our purposes, are post-structuralist or practice-theory arguments about the role of writing in intellectual traditions as well as in everyday social life. Central to the post-structuralist or the practice-theory argument is the claim that writing is usually associated with power, and particularly with specifically modern forms of power. But in taking up this claim – that literacy is shaped by power – we have been led to a further question "What is power?" This has in turn led to some interesting positions. Most basically, and of greatest relevance for understanding the puzzling legacies of literacy, it has become clear that power is not just some concentrated force that compels individuals or groups to behave in accordance with the will of an external authority, be it parent, boss, or public authority. Instead, power has "microscopic" dimensions, small, intimate, everyday dimensions, and these are constitutive as well as regulative; they are the stuff out of which senses of identity, senses of self as a private individual as well as a social entity in a given time and place, are composed and recomposed.

As we grapple with the unresolved dichotomies of literacy research while also exploring questions of text, power, and identity, we will of necessity develop a complicated argument. In order to do our subject justice, we proceed by presenting and criticizing influential texts, sometimes at considerable length, and by developing historical and ethnographic cases of differing scale. These cases will enable the reader to see how texts, power, and identity frequently intertwine. We also draw upon the work of French scholars associated with post-structuralism and practice theory – particularly, Jacques Derrida, Michel de Certeau, Pierre Bourdieu, and Michel Foucault – because they have been at the forefront of arguments about texts, power, and education. We use their work to engage with and reformulate a debate about literacy that, at least within anthropology and psychology, has been a largely Anglophone controversy. As we will see in the next chapter, certain concepts that have scarcely entered the literacy debate among anthropologists, such as de Certeau's notion of a "scriptural economy," provide a surprisingly apt lens through which to re-evaluate longstanding arguments about literacy, social development, and rationality.

Plan of the book

Our next chapter addresses the general debate about literacy, but it begins with a brief description of a Native American language revitalization program in which the question of an appropriate writing system was particularly vexed. The way in which politics, spelling, and history play out in this particular case provides a useful entree to the heart of this chapter, which is an assessment of arguments about the "consequences of literacy" (Goody and Watt, 1963). We focus upon the arguments and evidence that comprise "the literacy thesis": that there are unified, cumulative effects of literacy, in social and cognitive development. Put more bluntly, we assess claims that literacy underpins the uniqueness of the West and the superiority of Western minds. Our account develops by examining and critiquing claims about literacy and development, especially those presented in two influential books – Jack Goody's *The Logic of Writing and the Organization of Society* (1986) and David Olson's *The World on Paper* (1994). The former presents a standard account of the role of literacy in the development of social complexity, while Olson's arguments about the development of knowledge and the self begin by disavowing strong versions of the literacy thesis, but then return to sweeping claims about the historical consequences of reading practices. The central claims in these works have at their root an untenable literacy/orality contrast with implications for how we think about culture, language, and mind. It is important to understand the tenacity of this untenable contrast, however, and in this regard we turn to de Certeau (1984), whose exploration of "everyday life" also connects to the ongoing ethnographic critique of the literacy thesis.

Early counter-arguments to literacy thesis claims occurred in research advocating and demonstrating an ethnographic approach to the study of literacy. Prominent among such work was that of Shirley Brice Heath, Ruth Finnegan, and Brian Street. By illustrating the multifaceted, dialectical relations that hold between texts and social forms, their research and writing called into question many of the general consequences initially claimed for literacy. Although chapter 3 deals with numerous situated studies, it focuses on the analytical and empirical contributions of Heath's arguments about language socialization and "literacy events," Finnegan's "performance" approach to unifying talk-and-text, and Street's proposals concerning an "ideological model" of literacy. Detailed examples from each researcher's *œuvre* are presented, in order to illustrate the real advances of these ethnographic approaches to literacy and orality, but also to identify the limitations of such approaches. Chief among the shortcomings we discuss are underdeveloped conceptions and analyses of text and power.

In order to explore how literacies are implicated in the operations of social power, in our fourth chapter we present an extended historical case study of the uses of literacy, the development of modern nation states, and the emergence of universal education. More specifically, this chapter discusses in detail the complicated dialectic between textual practices, political subjectivities, and economic dynamics in early and mature stages of the American nation. In this account, the public school system plays an ever more central role in defining and distributing an official literacy. Our analysis of schooled literacy provides a relatively familiar account of expanding educational participation and rising literacy rates while also exploring the less-often-noted exclusions, resistances, and forms of gender, race, and class domination that accompanied the spread of modern schooling. As we will see, subtleties, transgressions, and subterfuges are an ongoing *sub rosa* accompaniment to the "official story," whether we deal with the nineteenth, twentieth or twenty-first centuries.

The official story has been optimistic about the transformative powers of literacy and education, perhaps the most durable element of an otherwise battered modern liberalism (Graff, 1979). In liberal thought, if literacy and education were to be the means for enlightened social progress, it was to be through a merging of social development and individual growth and autonomy. However, this joining of the social and individual has grown increasingly problematic. Indeed, in our current late modern or postmodern era it often seems that social developments and individual growth proceed along different vectors. In chapter 5 we analyze the relation between literacy and identity in order to explore the fault lines of self, inscription, and the social in both modern and postmodern America. As in other chapters, we proceed with an anthropological sensibility, via examination of detailed cases. In particular, we discuss ethnographies and educational memoirs dealing with literacy, education, and social identity, which also articulate an increasingly problematic view of salvation through education. In critically examining these studies, as well as confronting them with a set of feminist counter-cases, we are led to see how the social exchanges surrounding and carried out through acts of reading and writing necessarily involve the dynamics of class, gender, and race in contemporary America.

In the sixth chapter we explore the articulation of inscription, power, and identity in colonial and postcolonial contexts, presenting a number of analyses which show how the "uses of literacy" in non-Western settings both draw upon and transform Western textual legacies. In particular, we will analyze how among indigenous and subaltern peoples of North and South America, as well as the Caribbean, literacy, religion, and the secular salvation promised by education form a colonial and postcolonial terrain for conflicts over identity, authority, and visions of the self and the future. In dialogue with arguments developed in previous chapters, chapter 6 focuses upon the interplay between literacy practices and identity dynamics, but in substantially different historical settings. For example, across a diverse range of historical and contemporary cases, it explores the commonalities involved in constructing and subverting religious as well as educational authority.

Our book ends with a beginning, for in the seventh and concluding chapter, we return to the theme of the origins of literacy in prehistory, in literary and cinematic imaginings, and in ethnographic and ethnohistorical cases. Picking up the thread of Derrida's deconstruction of the idea of origins, his expansion of the concept of writing, and his links between inscription and power, we discuss again the Tolowa language revitalization program. This program and its ethnographic setting provide an example of the "beginning" of writing in which writing as practice and ideology is already long presupposed, in which contemporary identity politics are paramount, and in which the minutiae of transcription reflect familial as well as institutional rivalries. Understanding such a case requires a post-structuralist as well as ethnographic understanding of literacy. Such understanding neither accepts text/talk polarities nor ignores the cumulative, value-laden role of such polarities in the development of Western thought and its effort to understand and control civilization's marginalized or disenfranchised "Others."

Drawing out the implications of this insight requires us to return to Goody's arguments about archives and power. Made in his earliest essays, these are also made in his latest contribution to the literacy debate (Goody, 2000), in which he challenges Derrida's views on writing and archives. That debate raises anew the question of technology which, as we show, has ongoing implications for questions of power, for claims about the "end of literacy," and for understandings of identity, especially in the globalized world of so-called electronic literacy. The nature of such computer-assisted literacy is the newest topic in the ongoing debate about technology, communicative practices, social arrangements, and the human condition. The shifting, imprecise, yet value-laden notion of literacy has been a central trope in such discussions for over four decades.

2

THE LITERACY THESIS: VEXED
QUESTIONS OF RATIONALITY,
DEVELOPMENT, AND SELF

The invention of writing was the greatest movement by which mankind rose from barbarism to civilization. How vast its effect was, may be best measured by looking at the
low condition of tribes still living without it, dependent on memory for their traditions
and rules of life, and unable to amass knowledge as we do by keeping records of events,
and storing up new observations for the use of future generations. Thus it is no doubt
right to draw a line between barbarian and civilized where the art of writing comes in,
for this gives permanence to history, law, and science. Such knowledge so goes with
writing, that when a man is spoken of as learned, we at once take it to mean that he has
read many books, which are the main source men learn from.

(Tylor, 1898, pp. 179–180)

Introduction

Debates about the nature of literacy have been politically important because
they involve claims about "great divides," that is, about fundamental differences
in humankind, in particular in the social, cultural and cognitive development of
literates and nonliterates. This can be seen in the quote above from E. B. Tylor's
Anthropology: an Introduction to the Study of Man and Civilization which
clearly expresses the social-evolutionary thinking that held sway a century
ago. As might be expected, such sweeping claims and broad debates have led
to numerous specialist controversies as well as policy-oriented studies. There
have been longstanding controversies about the formal differences and similarities between spoken and written language, which are supposed to underlie
many educational problems (for example, Purcell-Gates [1995]; Tannen [1982];
Whiteman [1981]). There have also been ongoing discussions of the role of literacy in economic betterment, whether concerning historically prior periods
(Cipolla, 1969; Graff, 1981b), developing nations within the post-World War II
economic order (Freebody and Welch, 1993; Prinsloo and Breier, 1996;
UNESCO, 1957; Wagner, 1987), or marginalized populations within the world's
developed economies (Canada, 1996; Farkas, 1996; Friedmann, 1960; Ohmann,
1987).

These debates have largely been inconclusive. Where there have been substantive advances, such advances have depended upon reformulating the terms
of the debate – as in Biber's (1988) demonstration that the formal linguistic

9

differences attributed to spoken versus written language modes are either nonexistent or due to genre rather than mode. In Biber's case, he directly questioned and empirically demonstrated the invalidity of the oral/written contrast, rather than disputing the consequences after the conceptual dichotomy has been granted. Such reformulation is quite difficult, however, and frequently of limited impact – Biber's research, for example, appears to have had little influence on discussions of literacy. As we will see, the tenacity of the spoken/written dichotomy, despite its questionable empirical basis, is due to the way in which acts of reading and writing are intertwined with how Western intellectual culture understands itself as distinct from, yet related to, others: other races, other classes (the "folk" or "masses"), and those more shadowy others, primordial and sexualized, that constitute the psychic sense of self.

As the Tylor quote shows, it is an old argument within Western thought that there are fundamental differences or "great divides" in human intellect and cognition, differences tied to stages of civilization, grammatical elaboration, or racial order (Lévi-Bruhl, 1926; Stocking, 1968). The criticisms of such views are also longstanding and are or should be well known (Boas, 1911; Gould, 1981; Lévi-Strauss, 1966). Nonetheless, intellectual concern with essential differences between human populations remains a current topic, for various ideological reasons, as attested to by the recent "hereditarian" controversy about race, intelligence, and inequality in the United States (Fischer, 1996; Herrnstein and Murray, 1994; Lewontin, 2000; Patterson, 1997). In the discipline of anthropology in the post-World War II period, "great divide" theories were reformulated. Fundamental differences in human cognition and human social and cultural conditions were attributed not to differences in human nature, or stages of civilization, but rather to literacy, conceived as a "technology of the intellect."

The reformulation was only partial, however, for it has proven difficult to disentangle arguments about literacy from Tylorian assumptions about progress and the direction of history, about civilization and modernity. This is because the connections are both deep and pervasive. Our very concept of civilization has taken writing as essential.[1] The existence of writing has been presumed to be a feature which distinguished civilizations, with their cities, advanced economies, and specialized arts and technologies, from simpler forms of human societies which, lacking cities, social classes, and differentiated realms of politics and law, religion and art, were deemed primitive (Friedman, 1994; Gelb, 1963; Lévi-Strauss, 1964). To provide education and literacy was one aspect of the *mission civilatrice* that European colonial powers proclaimed as they secured control of much of the globe. As we will discuss more fully in chapter 6, such education was typically in a European language and script, and it was consciously viewed as a way to transform, to remake the morals and minds of, colonized peoples (Asad, 1992).

The colonial civilizing project always had its internal critics, and there have for centuries been efforts to document, provide books and dictionaries in, and variously inscribe native languages (Goddard, 1996). Oftentimes these efforts were undertaken merely as a more efficient means of securing conversion – as, for example, with the widespread Bible-translating efforts of the Summer Institute of Linguistics, which has produced translations of Christendom's holy text into hundreds of indigenous languages (Colby, 1995; Grinevald, 1998; Wallis, 1964). In recent decades, however, there has been a worldwide shift in understanding of how native or indigenous or "Fourth World" peoples fit within the overall political scheme of nations and the world. In particular, the assertion of cultural rights has been salient among the political strategies of native peoples, and specification of these rights has included preservation of the traditional language and at least some education for children in these languages (Friedman, 1994; Hornberger, 1997).

This more recent rights-based effort has provided the context for hundreds of language maintenance and revitalization efforts among native peoples in North and South America, Australia, Africa, and Asia (Grenoble and Whaley, 1998). Such efforts always involve "writing the language," that is, developing an orthography and preparing grammars, dictionaries, and other pedagogical tools. They thus provide numerous examples of the "origins of writing," cases in which ostensibly unwritten languages are rendered into written text.

The origins of writing, the ideal of transcribing: a Native American case

Such originary events can be of considerable interest, in part because of the baggage they carry and the conflicts they engender. The baggage has to do with pervasive assumptions about the origins and consequences of writing. Briefly put, writing is supposed to appear suddenly and from the outside, to transform a language and a people. With the advent of writing, native peoples, previously traditional and outside civilization, are seen as entering the modern world. If the beginning of writing induces epochal change, previously from primitive to civilized, and now from traditional to modern, this is because writing has consequences. These consequences are usually told as a narrative of progress: writing, and literacy more generally, leads to social development and individual improvement. In the cases at hand, language revitalization efforts, writing enables the preservation of valued tradition and the (re)integration of people with their cultural tradition. The given linguistic–cultural tradition, previously in danger of "death" from disuse, can now, rendered into written text, be used in the contemporary world.

In order for such good things to occur, however, writing must be done right; it must be "correct." And herein lies the focus of much conflict in language documentation efforts. A written text, whether an account of the past, a story, or a single word or sentence, is a representation. The question of representation – how one thing "stands for" another – has occasioned centuries of discussion and debate in philosophy, politics, religion, and literary studies, and, more recently, in a range of social science disciplines such as anthropology, sociology, and history (Bourdieu, 1984; Clifford, 1988; White, 1987). In language renewal efforts, the conflicts concern the best way to write a language. The passions aroused by such questions are due in part to the ideal, or dream, of an absolute transcription, of a "fully explicit" text, in which language and meaning are fully captured, fully present, and hence requiring no sense of context or other inter-pretive intermediaries (Derrida, 1976b). But passions are also aroused because orthographies-as-representations are also about affiliations, about who "we" are that write these ways and give these accounts, and also about authority, about struggles to secure "our" writing and our accounts against "theirs" (Collins, 1998a; Schieffelin and Doucet, 1998).

These issues can be made more concrete if we consider a single case, that of the Tolowa of northern California. Originally a small-scale, decentralized society, the Tolowa lived as hunters and gatherers, or, more precisely, as fishers, hunters, and gatherers, along the Smith River drainage and a nearby coastal plain in the northwest tip of the current State of California. Conquest by Euro-Americans, after the 1849 Gold Rush, was bloody, involved military internment, massive land loss, and much dying. By the beginning of the twentieth century, an estimated precontact population of 2,000 (Gould, 1978) had declined to 121 persons registered on a 1906 federal census of Indians. The population slowly rebounded throughout the century, but so did pressures to assimilate: get cash jobs and give up fishing; learn English and forget Tolowa; convert to Christianity and foreswear "Indian dancing" (Bommelyn, 1994; Collins, 1998b).

In the 1960s, however, as part of a general ferment involving educational re-form, civil rights, and cultural reassertion, the Tolowa began a process of lan-guage maintenance which has now continued for over forty years. It began with some Tolowa people, women in particular, who were concerned over the loss of knowledge about kinship, story lore, and the language. Encouraged by a com-munity development center at a university in the region, the Tolowa Language Committee, as they came to be known, began by calling together elders fluent in the native language, collecting lists of words and sentences, compiling story booklets and vocabulary and, later, publishing a dictionary with a grammar and specialized cultural appendices (Bommelyn and Humphrey, 1984).

Controversy dogged the program, however, as it did other native language revitalization programs in the area. At the heart of the controversy was the writing system. The orthography the Tolowa Language Committee had adopted, the Unifon Alphabet, had been provided by the founding director of a local community development center that helped provide funding, secure teaching credentials, and otherwise support the language program. The Unifon Alphabet was itself adapted from a scheme for teaching urban minority children to read via

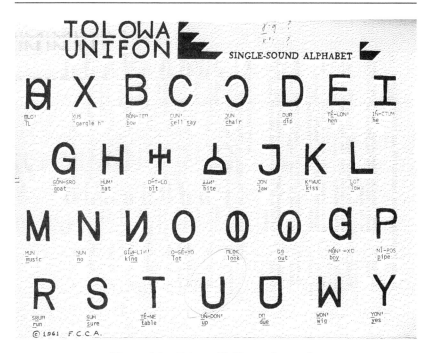

Figure 2.1 *Tolowa Unifon orthography*

a phonetic method. Like the transcription systems used by academic linguists, such as the International Phonetic Alphabet (IPA), the Unifon system strove for one-to-one sound/symbol consistency (as in "each time the sound 'bee' occurs, use the symbol '*b*' "). In this sense, both IPA and Unifon are alphabetic. They attempt to represent the discrete sound units – technically called phonemes – that make up a spoken language but not to represent the syllables of the spoken language, as do syllabaries, such as the Japanese writing system, nor to represent morphemes, as do logographic systems such as that of Classical Chinese.

The Unifon Alphabet was based on the English alphabet, but with modifications to provide unique symbols for vowel and consonant sounds. (The IPA also aspires to such uniqueness of sound representation, but it is based on a wider set of elements, drawn from a range of European and other languages.) The Unifon Alphabet for Tolowa is presented in figure 2.1. As we can see, some of the symbols look curious if we are accustomed to the "roman" alphabet in which English and many other languages are written. Consider, for example, ◬ for the sound "I" in "bite" (IPA *ay*); ◖ for the sound "oy" in "boy" (IPA *oi*); and Ɔ for the sound "ch" in "church" (IPA *c*). In addition, the Unifon Alphabet, being derived from English, was somewhat unsuited for Tolowa. It gives considerable attention to vowel differences, but the vowels used in Tolowa are fewer than those used in English. On the other hand, the Tolowa language uses a range of consonants that English does not employ – for example, the glottalized series t [t'], ch [c'], k [k'], and kw [kw'] – and these the Unifon script could not provide for without some jerryrigging.

Although the Unifon system, like a possible IPA system, aspired to alphabetic principles, it caused controversy as a representation of the language. Some Tolowa people, familiar with English writing, found it strange looking and hard to learn. Academic linguists argued (usually in personal communications rather than publications) that the Unifon did not adequately represent the structure of the language (see discussion in Collins [1998a]). Conversely, other Tolowa people, who had given years of their lives to developing the program, recording the language, and preparing texts for classroom use and publication, or perhaps had merely taken a course at the local high school, felt that Unifon was their writing system. They felt it was adequate to the task at hand and more appropriate for an "Indian language" since it did not look like English or other European writing systems. For their part, they resented the pressure from "outside" linguists to use IPA-derived systems. Such linguists might have an institutionally certified authority (an advanced degree in the discipline, known publications), but they had not demonstrated commitment to the local effort at language preservation. That is, the Tolowa language activists gave priority to local ties and traditional authenticity over the authority claims of academic position and recognition.

The case of Tolowa writing entangles questions of allegiance, authority, and representation, or, otherwise put, questions of identity, power, and text. It thus provides a rehearsal of themes found in the more general debate about the "nature of literacy" and a foreshadowing of the focal themes of this book. Was it more important that one used an IPA or Unifon alphabet, each with somewhat different capacities for representing, notating, the structure of the language? Or, was it more important that one system had university-academic approval, the seal of science, while the other had the approval of local language activists, those doing the lion's share of work documenting and teaching the language, that is, the social loyalties of those most directly engaged? In the debate about the nature of literacy, claims about the consequences of literacy are intertwined with assumptions about the emergence of Western modernity, and arguments about the superiority of alphabetic representation figure centrally in claims about the sociological and cognitive distinctness of writing and written traditions. In the Tolowa case, what initially appeared to be a purely technical question, "What alphabet to use?", turned out to be considerably more complicated. The question of textual form, whether to use Unifon or IPA, had implications for claims to identity, that is, affiliations with different families and with varieties of tribal identity. These questions in turn brought into play a politics of tribal recognition and academic authority, of powers desired and feared in practices of writing and styles of representation. Who gets to decide on an adequate representation of a language, at a time when the existence of that language, in objectified written form, and one's relation to that language, that is, one's ability to understand or use it, can be important aspects of claims to traditional identity? Although the literacy debate has been, and continues to be, powerfully shaped by accounts which separate out politics, subjectivities, and textual form, stressing instead an autonomy of the technical, matters are never quite so simple.

The literacy thesis

In a classic essay entitled "The Consequences of Literacy," Jack Goody and Ian Watt (Goody and Watt, 1963) argue that momentous consequences derived from the alphabetic literacy that first flowered in Greece and subsequently developed in medieval and modern Europe. Among the consequences of literacy they depict are basic transformations in the nature of knowledge and cultural tradition, in particular (a) a distinction between myth and history; (b) a distinction between opinion and truth (formalizable inquiry or logic); and (c) a distinction between acceptance of received tradition and a skepticism about tradition, this last leading to individuation and democratic social forms.

Their argument can be briefly summarized as follows. Whereas oral accounts of the past (myth) are inherently perspectival, history depends upon and emerges from a critical synthesis of differing accounts, a synthesis relying on written accounts and transcending perspectives. Oral or mythic accounts of the past are by their very nature presentist: bound to the immediacy of speech, they provide representations of the past continuously adjusted to current realities. At bottom, this is the claim that memory, whether individual or social, is adapted to, and largely shaped by, present exigencies. History, however, is a qualitatively different and superior representation of the past. Methodologically based on a comparison of written sources, it attains a distance in its account – for written texts are manipulable and endurable and thus detachable from the immediate present in a way that speakers and their spoken texts are not. Further, it attains a superior reliability from its sources, for written texts are supposedly permanent repositories of meaning, whereas spoken words are inherently ephemeral.

Put otherwise, for Goody and Watt history contrasts strikingly with the mode of remembering characteristic of nonliterate or preliterate societies, where knowledge of the past is transmitted orally. History, in their view, is not based on collective memory, which is always subject to current pressures and to forgetfulness, but on the accumulated documents of the literate segments of civilized societies. Accounts (interpretations) of past actions and events, written histories, can be tested against the documentary evidence; but the past events cannot be altered, they are as they always were, because written sources are available to verify the accounts.

Turning from history to epistemology, Goody and Watt argue that whereas opinion and common sense are tied to intersubjective group membership, systematic inquiry and truth-seeking depend on their transcending particular circumstances or interests, a detachability from context aided by written procedures for reasoning and argument. They discuss as examples the Aristotelian rules of logic, such as deductive reasoning in the form of syllogisms, which they see as a literate, context-independent mode of inferring and reasoning about things in the world. A syllogism has a major (a) and a minor premise (b) which necessarily lead to a conclusion (c), a conclusion which may override real world knowledge. For example: if (a) all faculty members are men; and (b) Mary is a faculty member; then (c) it follows that Mary is a man – notwithstanding what the proper name might suggest.

Addressing the sociopolitical consequences of literacy, Goody and Watt argue that whereas socialization through (oral) language makes us human by binding us to groups, it also inclines us to adherence to authority, received wisdom and common sense. In a word, it makes people conservative conformists. Indeed, they refer to orally transmitted knowledge and practice as "homeostatic," or self-regulating, a functionalist term drawn from the equilibrium models of 1950s sociology, conjuring up images of static, small-scale societies which lie outside the tumult of modern history. Literacy, and literate socialization, by contrast, are seen as providing alternate accounts of events, thus encouraging and sustaining skeptical attitudes to authority as well as greater individuality – both hallmarks of a so-called modern mentality.

These claims have come under considerable scrutiny and criticism in the past three decades, and they have been variously modified. For example, in an early and important critique, Gough (1968) drew on material from Ancient India and China to challenge the consequences argument on numerous grounds. At issue was the distinction between "full" and "restricted" literacy and the social powers attributed to alphabetic script. Goody and Watt had explained the anomaly of ancient and longstanding literate traditions which did not produce the expected consequences by postulating a distinction between full literacies, which had the predicted results, and restricted literacies, which did not. A major cause of restricted literacy, in their account, was lack of an alphabetic script. Hence Ancient India, with a syllabary writing system, and Ancient China, with a logographic system, were among their examples of "restricted" literacy traditions. However, as Gough shows, their claims about the superior spread of alphabetic literacy do not hold, as both India and China had a similar scale of (nonalphabetic) literacy to Ancient Greece with its alphabetic literacy. Claims about literacy causing historical consciousness also do not hold, for China has a historiographic tradition, while India does not, yet both had literate traditions. Finally, claims about Western literacy, concern with systematic truth and the development of science, do not hold, for China developed impressive traditions of systematic science without alphabetic literacy. Gough's essay supports the insight implicit in the idea of "restricted literacy" – that is, that social conditions shape the practice and meanings of literacy. What it does *not* support, and indeed challenges, is the idea of a sociologically "unrestricted" literacy, a communicative technology endowed with transformative powers.

We will look again at other aspects of the consequences argument and at other criticisms; suffice it here to say that in essential respects the account has not changed. Instead it has developed in numerous works by Goody, by literary scholars such as Walter Ong, and by psychologists such as David Olson, into what Halverson (1991, 1992) calls the "the literacy thesis." Although the details differ, the central claims of the thesis are that writing is a technology that transforms human thinking, relations to language, and representations of tradition, a technology that also enables a coordination of social action in unprecedented precision and scale, thus enabling the development of unique social and institutional complexity.

Many of the claims of the literacy thesis are intriguing, and they have an initial plausibility. A literate bias is part of our academic common sense as well as our schooled and media-saturated common culture, and so it makes sense to view inscription, text, and print as momentous practices and technologies. The assumption that literacy develops a modern mentality underlies the numerous calls for literacy campaigns in the United States and United Kingdom, whether in the 1970s or the 1990s (Edmondson, 2000; Lightfoot, 1998; MOE, 1998). Similarly, from the UNESCO documents and campaigns of the 1950s (Philips, 1979) to the Cuban and Nicaraguan postrevolution literacy campaigns (Arnove, 1980; Kozol, 1978) to the recent internationally funded South African literacy campaigns (Prinsloo and Breier, 1996), it is frequently assumed and asserted that widespread literacy leads to, and is necessary for, modern economic development and full political participation.

What is crucial to understand, however, is that the plausibility of such claims depends on how the dichotomy oral versus literate is presented and secured. Although the literacy thesis is essentially about semiotic means, about a communicative modality supposedly reshaping cognitive and social processes, it depends on various bracketing operations to establish comparability and provide historical trajectory. In what follows, we will examine specific works on literacy, social development, and cognitive development in detail, in order that we might appreciate both the appeal of the literacy thesis, its reasonableness, and also the way in which it emerges from and is bound to very problematic assumptions about inscription, social evolution, and language.

Literacy, rationality, and social development

We will come at these issues by first looking at a body of work that is indirectly concerned with what we would recognize as the modern era. We speak here of the arguments by Goody that literacy is a "technology of the intellect" which leads to basic changes in thinking as well as providing the foundations for basic "transformations of social organization." We want to address first the theme of writing as essential for certain "transformations of social organization." That is the subject of a book-length treatment by Goody, *The Logic of Writing and the Organization of Society* (1986). Unfortunately not as well discussed as other works by Goody (1977, 1987), it nonetheless lays out the argument about literacy and social evolution in its clearest and most sustained form.

LWOS is an exercise in historical and sociological comparison. The uses of writing in states of the Ancient Near East (for example, Mesopotamia, Sumer, Egypt) are compared with the complementary uses of orality in nonliterate states and kingdoms in West Africa (for example, the Lo Daaga, the Asante, and the Dahomey). Unlike Goody and Watt's "Consequences" essay, the temporal frame of *LWOS* extends several millennia prior to Classical Greece, and the analytic concern is not to explain continuities between the literate traditions of Greece and the modern West, but rather to compare complex nonliterate societies (Western Africa) with complex, literate, but premodern societies (Ancient Near East). The analysis investigates the role of writing in religion, economics, politics, and law. In each domain there is what we may call a general effect of a system of transcription: writing provides relatively permanent representations, establishing a new form of textual or scriptural authority, and enabling both the central storage and widespread dispersal of inscribed messages. There is a familiar theme developed in each chapter, writing leads to a transition from particularism to universalism, and this is part of a general Weberian theme in which writing is causally linked with instrumental rationality in religion, economy, politics, and law.[2]

In a chapter entitled "The word of Mammon," Goody discusses the role of writing in the organization of the economy. It appears that in Ancient Near Eastern social formations, the temple controlled a substantial portion of the economy, and temples kept extensive records of endowments and income, developing a tradition of bookkeeping and auditing. Parallel to the "temple economy" was the economy of the royal household, the "palace economy," which reveals the concern of states with taxation, census, and conscription. These concerns are not unique to states based on writing, for taxes were collected in nonliterate redistributive state economies, whether in Africa or elsewhere (Polanyi, 1957; Sahlins, 1972). However, as with religion, writing permits an apparently unprecedented scale to economic record keeping. This is attested to by archives from centralized palace economies in Mesopotamia in 1700 BCE; detailed ledgers of textile production, from a similar period; and even earlier trade records, such as in the Eblen archive, from Mesopotamia in 2400 BCE, in which an estimated 70 percent of texts are bookkeeping lists (Goody, 1986, p. 70).

In addition to temple and palace, extensive record keeping was also found in a third economic sector: commerce and banking. This "mercantile economy," dating from third-millennium Mesopotamia onwards, is attested to by extensive records of shareholding in trade ventures and of letters of credit (the latter allowing textual "IOU"s to serve as an early monetary form). Written evidence of individual transactions from this period includes records of transfer of property and title to land – a written form of title aiding, in Goody's view, the seizure of common land by private individuals.[3] In an interesting argument, Goody suggests that writing provided the prototype for money. Scholars of the prehistory of writing (Gelb, 1963; Schmandt-Besserat, 1978, 1989) have argued that writing in Mesopotamia emerged from an urban accounting system in which tokens were used to keep records of stores and transactions. The system of writing became more abstract as the inscriptions, materials, and messages were differentiated.[4] Taking the analysis one step further, Goody argues for a further abstraction: as writing and bookkeeping developed in ancient economies, written script became a primitive monetary form, a generalized medium of exchange represented by IOUs and letters of credit, permitting economic coordination on a scale previously unattainable.

One distinctive theme in Goody's discussion of writing and the economy, as in the discussion of writing and the state, is the emphasis on writing as an instrument of power and domination. This mutes the optimism of the earlier "Consequences" essay, in which literacy led to democracy. In this regard *LWOS* joins the line of argument put forth by Lévi-Strauss in *Tristes Tropiques*, some twenty-five years earlier, that contrary to Enlightenment optimism, the historical record of literacy was more of enslavement than improvement: "Writing is a strange thing...The one phenomenon which has invariably accompanied it is the formation of cities and empires: the integration into a political system, that is to say, of a considerable number of individuals, and the distribution of those individuals into a hierarchy of castes and classes...It seems to favor rather the exploitation than the enlightenment of mankind" (Lévi-Strauss, 1964, p. 291).

These are, of course, very broad generalizations. In response we may rightly ask to what extent literate domination is based on literate bookkeeping versus the religious-monumentalist "magic" of inscription reported for many ancient states (Harbsmeier, 1988). Or, following Derrida's (1976c) critique of Lévi-Strauss, we may ask in precisely what ways domination by writing differs from domination by speaking. More directly germane to Goody's analysis, we may also inquire about modes of economic coordination and control in which writing is not primary. This latter comparison of "literate" and "oral" economic coordination is, however, poorly developed in *LWOS* – a point to which we will return.

A general virtue of *LWOS* is that it provides constant reminders of the semiotic dimensions of social complexity. An endless keeping of lists seems to accompany social undertakings of any significant scale: censuses of population undertaken by states and lists of priest-officiants maintained by temples are prime examples. Bookkeeping emerged early as a primary function, if not *the* primary function of inscription in Mesopotamia, and it figured in subsequent temple, palace, and merchant economies in the Ancient Near East. It is also undeniable that writing – inscription "to assist the user in an act of recognition" in Havelock's definition (1982b, p. 54) – lends itself readily to the ubiquitous social desire to control representations (Bourdieu, 1977; Silverstein and Urban, 1996). This appears particularly true in religious domains, where prayers, rituals, and myths are inscribed in order to preserve, and also in order to control, their form (Basso, 1990a; Probst, 1993).

That writing helps to coordinate social action at a distance, and that it plays a role in symbolically complex representations of space, time, and identity, has led classical (Durkheim, 1960) and contemporary social theorists (Bourdieu, 1977; Habermas, 1987) to join Goody in attributing epoch-defining status to literacy. Having stated this, we must note that what is striking, alongside the symbolic richness of written social complexity analyzed in *LWOS*, is how threadbare seems the symbolic wherewithal of "nonliterate" or "oral" societies. It is our conviction, however, that this is a mistaken impression, due not to what we know about the communicative resources of primarily oral societies, but rather to the organization of description and comparison in *LWOS*.

Although the nonliterate societies of Western Africa are a cardinal point of comparison in *LWOS*, the book simply does not say very much about oral resources for religion, economic organization, or political undertaking. This paucity of description can be highlighted by comparing Goody's treatment of "oral societies" with other treatments of oral traditions, whether contemporary or historical. As is discussed more fully in our next chapter, among the primarily oral Limba of Senegal, Finnegan (1988) finds a highly developed and self-conscious poetics and oral literature, with complex feats of memory and composition. Similarly, she also analyzes and reports a sophisticated philosophy of language, experientially based in multilingual language awareness and focused upon a regional conception of speech-and-action. From a different historical era, but dealing with the relevant oral/written contrast, Lloyd's (1990) discussion of the conversational dimensions of political dispute and scientific inquiry in Classical Greece brings out important issues. In particular, Lloyd shows that subtle assumptions and practices regarding face-to-face argument, in the historical context of pervasive concern with justifying positions and claims, underlay the famous Greek proclivity for "writing up" systematic treatises on rhetoric and natural history. Similarly, Havelock's early work on pre-Homeric story traditions (Havelock, 1963) and his later (1982a, 1986) discussion of the richly intricate relation between speaking and writing in pre-Socratic Greece reconstruct intricate and complex traditions of speech. Compared with any of these, *LWOS*'s oral/literate dichotomy is stark, and the description of orality is thin.

The tendency to slight description and analysis of oral-based social organization goes hand in hand with problems in historical periodizing and the scope of comparison. Much of the argument about writing in *LWOS* collapses some three thousand years of development into generalizations about "written society." This flattens out significant differences among ancient social formations. As noted earlier, Goody accepts and elaborates Schmandt-Besserat's (1978) arguments about the origins of writing in economic accounting systems – a straightforward account of the co-development of writing and the instrumental rationality of market accounting. This argument may hold for Mesopotamia, but as Larsen (1988) and others (Harbsmeier, 1988) have shown, it is not adequate for Ancient Egypt, where ritual–political inscription dominated, in both kind and quantity of writing. What this means is that the instrumental rationality Goody sees as fundamental in the development of writing and social complexity needs a more nuanced treatment. The argument that the primary function of writing is to record, store, and organize *information* undoubtedly captures an important truth, but cannot do justice to the symbolics of monumental display, to the "magic" of writing that typically accompanies, and can overshadow, the "reason" of writing.

An unbalanced comparison is most evident in *LWOS* in "The word of Mammon." As discussed above, this chapter provides extensive, detailed descriptions of temple, palace, and merchant economies and of uses of writing in individual economic transactions. These comprise a total of some thirty-seven pages in print. We then come to the point of comparison in a section entitled "Writing and the economy in Africa," but the comparison never occurs. We are told that "many African communities have been involved in long-distance trade for a very long time" (p. 83); however, we are told nothing about the temporal, spatial, or semiotic dimensions of that trade. Instead, we are treated to an off-hand remark about *contemporary* traders, "the Ghanaian ladies observed by Hart who provided food on credit to transport workers" (p. 83), who did not keep written records and so, apparently, limited their transactions and customers. Then we are given a brief, paragraph-length description of a Vai merchant keeping his account books, though again there is no indication of scale or complexity of trade. After speculating about cognitive effects of keeping account books, Goody then alludes in a sentence to assumptions about literacy and modernization, "about levels of literacy required for 'development' " (p. 84). The argument then shifts to a page-length discussion of writing and knowledge in seventeenth-century China, and another page on fifth-dynasty Egypt, before concluding – though in less than half a page – that the "indigenous states in Africa . . . lacked the availability of such a catalytic agent" (p. 86) as literacy, and that for this reason they were more vulnerable to colonialism and neocolonialism.

This slapdash comparison is all the more puzzling when we realize that Goody has himself written carefully about oral-and-written practices in Africa. For example, his analysis of a Ghanaian scribe (1968) is a thorough historical ethnography of literacy which is reasonably sensitive to the relation of speaking to writing. The problem lies, we would suggest, more in the conceptual framework used than in the lack of relevant material. In particular, the overarching argument in *LWOS* is built upon a series of oppositions: theoretical (writing versus orality); regional (Ancient Near East versus West Africa); and evidential (sociological comparison versus ethnography). The former term in each pair is handled carefully, the latter term is treated casually. As noted, writing is described and analyzed extensively, oral resources are typically characterized in a general fashion. The analysis of written and nonwritten economies just discussed is symptomatic of the treatment of the Ancient Near East *vis-à-vis* sub-Saharan Africa. Although the chapter on the economy is the most extreme, it is typical of the book as a whole that extensive discussion of the ancient societies, buttressed with comparison to medieval and modern Europe, is paired with much terser descriptions of African religion, political organization, and law. Finally, ethnographic evidence is used in *LWOS* to report on orality and Africa, but ethnography is not used to present a complex account of orality-and-literacy in a given social formation. Instead, ethnography supplies anecdotes. For example, during a discussion of writing and religion, we are suddenly told about LoDagaa views that funerals are not private affairs (p. 42) but nothing about how the rituals of death are communicatively organized, which is the ostensible topic of the paragraph.

What are we to make of this odd binarism, in which writing and the Ancient Near East are defined and articulated, while orality and Black Africa are left underspecified? What are we to make of a work by an anthropologist in which comparative historical evidence is handled with care, while ethnographic evidence is presented as offhand examples rather than in theoretically informed descriptions and analyses? In order to begin an answer to these questions we will have to delve more deeply into the oral/literate dichotomy. It is a momentous distinction in our received intellectual traditions, and it is a dichotomy that structures most discussions of literacy, including, as we will shortly see, discussions of literacy and cognitive development. For our present purposes, however, in order to draw a provisional balance sheet on the arguments about social development and writing in *LWOS*, let us note the general criticisms. The emphasis on instrumental rationality in development, a technical–rational view of ancient written society, is belied by variation among these ancient societies and the dominance in some of ritual, monumental aspects of inscription over instrumental function. In the comparative exercise, writing is overgeneralized, while orality and "mainly oral" societies are underanalyzed.

We are left unable to gain a dialectical rather than reductionist view of the "consequences of literacy." That is, we are unable to gain insight into the interactions whereby semiotic and social complexity, writing and the organization of society, mutually constitute one another. This problem is also found when we turn to the second major theme: the discussion of rationality, self, and development in the literacy thesis.

Literacy and cognitive development

In addition to broad historical and cultural claims about literacy and social development, arguments about the consequences of reading and writing for cognitive development have also been prominent parts of the literacy thesis. Such arguments have significant historical antecedents. Thinkers of the Enlightenment equated literacy with civilization and the development of reason, as well as with alienation and oppression. James and John Stuart Mill believed in the empowering effects of literacy and schooling on the individual as well as the wider society (Cook-Gumperz, 1986; Donald, 1983). Jean-Jacques Rousseau equated writing and reading with the development of reason but also with alienation from mankind's natural state and the corruptions and oppressions of civilized society (Derrida, 1976c; Rousseau, 1998). In nineteenth-century North America and England, as provision for mass public education became a significant part of the social structure, and as the shocks of industrial capitalism and class conflicts made the question of social order prominent, there emerged what Soltow and Stevens (1981) call "the moral economy of literacy." In this ideological discourse about and within an increasingly schooled society, literacy was equated with morality, economic prospects, and civic virtue. Illiteracy was paired with the opposites: criminality, poverty, and political apathy. In all three cases literacy is seen as an essential attribute of individuals, as a requisite or formative part of a *mentalité* or mode of thought characteristic of a civilized epoch, whatever the associated social consequences. Illiteracy or nonliteracy signified a different state of affairs: a natural mind, undeveloped or needing development for Mill or Rousseau; unsuited for modern life and society in the dominant nineteenth-century view.

As noted earlier, the view that literacy is essential for economic and political development, which depended on a particular cognitive and dispositional infrastructure – a modern self or subjectivity we might say – has been commonly assumed among elites in the post-World War II period. It is reflected, for example in UNESCO reports (Philips, 1979; UNESCO, 1957), as well as in the neoliberal arguments about literacy and the modern workforce made, for example, by the current US and UK governments (Fox and Baker, 1990; MacLeod, 1998; NCEE, 1983). The equation of literacy with civilization and modern states of mind was explicitly addressed in Goody and Watt's (1963) seminal essay. As we have discussed earlier, they had sought in the consequences of reading and writing a motor of history that would explain some of the differences of the West *vis-à-vis* the rest of humankind without recourse to racial hierarchies. They also sought a mechanism accounting for the sociocultural and cognitive developments – such as modern science – that apparently distinguished Western from other large-scale civilizations. In their arguments they postulated key elements of a literate mentality including (1) the capability of thinking historically, that is, being able to construct synthetic historical accounts, and (2) the capability of distinguishing truth from opinion, which involved formalizing modes of reasoning about evidence and justification.

As we have also noted, the "Consequences" essay was followed by a steady stream of work advocating and criticizing the argument (Bloch, 1989; Gough, 1968; Greenfield, 1972; Ong, 1982). Goody himself fleshed out the argument in subsequent monographs (Goody, 1977, 1987). Here, however, we want to focus on two influential works by the psychologist David Olson. These also argue, in a somewhat more focused fashion, for cognitive transformations wrought by literacy, and they are widely regarded by critics as a second pillar of the literacy thesis (Foley, 1997a; Halverson, 1991; Street, 1984).

The first of these works, "From Utterance to Text: the Bias of Language in Speech and Writing" (Olson, 1977), advanced a strong version of the thesis. Picking up the "alphabetization of mind" theme found in Goody and Watt (1963) and in the work of classicists such as Havelock (1963) and Ong (1967), Olson developed one strand of the argument: that the alphabet made the sound structure of language fully explicit. The idea of orthographic explicitness we have already encountered in the discussion of conflicts over writing Tolowa; what Olson does is suggest why explicitness should become a language ideal associated with certain visions of modern life and mind. According to Olson, explicitness of spelling had the consequence that readers become more aware of language form *per se* – of form as well as function or communicative purpose. In addition, and related to the first consequence, literates become more aware of strict or literal meaning, that is, of what the text specifically says, as against pragmatic or contextual meaning, that is, what the given text might be understood as actually meaning, "in so many words," given the circumstances in which it was uttered and heard or composed and read.

This emphasis on language itself as a bearer of propositions, referring to the world but not reducible to empirical knowledge of the world, is for Olson the basis of a scientific attitude toward the world. This attitude is prepared for in the textual practices of seventeenth-century essayists: philosophers such as Montaigne, Locke, and Hume developed a style of explicit argumentation, with propositions advanced and carefully justified, over hundreds of print pages. For Olson this essayist tradition underpins and develops the *mentalité* characteristic of modern science: logical, skeptical, and concerned with counterfactuals (the famous negative hypothesis) rather than common sense. The extended essay represents the apogee of the ideal of an "autonomous text," a text whose meaning is wholly self-contained.

The "bias" from spoken utterance to written text, as repository of meaning, thus results from an historical development. A text-based mode of thought, which is deemed modern and scientific, emerges out of but is distinct from an utterance-bound mode of thought, which is deemed premodern and prescientific. In Olson's account, a central characteristic of this modern mentality is its readiness and ability to distinguish strictly literal meaning, the propositional content and logical entailments of an utterance, from contextual meaning, that is, from all that depends upon circumstances, intertextual associations, and participants' histories and intentions (Hanks, 1996b).

The "bias" argument, with its historical construction of the semiotic underpinnings of a modern style of thought, and its bipolar contrast between text-based and utterance-based modes of thinking, presents a fairly blunt statement of a cognitive "great divide" wrought by literacy. On one side of the divide is the realm of the nonliterate, in which are found direct experience and apprehension of language, a tendency toward concreteness of perception and expression, awareness solely of contextualized meaning, and lack of awareness of language form. On the other side is the realm of the modern, alphabetic, print-based literate, in which there are mediated experience and apprehension of language, a tendency toward abstraction in perception and expression, awareness of autonomous or strictly literal meaning and, concomitantly, of language form as well as language function. There are numerous serious problems with these claims, as critics have noted (Bauman and Briggs, 1990; Foley, 1997a; Halverson, 1991; Street, 1984). Before taking up criticisms, however, let us first consider a major development of Olson's argument, containing significant revisions, which appeared nearly two decades later.

With the publication of *The World on Paper* (Olson, 1994), we have a significantly modulated version of the literacy thesis. *TWOP* contains revisions of earlier claims, which had come in for considerable criticism, but the fundamental line of inquiry remains unchanged. This book also explores the relation between literacy, the history of Protestantism, and the development of science. Now, however, certain emphases are sharpened, while earlier claims are modified or abandoned. As if in complement to Goody's *LWOS*, a monograph on writing, *TWOP* focuses on histories, philosophies, and practices of reading, and not on literacy in general. The earlier and rather simplistic claims about written text and meaning are changed to more perspectival claims about representations. For example, instead of arguing, as in "From Utterance to Text," that Greek and European alphabetic literacy provides a uniquely explicit representation of language, Olson grants that *all* scripts provide representations. What is now at issue is the existence or not of a script-based representation of language, and not a calculation of more or less explicitness. A written textual representation, whether alphabetic or other, is important not because it is explicit in some truth-semantic sense, but because it provides *a* model of language. This model, by its very existence, inclines users (a) to become aware of the dimensions of language represented (say letters and words) and (b) to become troubled by what is not represented, that is, by what is left unsaid.

Olson argues that this different semiotic conundrum, not of more or less explicitness, but of the said and unsaid, develops in European religious-intellectual history in a particular way. In tracing this history, *TWOP* abandons the earlier claim that text in itself represents full, explicit meaning, advancing instead a more nuanced argument that allows for the communicative intentions of a speaking/writing subject. In the history of reading that *TWOP* constructs for the medieval, early modern, and contemporary West, the problem of the said/unsaid leads to textual features becoming increasingly important. The result is not full explicitness, that is, the idealized transparency of written meaning argued for in the earlier essay, in which all "meaning is in the text." Instead, it is a situation in which text features, while not providing full meaning, do provide significant clues, which it is the interpreter's task to flesh out.

In Olson's account, this model of reading-faithful-to-the-text, which emerges out of medieval and early modern religious debates, subsequently informs modern science. This is because it animates the debates in sixteenth- and seventeenth-century science about proper ways to read the "Book of Nature." And the best way to "read" said "Book" is to have careful descriptions. Hence there emerges, from Francis Bacon onwards, a concern with precise records, in an unadorned style, in experimental and other natural scientific inquiry.[5] The modern concern with realistic, replicable representations of the natural world takes form in seventeenth-century representational media: portrait painting, map-making, and botanical drawing. Thus, a "world on paper."

Importantly, the world so known is not just an external world. Interwoven throughout *TWOP* is the argument, found also in the earlier essay, that the cultural–historical literate development is paralleled by ontogenetic development. Olson reports that under experimental conditions, children at the age of five do not reliably distinguish speaker intent from what is said. They focus on the intent, what was palpably meant, and ignore how it may differ from what was strictly said. Seven-year-old children do make such distinctions, revealing an adult-like awareness of internal intention versus public statement. This ontogenetic-and-literate sophistication about communicative intent and internal states versus overt or literal utterance develops into a special form of consciousness. *TWOP*'s concluding chapters argue that literacy develops an internal subjectivity, a consciousness and discourse of thoughts and feeling, both in contemporary children and in the long history of what is often called "Western thought." Olson argues that whereas preliterate Homeric Greeks thought that the passions and intentions came from the outside, literates, beginning with the Classical Greeks and continuing through to our very times, have developed a rich theory of an internal self, a mind, which stands in contrast to the world. In *TWOP* the development of the sense of inwardness, the awareness of internal states, and of other minds, depends crucially on the development of a model of reading, of text and interpretation, which takes as problematic the relation between text and intended meaning.

As the reader can see, the set of arguments comprising "From Utterance to Text" and *TWOP* are frequently thought-provoking. The essay and monograph contain rich descriptions of semiotic means – of utterances, text features, and pictorial representations. In addition, Olson's historical analyses of the "folk philosophies" of language, the speech act assumptions built into dominant European models of reading and the associated theories of sacred and scientific truth, are informative and suggestive. Nonetheless, as with Goody's *LWOS*, the overall argument is burdened with problematic dichotomies. These are overtly presented in the "Utterance" essay and covertly but persistently employed in *TWOP*.

"Oral" versus "literate" is still the fundamental contrast, in 1994 as in 1977, and from this contrast subsidiary claims and distinctions emerge. Consider, for example, Olson's semiotics of absence and presence: these centrally involve the claim that texts are more context-independent, while utterances are more context-bound. This is undoubtedly true of some written texts and spoken utterances – the cliched contrast is between a written academic essay, reasonably independent of context, and a casual conversation with an intimate, likely to be highly dependent on shared background. However, it is just as likely to be untrue of others – say, an electronic chatroom posting, requiring prior context, versus a spoken political speech, made without notes, and not requiring much prior knowledge for understanding. Biber (1988) argues persuasively, by means of extensive quantitative analysis of spoken and written corpora, that the context-dependence or context-independence of texts or utterances is a function of *genre* – socially differentiated uses of language – rather than of the spoken–written contrast *per se*. Critics of Olson have made similar points by developing particular cases (Halverson, 1991; Street, 1984) rather than extensive corpus analysis.[6]

The equation of speech with presence and writing with absence leads to a further problematic issue. In *TWOP* the emergence of representational writing depends on the routinizing of hermeneutics: "the invention of graphic and lexical devices for indicating not only what was said but how it was to be taken" (p. 182). But the account Olson provides of written versus oral hermeneutics is itself flawed. The argument that written hermeneutics must grapple with the unsaid, that is, with the reconstruction of pragmatic intention in the face of the incompleteness of verbal representation, points to a general feature of all communication and not a problem specific to writing. Olson is aware that oral utterances also pose problems of interpretation, and his discussion of "oral hermeneutics" allows that the interpretation of spoken utterances can attract institutionalized expert attention. He strains at credulity, however, when he argues that hermeneutics in an oral context occurs only on special occasions: "In the oral societies we have discussed, interpretation belongs only to particular, marked genres of discourse such as oratory and poetic discourse and ceremonial occasions ... [while] [i]n literate culture, special procedures have evolved for dealing with the information which is lost in the act of transcription, namely, with illocutionary force, the putative audience-directed intentions of the author" (1994, p. 141).

Certainly, in nonliterate societies, or perhaps more precisely, societies in which literacy is not pervasive, some genres and occasions of talk attract greater than usual attention and interpretive anxiety, as the ethnographic record richly attests (Bloch, 1975, 1993; Brenneis and Myers, 1986; Briggs, 1993, 1998; Kulick and Stroud, 1993; Lederman, 1986).[7] And it is also indisputable that in European and contemporary North American institutional traditions, interpretations of written text attract great hermeneutic care; law and theology provide two prime examples (Palmer, 1969). Nonetheless, in between these extremes there is a great deal which is shared, whether in primarily nonliterate or highly literate social formations. Neither the oral nor the written are the special province of the hermeneutic/interpretive impulse. Language, whether spoken or written, requires interpretation, and this may be done casually or with great care. As Swearingen (1988) has noted of the classical German hermeneutic tradition, the relation between oral and written utterances, their intermingling, was a primary concern. It is significant that Havelock's (1963, 1982a) work on Classical and pre-Classical Greek literature and philosophy, often cited in support of the "alphabetizing of the mind" thesis, in fact emphasizes the complex intermingling of oral modes of expression and written composition, together with the interpretive puzzles coexisting, in written and spoken modalities, for historical participants as well as later analysts (see also Illich and Sanders, 1988).

Finally, there are a clutch of issues raised by equating child and nonliterate, adult and literate. Developed in embryonic form in the "Utterance" essay, this equation emerges in full dress in *TWOP*. There it informs the discussion of the development of awareness of illocutionary (practical) versus locutionary (strictly representational) functions in language and, more generally, of the development of self-consciousness. The difficulty with Olson's argument in this case is to know what to make of the research finding that somewhere between the ages of four and seven years children develop a distinction between speaker intention and what is strictly said. We are never told that non-Western societies lack this distinction, but rather that they may be more or less circumspect about expressing it. For example, Olson notes that "[t]he Mangalese [of Highland Papua New Guinea] avoid open displays or discussions of intention" (p. 138). In this matter we may be dealing with capacities that all humans develop, as they develop grammatical competence (Chomsky, 1988), narrative abilities (Gee, 1996), and metalinguistic insight (Lucy, 1993), capacities which are nonetheless culturally shaped in their emphasis and expression. So also we can imagine a universal awareness of communicative intention versus what is strictly said. If such is the case, however, then we must ask in what sense awareness of such a distinction is due to literacy or a particular literate tradition.

A similar set of concerns holds for the closely related claim about literate traditions and the development of internal self-awareness. The link between literate practices and the development of self-consciousness is a longstanding argument among literacy thesis proponents; it supposedly begins with the

Greeks, is revived in the European Renaissance, and reaches full flower in recent modernity (Havelock, 1963; Ong, 1982; Sanders, 1994). There are doubtlessly merits to specific arguments about literacy practices and newly emerging expressions of self. Most of us in the bookish zones of contemporary culture, who read and write a great deal, probably feel that we are fundamentally shaped by these activities. The difficulty, however, is with sweeping claims of causality. For example, the literate inwardness that Olson attributes to modern theories of reading, the historian Marc Bloch (1961), in his classic *Feudal Society*, locates earlier in European history and attributes not to literacy or ideologies of reading *per se* but instead to institutional conflicts, such as the Gregorian Reform, and related developments, such as the revival of jurisprudence. Second, as Schieffelin (1995) has argued, there are numerous ethnographic counterexamples to Olson's view that self-awareness and an explicit conception of mind are specifically modern and Western/literate characteristics (Foley, 1997b; Ochs, 1986; Rosaldo, 1986). Referring to her own work among the Kaluli of Papua New Guinea, Schieffelin argues that children in this traditionally nonliterate society have little trouble distinguishing intentions from what is said but that they learn not to speculate about such intentions. This restraint among the Kaluli, recalling that of the Mangalese, "has to do with local notions of a self which has boundaries and definitions that differ from the Western view" (p. 7). Finally, as Olson acknowledges, recent work in cognitive science (Hirschfield and Gelman, 1994) suggests that the attribution of intentionality and internal states to self and others is something that human minds do very early and consistently. Notwithstanding the variety of ways in which individuals or cultures handle the distinction between communicative intent and overt utterance, a "theory of mind module" (Sperber, 1996, p. 147) may be something generic to humans, rather than the product of experience with a paper world.

A practice alternative to the literacy thesis

We are faced with assessing remarkably steadfast lines of inquiry in the preceding arguments which impute causal or enabling roles to literacy in social and cognitive development. In the work of Jack Goody and David Olson considerable erudition is brought to bear in constructing analyses and argument which range from the fourth millennium BCE to the last decade of this century, from the Ancient Near East to West Africa to the Greek/European axis we typically construct as "the West." The entire literacy thesis rests on sets of dichotomies which flow from a momentous but transhistorical contrast: "written" versus "oral." This contrast carries with it considerable evaluative baggage, for what is striking in the literacy thesis, both in the work of its main proponents and in that of the secondary disseminators, is the way in which the "consequences of literacy" invariably point to elite institutions and outcomes. In Goody's work the dominant institutions of society emerge rationally from practices of writing;

in Olson's, theories of reading produce science as well as modern philosophies of mind.

Perhaps it is therefore understandable that a work devoted to subaltern or "common" lifeways should provide us with an alternative perspective on the literacy debate. In *The Practice of Everyday Life*, de Certeau (1984) sets out to explore the ordinary life, which is typically ignored in favor of the elite life, and the arts and techniques of living, which are often given short shrift in favor of theoretical or industrial-engineering knowledge. This line of inquiry requires an unearthing, deciphering, and reconstruction, for practical or ordinary life, the prosaic or mundane, is usually not the object of systematic description and analysis, and while the practical has its "reason," it is not usually organized along consciously rationalized or systematic lines (Scott, 1998).

The relevance of the neglected ordinary for our thinking about literacy becomes apparent in de Certeau's analysis of "the scriptural economy." Regarding this economy, he argues that the salience of the scriptural, of writing, in modern social formations is due to two developments: one is based on an institutional development – the system of intense, pervasive recording in medicine, public health, education, psychology, and the penal system that Foucault (1975, 1978) called "disciplinary power." The other is a technical–productive development, in particular, printing within the matrix of capitalist development, what Anderson (1991) has called "print-capitalism." Arising from these linked institutional and political–economic developments, the scriptural economy reflects and contributes to double isolations: (1) the separation of "the people" from the bourgeois in matters of culture and sentiment as well as class interest (Davis, 1975; Thompson, 1963) and (2) the separation of "voice" from the written, a fundamental cleavage of knowledge from language, presence from absence, other from self (Derrida, 1976b).

De Certeau argues that in the regulation resulting from this double separation, there is no pure voice. Instead "orality insinuates itself, like one of the threads of which it is composed, into the network – an endless tapestry – of a scriptural economy" (de Certeau, 1984, p. 132).[8] Taking his lead from Derrida's (1976a, d) meticulous explorations of how the contrast oral versus written informs much Enlightenment and post-Enlightenment literature, philosophy, and social theory, de Certeau argues that writing and orality refer not to opposed or equivalent terms but to *complementary* terms. What he means by this is that one term or concept is the necessary counterpart to the other, adding that often-mysterious extra that the better known or the more fully represented somehow lacks. As complementary terms, "the definition of one presupposes that the other remains undefined" (p. 133). In this historical pairing, writing is associated with the productive, the predominant, the articulated, while orality is associated with the inert (e.g. "homeostatic" minds and traditions), the subordinate (contrast the "folk" or "the people" with the bourgeois), and the opaque ("the forgotten history of common people," "the inarticulate masses").

It should be apparent from the foregoing discussion of research on literacy and development that "literacy" and "orality" function in description and analysis as complementary terms, despite their being presented as equivalent terms. In Goody's *LWOS* orality remains the undefined complement, the taken-for-granted background against which the figure of inscription stands forth. So also "Black Africa" provides the diffuse long-distance trade against which the temple and palace economies of the Ancient Near East attain descriptive precision and institutional salience. Ethnography, reporting and recording the unwritten, signifies the subjection and opacity of everyday West Africa by its casual, incidental use in *LWOS*, where it is an anecdotal adornment to the serious work of historical and sociological comparison.

With Olson's "From Utterance to Text" and *TWOP* we have the scriptural economy telling its own sanitized life story. There is print galore in these accounts, but nothing so unruly as capitalist marketeering as motive for, say, the desire to map the world; nothing so unruly as class divisions and conflicts influencing the forward march of theories of reading, the development of genres, or the procedures for quoting others' voices and texts – even though the relation between written text, quotation, and class relations is the subject of a rich philosophical and critical literature (Bakhtin, 1981; Voloshinov, 1973; Williams, 1983). Instead, in this account everything depends on textual precision versus the laxness of utterance. An axis of development connects Classical Greece to modern Europe, and the centuries of oral/written mixing which preceded "literate Greece" (Havelock, 1982a) are given short shrift, as are medieval practices of memory (Carruthers, 1990) and other self-forming discursive practices (Bloch, 1961). Lastly, literate adults stand to children and nonliterates as self-conscious Mind to civilizational Other.

In addition to stressing the inherent asymmetry and nonequivalence of such terms as oral/written, de Certeau argues that their analysis must always be historical: "These [apparent] 'unities' (e.g. writing and orality)...cannot be isolated from the[ir] historical determinations or raised to the status of general categories" (1984, p. 133). What this means in terms of our general argument is that what we denote by terms such as "reading" and "writing" or "speaking" and "hearing" are not the same things in distinct historical periods. What we denote by such terms are communicative practices, defined in changing relation to each other, according to historically specific institutional developments and cultural concerns.

Bearing in mind the injunction that such contrasts "cannot be isolated from the[ir] historical determinations" we can assess another fundamental problem with the literacy thesis. Put bluntly, despite its broad temporal sweep, Goody's *LWOS* is notable for its lack of historical sensibility. Despite the rich record of Ancient Near East ecological and agricultural dynamics, internecine intrigue and dynastic warfare (Larsen, 1988), the only cause of historical development in *LWOS* is a transcendent will to rationalize. Such an approach gives no purchase to basic questions such as why the function of writing is primarily economic in one ancient state and ideological or legitimatizing in another (Harbsmeier, 1988).

Olson's *TWOP* is a more self-consciously historical undertaking, within a more manageable temporal compass. In this case, however, what is not taken into consideration is that the terms of analysis – "reading" versus "hearing" – might be reciprocal and historically variable in their relationship. Olson frequently cites Clanchy's (1979) groundbreaking history of changes in forms of literacy in Norman England. But Olson's analysis gives little indication that the verb "to read" denoted, throughout the medieval period of Clanchy's analysis, a public, collective, and necessarily "oral" event, rather than the private, individual, in-the-head encounter that is central to our modern conception (D. Boyarin, 1993; Howe, 1993). Similarly, we know that various forms of collective or collaborative reading were part of the "popular literacies" that emerged in seventeenth- and eighteenth-century France and England, in work sites, dissenting churches, modest households, and early labor organizations (Chartier, 1989; Cook-Gumperz, 1986; Davis, 1975; Thompson, 1963). But we have no idea whether or how this everyday literacy affected or was affected by the theories of reading that Olson discusses and that he attributes to the dominant theological and scientific debates of the time.

Conclusion: intimations of textuality and power

Attempting to characterize the scriptural economy of the modern, capitalist West, de Certeau posits three defining elements or operations of a "practice of writing": (1) a presumed blank space or tabula rasa, on which inscription operates; (2) a text constructed in or upon this place of blankness; and (3) a strategic intention to dominate or transform. Of this last, de Certeau says: "[writing's] goal is social efficacy . . . either an item of information received from tradition or the outside is collected, classified, inserted into a system and thereby transformed or the rules and models developed in this place . . . [of writing, the blank page] allow one to act on the environment and transform it" (p. 135).

This set of operations, which define a model of modern writing, apply suggestively to parts of *TWOP* and *LWOS*, and they anticipate some of our later arguments. In *TWOP* the unknown world is mapped, via a formalization and mathematization of space, in order to explore and conquer; the practice of literacy transforms childhood – viewed as a cognitive blank slate – into self-aware and self-conscious adulthood. As we will see in subsequent chapters, belief in the morally and cognitively transforming effects of literacy is a theme that runs through early nineteenth-century arguments for universal education as well as late twentieth-century debates about identity and schooling. Although the modern era is not its primary focus, *LWOS* contains several informative discussions of colonial and postliberation national uses of writing in Africa. For European colonial powers, to know "the Dark Continent" was to conquer it, literally as well as figuratively; a profusion of records accompanied the effort to extract material resources, transform farmers and pastoralists into wage laborers, and win young hearts and minds both to Christendom and clerking (Fabian, 1991; Probst, 1993). In our sixth chapter, we analyze how colonial powers in the Americas imputed to their conquered populations a textual blankness – often in the face of considerable evidence otherwise – and by inscribing this blankness with the literal "scriptures" they sought to transform colonial subjects.

We have now discussed the usefulness of de Certeau for thinking about puzzling aspects of the literacy thesis: not just the untenability of arguments but the way in which they are constructed. We have also noted connections between de Certeau's model of writing and arguments we will develop in subsequent chapters. In closing, let us also comment briefly on two general features of his approach which have implications for our subsequent argument.

First, we should recall his questioning of the pure voice, his assertion that "orality insinuates itself... into the network... of a scriptural economy" (p. 132). As noted, this insight and argument are drawn from the philosophical investigations of Derrida who, perhaps more than any contemporary thinker, has problematized our received ways of thinking about "text," "voice," "the people," "writing," and "civilization." In his emphasis on the complexity of orality and its inseparability from writing, de Certeau shares these Derridean themes, and he also shares affinities with recent approaches to the anthropology and history of literacy. However, as we will see in the next chapter, despite advances of situated approaches to literacy, the question of text, of the binary written/oral, is often inescapable even in the most careful ethnographic description. Second, de Certeau's approach is also congenial to our general argument because it takes up the question of *practice*. This emphasis, found also in the work of Bourdieu and Foucault, enables us to inquire into the relation between everyday language use (including literacies) and institutionally regulated use, without forgetting that the one always informs the other. The emphasis on practice, on the everyday as well as the institutional or schooled, is shared with sociocultural approaches to literacy and by the more specific ethnographic tradition we will next discuss. This tradition emerged in response to the literacy thesis and, like de Certeau, its practitioners focus on everyday life, rather than the dominant perspective or major institution, on the ordinary or popular rather than the elite. What de Certeau, or a post-structuralist perspective, also insists is that the question of text and practice cannot be separated from considerations of history and power.

3

SITUATED APPROACHES TO THE
LITERACY DEBATE

Literacy is an activity of social groups, and a necessary feature of some kinds of social organization. Like every other human activity or product, it embeds social relations within
it. And these relations always include *conflict* as well as cooperation. Like language
itself, literacy is an exchange between classes, races, the sexes, and so on.

(Ohmann, 1987, p. 226)

Introduction

From the very beginning, soon after Goody and Watt's (1963) classic paper,
the arguments of the literacy thesis had been challenged. In a volume entitled
Literacy in Traditional Society Goody (1968) reprinted his article with Watt
along with a series of articles which criticized various of the claims made in that
early paper. These included, for example, Gough's article on literacy in Ancient
Indian and China and how those literate traditions undermined arguments about
"alphabetic" and "restricted" literacy (Gough, 1968). During this same period –
from the mid-1960s into the 1970s – a number of anthropologists were engaged
in ground-breaking research based on extensive fieldwork in areas as diverse
as the southern US, Iran, and West Africa. The results of this research, the
strongest ethnographic challenges yet to the Goody–Watt thesis, were to appear
in publications in the early 1980s. This work provided alternative models for
understanding literacy, and has had considerable influence on subsequent work
by educators, anthropologists, and historians. Among the many works from
that period contributing to our understanding of literacy, three stand out as the
most influential: Shirley Brice Heath's *Ways with Words* (1983); Brian Street's
Literacy in Theory and Practice (1984); and Ruth Finnegan's *Literacy and
Orality* (1988). The influence of these works is pervasive and clearly seen in the
subsequent important collections edited by Goelman, Oberg, and Smith (1984),
Schieffelin and Gilmore (1986), Kintgen, Kroll, and Rose (1988), Barton and
Ivanic (1991), Boyarin (1993a), Street (1993), and Prinsloo and Breier (1996).

While all of these researchers share Goody's concern to address the neglect
within anthropological studies of serious attention to reading and writing in society, they differ with him in fundamental ways. Where Goody focuses on the nature of literacy and its consequences – cognitive, cultural, and historical – these

34

writers begin by asking what reading and writing are for, how they are conducted, and how they are judged. While at first this may seem a subtle distinction, its importance is evident in the approaches to the study of literacy to be discussed below. It should be emphasized that for Goody and Watt and like contributors to the literacy thesis, what literacy is in itself is noted in general terms and primary attention is given to its consequences. The nature of literacy, once established, is treated as fixed. Wherever it is found, it will have the same essential character. It is, in short, a stable technology, relatively unchanging in any given social environment, although its distribution within a society or region may run the range from restricted to pervasive.

The anthropologists whose work we will consider in this chapter take a different approach. They come to a definition of literacy inductively through careful fieldwork on "the *social meaning of literacy*: that is, the roles these abilities [reading and writing] play in social life; the varieties of reading and writing available for choice; the contexts for their performance; and the manner in which they are interpreted and tested, not by experts, but by ordinary people in ordinary activities" (Szwed, 1981, p. 14, original emphasis). This perspective, from an anthropologist, is not in the least surprising. To discover the meaning of activities in the lives of "ordinary people" is a *sine qua non* of anthropological method.

Granting the value of this methodological orientation, we would argue, nonetheless, that it is not sufficient simply to proceed inductively and with a focus on everyday life. In order to anticipate some of the complexities which "ethnographies of literacy" face, let us recall de Certeau's comments on writing and "the ordinary." De Certeau views the realm of ordinary lives and ordinary people as a historically constituted domain profoundly shaped by its separation from elite classes, dominant institutions, and systematic–formal procedures. In this realm of situated, provisional ways of living, mundane practices of speaking and writing are densely intertwined – and typically either ignored by or in opposition to institutionally motivated and recognized literacies.[1] That is, questions of power and knowledge are unavoidable aspects of "the ordinary." In addition, let us recall that de Certeau's theme of the unavoidable intertwining of speech and writing was first developed by Derrida (1976a, d), who has made his own contributions to an anthropology of literacy, albeit, typically, by pointing out the problematic nature of received categories and the difficulties of analysis and description, rather than by advancing a positive research program.

In an essay entitled "The Violence of the Letter: from Lévi-Strauss to Rousseau," Derrida (1976c) examines very closely a famous description by Lévi-Strauss (1964) of the introduction of writing to the Nambikwara, an isolated hunting and gathering society living deep in the Amazon. Derrida's criticism of Lévi-Strauss' account contains several points that fit well with our prior discussion of Tolowa conflicts over alphabets and "original" writing, and these points are even more germane to full-fledged ethnographies of literacy.

First, he argues that anthropological analysis, however well intentioned, is suffused with confrontation and power, signified in Lévi-Strauss' account through an imagery of violence, military campaigns, trickery, and domination. Second, he argues that Lévi-Strauss shares with philosophical forebears such as Rousseau a tendency to sentimentalize non-Europeans, to depict them in scenes of unlettered primitive harmony which contrast with the inauthenticity and conflict of overly civilized European literates. Third, he argues that rigid assumptions about what is writing and what speech ignore evidence of inscription practices among "nonliterate" peoples, such as the Nambikwara, contributing to a corollary tendency to see them as essentially different, as a primitive "Other" to our cultured, civilized selves. What de Certeau's and Derrida's arguments remind us is that conceptions and practices of literacy and orality are inextricably intertwined, historically variable, and fraught with the inequalities and power relations of social life. We should see these arguments as cautionary for an ethnography of literacy as well as critical of the literacy thesis.

Having registered these concerns, let us return to Szwed's proposals for literacy research. Perhaps reacting to the neglect of "ordinary life" in literacy studies prior to the 1980s, Szwed makes very strong methodological claims for ethnographic approaches. As he puts it: "One method of studying literacy – ethnography – represents a considerable break with most past research. I would contend that ethnographic methods, in fact, are the only means for finding out what literacy really is and what can be validly measured" (Szwed, 1981, p. 20). The research on literacy discussed in this chapter will provide us with three examples from which to assess Szwed's claims for the strength of ethnographic methods. The models proposed by Heath, Finnegan, and Street are what we will term "practice models." Although they deal with literacy in action, with the practices of literacies, they were not initially formulated in dialogue with the post-structuralist practice theory we have treated in earlier chapters.[2] The Heath, Finnegan, and Street models focus on what we can do with literacy, what we can accomplish with the use of scripts and texts; they shift emphasis from the consequences of literacy for society to the study of its uses by individuals and its functions in particular groups. They view literacy not as an advance over oral uses of language, but as complementary to it. Literacies in context are situated within the realm of everyday life, and in such quotidian realms the written interpenetrates but does not supersede the oral; or, we might say that oral language is the context for written language.

Heath

In *Ways with Words* (1983), an extensive, nearly decade long (1969–1978) study of three communities in the Piedmont region of the southeastern United States, Shirley Brice Heath addresses a lacuna in the research literature. Goody had called for examining "the concrete context of written communication" in traditional societies in order to assess "the nature of societal and cultural factors on literacy and its uses" (1968, p. 4). Heath's "ethnography of literacy" extends the analysis to modern societies as she addresses questions central to the work of anthropologists, sociologists, historians, educators, and others concerned with literacy:

> Where, when, how, for whom, and with what results are individuals in different social groups of today's highly industrialized society using reading and writing skills? . . . Does modern society contain certain conditions which restrict literacy just as some traditional societies do? If so, what are those factors, and are groups with restricted literacy denied benefits widely attributed to full literacy, such as upward socioeconomic mobility, the development of logical reasoning, and access to the information necessary to make well-informed political judgments? (Heath, 1982a, p. 93)

As a formal means of describing literate practices, Heath adopts Hymes' (1972) sociolinguistic analysis of speech events and refashions it to empirically examine "the actual forms and functions of oral and literate traditions and co-existing relationships between spoken and written language." For Heath the "literacy event" is "any occasion in which a piece of writing is integral to the nature of participants' interactions and their interpretive processes" (1982a, p. 93). She wishes to discover the "socially established rules for verbalizing what [participants] know from and about the written material. Each community has rules for socially interacting and sharing knowledge in literacy events" (Heath, 1982c, p. 50).[3]

The purpose of the descriptions of literate practices comprising literacy events is to make comparison across contexts possible. Heath was interested in particular in comparing language socialization with language expectations encountered in formal education settings in three distinct communities "in a moderate-sized city of the Southeastern United States" (Heath, 1982b, p. 105). Heath investigated questioning at home and at school in the three communities she studied: "Roadville," a white working-class neighborhood; "Trackton," an African-American working-class neighborhood; and "Townspeople," a composite portrait of middle-class town residents of both ethnicities. In what follows, we will focus on a two-way contrast between Trackton and Townspeople. This will enable us to see the sharpest differences in language socialization and literacy practices which are valued and devalued in formal schooling.

In Heath's words Trackton was "an all-black residential group whose members identified themselves as a community both spatially and in terms of group membership"(1982b, p. 106), "whose older generations have been brought up on the land, either farming their own land or working for other landowners . . . [and have] in the past decade . . . found work in the textile mills" (1982c, p. 57). Heath had been invited into this community by a number of the older residents who were concerned that children in the community "were not doing better in school" (1982b, p. 106). Because Heath's research took place after legal rulings had forced desegregation of the public schools nationwide, white teachers who had formerly taught all white classes were now facing mixed classes of blacks and whites. Trackton parents reported that their children hated school and "felt there was little meaningful communication going on between teachers and their children in the classroom" (1982b, p. 107). The children's teachers, Heath found, agreed there were problems with communication and expressed a desire to understand the reasons behind these problems. Teachers felt that many students could not answer even the most basic of questions. Some accepted as plausible the explanation provided by research in linguistics that differences in the linguistic structures and uses of nonstandard English (Black English) and standard English caused difficulties in communication. Others believed: "the breakdown lay in the nature of interactions called for in school. The interactional tasks between teacher and child called for particular kind of responses from students . . . It was difficult, however, for teachers to pin down exactly what was called for in these interactions; thus they felt they could not help their students achieve success in these tasks" (1982b, p. 107).

   Heath suggested that, along with herself, the teachers collect data on their own uses of language at home with their preschool children. In addition, Heath was able to observe and transcribe the uses of language among children in Trackton "extensively over a period of five years" (1970–1975), including especially children who were beginning school. She was therefore in a position to *compare* the uses of language in and out of school and to note any difficulties potentially stemming from communication breakdown. However, careful research precluded an exclusive focus on preschool and early school-age children to the neglect of parents and other adult caregivers. Instead, Heath observed adults in a variety of encounters within and outside Trackton in interaction with teachers and other community members. This procedure was essential to ethnographic method, and key to her study:

> The context of language use, including setting, topic, and participants (both those directly involved in the talk and those who only listened), determined in large part how community members, teachers, public service personnel, and fellow workers judged the communicative competence of Trackton residents. *Proper handling of questions was especially critical, because outsiders often judged the intelligence and general competence of individuals by their responses to questions and by the questions they asked.*
> (1982b, pp. 108–109, emphasis added)

   As Heath's research ensued she discovered a disjunction between the uses and functions of questions within Trackton and in a number of settings outside Trackton. This provided a clue as to why Trackton children might be having difficulty negotiating the routines of school classrooms where: "questions had several functions relatively rarely used by residents [of Trackton]" (1982c, p. 109). Although *Ways with Words* is a classic ethnographic study of literacy, it gives considerable attention to language use generally, such as the use of questions. There are several reasons for this approach, two of which merit comment.

First, Heath wanted to understand literacy acquisition in those communities as part of general language acquisition. In any society in which literate practices are observed, even in those Goody would label "restricted," development of communicative competence involves the acquiring of some competence in literacy. That is, even an individual labeled "illiterate" by the established norms of that society has some knowledge of the uses and functions of literacy as part of his or her communicative competence. In becoming a competent member of a social group, one does not learn the forms of communicating common to family or community or society as separate packages which are only later applied to other arenas. Instead, the acquisition of communicative competence proceeds through immersion in cultural practices that include oral and written language modalities. Thus, Heath concludes from her observations in the homes in Trackton that:

In effect, these children achieved some mastery of environmental print *without being taught*. They learned names of cereals or the meanings of railroad names, not because these were pointed out each time or because their letters were sounded out, but because of their juxtaposition with a spoken word or an action that carried meaning. The relevant context or set of circumstances of the material was often recalled by the children when the word later appeared in a different context. For these children, *comprehension was the context rather than the outcome of learning to read*. They acquired the skill without out formal instruction or reading-readiness activities generally used by school-oriented parents with their preschoolers. (Heath, 1986, pp. 20–21, emphasis added)

Second, at the time of Heath's research there was little research on questions and questioning as such, although much language acquisition research reported that question forms comprised a bulk of the language input preschool children receive from adult caregivers. It had also been demonstrated that the uses of questions in language socialization varied cross-culturally (E. Goody, 1977; Schieffelin and Ochs, 1986). It was also known from the study of discourse patterns in school classrooms that the structure of lessons followed an Initiation–Response–Evaluation pattern, in which the teacher, controlling the flow of classroom discourse within the lesson, begins by asking a student a question, usually one to which she already possesses the answer. The student's response is compared with the expected or desired response and then evaluated by the teacher (Cazden, 1988; Mehan, 1979). Since questions comprise a most substantial portion of language interaction in classrooms, Heath's focus was warranted.

In light of such findings about questions, their cultural variability and institutional regulation, it is noteworthy that the teachers in Heath's study had informed her that students did not or could not respond appropriately to even the "simplest" questions or instructions. A comparison of the question forms used by teachers with their own preschool children versus those used by Trackton adults with their children revealed significant differences. What Heath discovered was that among the middle-class teachers of preschool children – that is, among "Townspeople" – questions comprised the largest proportion of the total utterances in adult–child interactions, near or above 50 percent. In addition, these parents used questions often when reading to children, even when (perhaps especially so) children did not themselves read. For example, the stimuli provided by the pictures in children's books would occasion a spate of questions of the type "in which the questioner has the information requested of the addressee" (1982b, p. 111). Heath summarized teachers' language use at home with their preschoolers as follows:

[Teachers] used questions to teach their children what they should attend to when looking at a book ("What's that?" "Where's the puppy?" "What does he have in his hand?"). The children were taught to label . . . to search out pieces of pictures, to name parts of the whole, and to talk about these out of context. As the children grew older, adults used questions to add power to their directives ("Stop that! Did you hear me?") and to call particular attention to the infraction committed ("Put that back. Don't you know that's not yours?"). Adults saw questions as necessary to train children, to cause them to respond verbally, and to be trained as conversational partners.   (p. 113)

But in Trackton Heath was to discover uses of language not in accord with those found in Townspeople homes or school classrooms. First, "questions addressed by adults to children occurred far less frequently in Trackton than in the homes of teachers" (p. 114) possibly because "adults did not attempt to engage children as conversational partners until they were seen as realistic sources of information and competent partners in talk" (p. 114). In Trackton questions were not directed at preverbal infants; adults chose other adults or verbally competent conversational partners and made statements about the infant to them. Importantly, such statements "conveyed the same information as questions directed by teachers to their children. Trackton adults would say of a crying preverbal infant: 'Sump'n's the matter with that child.' The equivalent in the teacher's home would be to direct a question to the child: 'What's the matter?' 'Does something hurt you?' 'Are you hungry?' " (p. 114).

   Such observed differences cannot be attributed to a diminished level of "linguistic input" to children in the home. Rather, as Heath notes, although "In Trackton, adults almost always had someone else around to talk to . . ." (p. 114) "children were not excluded from activities of adults or from listening to their conversations on any topic" (p. 115). However, there was a cultural prohibition on divulging information to nonintimates. Outside their home, on a porch or in the yard, children might be addressed by those not of the community, that is, strangers, who had business in Trackton. When, say, a utility serviceman would approach a child and ask his name he would most often receive no verbal response from the child. To answer a stranger was negatively sanctioned, and children who responded to outsiders' questions "would later be chastised by adults of the community. Children learned very early that it was not appropriate to report on the behavior of their intimates to strangers whose purposes in the community were not known. Likewise, outside the community, when non-intimates asked information about the children's family or living arrangements, they usually got no answer" (p. 115).

Here we can see a cultural influence on the school teachers' and other school personnel's assessment of the language ability of the black children of Trackton. Should a teacher ask a child, "Do you have any brothers or sisters?" and receive no answer, she would more than likely judge the child as "nonverbal" if not "a little slow." The child, however, would be behaving in accord with the rules of social interaction gained through preschool socialization. Rather than an uncooperative child, or one who does not know the meaning of the question, what we have is a child who is behaving appropriately in the context of her own Trackton upbringing. Difficulties arise for the child because her ways of behaving are not considered appropriate for the classroom by those making authoritative judgments. They do not meet teacher expectations, and, since the teacher was not knowledgeable regarding language uses in Trackton, she was likely to judge the child negatively. The question for the child does not have the same meaning as it does for the teacher.

Heath had found that the meanings of questions and their uses for preschool children in Trackton differed dramatically from those for preschoolers in the homes of Townspeople.[4] Not surprisingly, they differed also from typical questioning in school classrooms. The school thus became a site for experiencing new uses for questions in the context of learning school routines. If teachers' talk contained question types and questioning patterns novel to Trackton children, but similar to the children of Townspeople (and others of the same socioeconomic class background as the teachers), this placed an additional burden on Trackton children. When teachers in the early grades asked seemingly innocuous questions of their charges in order to get basic information ("What's your name?" "Where do you live?") children from Trackton answered with silence or gave nominal answers.[5] In short, Heath found that for Trackton children, "Their communicative competence in responding to questions in their own community had very little positive transfer value to [their] classrooms" (1982b, p. 123).

Heath's study of questioning demonstrates the strengths of ethnographic method in application to contemporary problems. By comparing the uses of questions in two groups of children both in their homes and at school, she was able to provide teachers with one explanation for the perceived failure of Trackton children at school. Rather than a deficiency in language-using abilities, Trackton children's language and social behaviors were manifestations of the rules of communicative competence acquired successfully in their community. They had acquired a set of question forms and uses *and* the meanings associated with them; these were competent children responding as they had learned was appropriate. But judged by the expectations and standards of the school, their responses were deemed inappropriate. Had the teacher's preschoolers been placed in settings in Trackton, their language behavior, appropriate in their own homes, would have been inappropriate in the African-American neighborhood – though without the same institutional consequences.

If Trackton children were being judged "non-responsive," "slow," even "stupid," how would this affect their acquisition of the school literacy necessary for academic success? Is it legitimate to extrapolate from such oral evidence to literate practices and activities? Adherents of the Goody–Watt thesis might argue "no" for they uphold a rigid categorical distinction between literate and oral means of communication, even in societies where both are present. Such rigidity is not, however, supported by Heath's ethnographic evidence. Uses of literacy can and do vary widely within the same society and are intertwined with oral language practices. Further, in their development and use, specific literate practices in home and community may or may not exhibit congruence with school uses.

In a widely cited article based on the same research, "What No Bedtime Story Means," Heath (1982c) describes "ways of taking meaning from written sources" in three communities: "Maintown" ("Townspeople"), "Roadville" and "Trackton." She then compares these communities' literacy practices with "*mainstream* ways [which] exist in societies around the world that rely on formal educational systems to prepare their children for participation in settings involving literacy" (1982c, p. 50, original emphasis).

Heath's study found that children in Maintown (Townspeople) homes were enmeshed in a print-rich environment, books were housed in bookcases, and the children had toys and pictorial representations of characters from books in their rooms. Very early, "as early as six months of age," children could "*give attention to books and information derived from books*" (p. 52, original emphasis). Among this group, Heath found culturally "mainstream" ways of taking meaning from text. Children beyond age two engaged in "book talk." They invented stories by using "*their knowledge of what books do to legitimate their departures from 'truth'*" (p. 52, original emphasis). While these stories may have been about objects in the children's real world, they were not about actual events, that is, having learned what storybooks do, the children then "fictionalized" their world. This inventiveness was encouraged by the adults around them as exhibiting creativity. There was, then, a bond forged between story reading and story telling.

As children reach the age of three, the nature of their participation in this literacy event [book reading] changed from one of an active questioner or question-answerer who interrupted the story flow at times throughout the reading, to an active listener, becoming a "proper" audience for the reader. Heath tells us that "adults jump[ed] at openings their children give them for pursuing talk about books and reading" (p. 53). From such responses to their behavior, children learned the importance of book reading and specific types of narration, those patterned on story structures of children's books. These do not vary widely from those of "the mainstream pattern" so necessary for school success, for what children face in school classrooms are questions familiar from these bedtime story events:

> In each individual reading episode in the primary years of schooling, children must move through what-explanations before they can provide *reason-explanations* or *affective commentaries*. Questions about why a particular event occurred or why a specific action was right or wrong came at the end of primary-level reading lessons, just as they come at the end of bedtime stories. Throughout the primary grade levels, what-explanations predominate, reason-explanations come with increasing frequency in the upper grades, and affective comments most often come in the extra-credit portions of the reading workbook or at the end of the list of suggested activities in text books across grade levels. This sequence characterizes the total school career.   (p. 54, original emphasis)

In short, during the entirety of their preschool years, mainstream children have engaged in "practice sessions in literacy development" for what they will later encounter in the classroom (Cochran-Smith, 1984).

But what of children from nonmainstream homes? Although Heath provides comparative data from two working-class communities, Roadville and Trackton, the latter has already been described and will be the focus of our comparison.[6] We have already seen significant differences in the patterns and meaning of questions in Trackton when compared to those in school. Were there significant differences found as well in the uses of literacy? In Trackton Heath had "recorded the literacy behaviors of approximately 90 individuals in community, work, school, and home settings" (1986, p. 19). She was particularly interested here, as in Roadville and Maintown, with "how the adults participated in preschoolers' experience with print" (p. 20). What she discovered was that in Trackton parents did not teach their children to read: "the adults did not read to the children, or consciously model or demonstrate reading and writing behaviors for them. Instead, the adults let the children find their own reading and writing tasks . . . and they [the adults] made their instructions fit the requirements of the tasks" (p. 20). The effect of this was that *prior to attending school children taught themselves to read. Their reading tasks were set by everyday life and these tasks were completed with the support of that context.*

One of the notable differences between school literacy and that encountered in Trackton was that reading for adults "was social activity, involving more that the individual reader. Solitary reading, in fact, was often interpreted as an indication that one had not succeeded socially" (p. 21). In schools, in comparison, sustained silent reading, an individual activity, is encouraged; in fact, it is promoted as the normal way to engage text (Bialostok, 1999). In addition, Heath discovered recurring uses of literacy in Trackton which both overlapped and differed from Maintown (and Roadville) patterns.[7] Perhaps most significant, the Trackton types did "not include those uses – critical, aesthetic, organizational, and recreational . . . – usually highlighted in school-oriented discussions of literacy uses" (1986, p. 22).

What we learn from Heath's work is that there is no universality to literacy; there are many literacies. To describe only one set of uses and functions (those associated with school or essayist literacy) is to miss the myriad other uses and functions found among the literacies of communities throughout the world. This is no mere academic issue. An acceptance of Olson-like essayist literacy as normative condemns those whose ways of making meaning and of taking meaning from text vary from the norm to a perpetual struggle to legitimate their own practices.

Szwed, in calling for ethnographic studies of literacy, had suggested that researchers emulate the methods of linguists by observing and recording in naturalistic settings the means and materials used in all reading and writing activities engaged in by members of a specific community. "The end product . . . should be an inventory of at least one American sub-community's literacy needs and resources, and should provide both the model for making other similar surveys elsewhere" (Szwed, 1981, p. 23). Heath's study of Roadville, Trackton, and Maintown carried out Szwed's suggestion admirably. *Ways with Words* is a major accomplishment, one that has yet to be surpassed in depth or influence. Her ethnographic methodology uncovered the meanings of literate practices that had to be observed in order to be made manifest. Her reports allowed for cross-cultural comparisons to be made easily and effectively. And, not least, the evidence mustered to demonstrate differing literacies and the complex mix of oral and literate means of communication in the communities undermines any claim to a set of universal uses and functions of literacy.

Notably lacking from Szwed's program for an ethnography of literacy, however, was any direct mention of power dynamics. It is present only in that class stratification and ethnic and racial differences in complex societies presuppose power relations. Heath's study exhibits the same neglect. Although *Ways* has been widely praised, critics have also noted that it avoids central questions of power in American society (de Castell and Walker, 1991; Rosen, 1985). Readers of *Ways* are often shocked when they reach the book's "Epilogue." After more than 350 pages of detailed description of language use, community life, and intelligent educational innovation, readers are suddenly told of federal and state-level political forces which reversed these innovations. Part of the Reagan Revolution as it unfolded in the American South, these forces removed the institutional space for educational reform, scattering and demoralizing local efforts at school-based desegregation. Readers are surprised because these actors – state legislatures and education departments – are absent from Heath's analysis until the very (and bitter) end.

One point persuasively argued by Foucault in various of his studies, including those of schooling systems (1975), is that power and knowledge are intimately wed. In the neoliberal movement for educational reform that has swept the US since the 1980s, beginning early in the Carolinas that Heath describes, we see a striking confirmation of the maxim that the ability to set standards – in this case what will count as literacy, how it will be assessed, etc. – is a very effective form of state power (Marvin, 1988). In the 1980s rollback of classroom reforms that elevated the everyday knowledge of African-American families and communities to "school knowledge," we can see an old American pattern, especially sharp in the South, of excluding, downgrading, and regulating the literacy practices of African Americans. We will further discuss the issue of state power and racial domination in chapter 4; here we may note merely that it is a significant absence in Heath's analysis.

At issue is something more profound than privilege or disprivilege. Rather, it is how along with the distribution of material resources, there is also a distribution of persons – of kinds of persons and social subjectivities. If we consider again the differing use of questioning in language socialization found in Trackton and among Townspeople, we have a useful illustration of what Foucault called "micro-power." Micro-power consists of small techniques – for example, ways of inducing, recording, and assessing behaviors – which were used to establish truths about individuals and groups so that they could be both trained in ways of being (and speaking) and positioned within quantitative series. In Foucault's account (1975, 1978), micro-power was fundamental to the new forms of power emerging with modern institutions, such as schools, clinics, and prisons, and central among the procedures of micro-power were questioning and the examination. However, the tactics of micro-power could also migrate, in unpredictable ways, to other social domains, for example, the workplace or domestic realm.

In the case at hand, we may say that the power-knowledge techniques of questioning, pervasive in schooling, have deeply penetrated the child-rearing practices of Maintowners, with the result that such children are "enabled." They are ready for questions from nonintimate adults about a range of activities and text-artifacts and often involving a fundamental artifice. Recall that school questioning is often rhetorical, for the adult already knows the answer. Rather, the questioning is part of an incessant testing, with which the child eagerly complies.

Trackton children, on the other hand, are socialized to a different fate. The discursive strategies of schooling have not penetrated as deeply into their homes or daily lives. They are in this way, and others, unprepared for school, and they are thus "disabled" when their nonresponse to questions is taken as evidence of ignorance or a difficult nature. Their practice of everyday life, in de Certeau's sense, has ingrained in them a different set of expectations regarding intimates and how they address one another, and a greater reserve when dealing with nonintimates, in institutional or neighborhood settings. In their case, discursive strategies which are enabling in the everyday lifeworld are disabling in the school encounter.

As Foucault, de Certeau, and other practice theorists such as Bourdieu have long argued, techniques of micro-power are related, in the final analysis, to broader questions of economic production, resource distribution, and the fate of populations. We will take up the question of that relationship later, for now it suffices for our purposes to have introduced the idea that power has multiple forms. It is not simply coercion or external force, nor even control of organizational standards; rather, it is also manifest in face-to-face exchanges, in intimate judgments, and in procedures of teaching and learning.

Finnegan

In a series of papers published as *Literacy and Orality*, Ruth Finnegan (1988) also challenged the generalities of the literacy thesis as articulated by Goody, Watt, and others. In this work, Finnegan was concerned with the many forms of communication found within any society or community, the technologies associated with them, and any claims as to how specific technologies such as writing or print affect the nature of thinking and the formation of worldview. Such claims are subjected to careful analyses, and counter-claims are made based on ethnographic examples from both Western and non-Western societies. These analyses complicate our understanding of writing and reading practices and undermine the neat, delineated categories "oral" and "literate" presupposed by adherents of the literacy thesis.

For such adherents, there are a chain of associations linking state civilizations to sophisticated thinking to literacy. First, the efficiency of writing-as-recording makes it possible to administer contemporary state societies, a point which Finnegan also concedes:

consider the crucial role of writing for the kinds of activities we tend to take for granted in modern society: publishing and implementing laws; issue of passports, driving licences or international vaccination certificates; circulation of newspapers and books; publicity and information leaflets; Open University and other distance teaching; postal service; medical prescriptions; country-wide examination systems; civil service and regular administrative functions.   (1988, p. 18)

Such a list points to the use of writing to *regulate* the behaviors of individuals in society; the power of the state over individual lives is implicated in each of the items listed. In addition, the processes of administration rest on the legitimacy of state power, and the ability to *write* (and *interpret*) history is of often of paramount importance in establishing such legitimacy. Any historical interpretation will require abstract reasoning ability, and supporters of the Goody–Watt thesis claim that literacy is *a necessary precondition for abstract thought*. They argue that due to a lack of literacy, those on the other, distant side of the Great Divide live in an existential present, their thinking characteristically simple and concrete. Although often challenged by anthropologists since Boas (1911), this claim has many adherents still.

Finnegan's ethnographic work with the Limba of Sierra Leone, carried out over a fifteen-month period in the early 1960s, provides a clear counterargument to any attempt to brand the thinking of nonliterate peoples as simple, concrete, and unreflective. The Limba, a tribal society of predominantly rice farmers, inhabit an area of approximately 1,900 square miles in the north of the West African nation of Sierra Leone.[8] Because the territory of the Limba is narrow, "seldom more than twenty miles across" (1988, p. 46), the Limba are in contact with many neighboring peoples who speak different languages. Many Limba who live near the areas in contact with non-Limba-speaking neighbors "are often bilingual, or at least able to understand a considerable amount of the neighboring language or languages" (p. 46). Also, due to the fact that many Limba travel extensively there is an increased awareness and knowledge of languages other than Limba, not to mention the fact that people speaking languages other than Limba live in settlements within Limba territory. As well, although "the Limba themselves are by and large non-literate, they have some contact with Arabic literacy, and there are a few elementary Koranic schools within Limba country, run and attended by members of the Fula and Mandingo communities" (p. 46).

One may conclude from this brief "linguistic survey" that the Limba must be aware of the place of their language as only one among many. Such awareness allows a heightened sense of distinctiveness of the Limba language among its speakers. Like peoples around the world, the Limba use their language as "the main mark by which they distinguish themselves from the many other peoples in the area" (p. 47). The Limba language and the Limba people are one:

> The native term is *hulimba ha*, "the Limba language." The prefix *hu-* is commonly used not only for terms referring to speech, words or language but as the normal prefix used to transform a root word into an abstract noun. *Hulimba ha* can therefore be interpreted to mean not only the Limba language but Limbahood itself. (p. 47)

And further:

> by their common use of *hu-* to turn any word into an abstract noun or concept . . . [t]he Limba are well aware of the possibility of considering a linguistic formulation in itself detached from its direct social or personal context. (p. 50)

This interpretation was validated numerous times over the course of Finnegan's research when the Limba explained her presence among them as " 'she has come to learn *hulimba ha*' " and since "[e]verything that connects directly with language is often assumed to be distinctively Limba . . . I was . . . continuously and spontaneously instructed in new vocabulary, stories, songs and the requisite greetings in the various dialects" (p. 47).

The language environment – Limba-speaking people living among or near others who speak mutually unintelligible languages – brings a heightened awareness of language use. The Limba are "self-conscious about their own language" (p. 48); they discuss differences among dialects of Limba as well as comparisons with other languages. The Limba use language self-consciously for joking and amusement, taking pleasure, for example "in representing bird cries in words . . . the *kokoro koo koo* of the cock at dawn" (p. 49).

The Limba also possess an elaborated philosophy of language and of life centered around the concept of "speaking," *gboŋkoli*. "Speaking" is central to Limba life, both in their everyday goings-on and in their formal events marked by rituals of initiation, or any number of ceremonial occasions. The congeries of meanings associated with *gboŋkoli* and related terms and phrases is large, covering all aspects of social, political, and religious life. It is in "speaking," or maybe speaking well, that the stability and harmony of Limba life is assured. To understand how this is so we need at least a brief discussion of *gboŋkoli*, "speak," whose root meaning, Finnegan tells us, "seems to be to speak formally, responsibly and carefully, most typically in the context of a formal law case or transaction. 'Speaking' is the quality of a chief in his role of reconciling people and thus bringing peace to individuals and to the chiefdom as a whole" (p. 53). Finnegan's findings echo those of others with knowledge of tribal society in Africa. Chinua Achebe, for example, points out that among the Kikuyu the word for "chief" is "good talker" (1975, p. 42):

["Speaking"] is also a desired attribute and activity of anyone with authority over others – a father "speaks between" his children, a household head between his dependents, an older boy among his juniors, a respected senior wife, among her younger co-wives, a *bondo* (women's society) leader among her followers. Formality of speech covers not only speaking to reconcile people but also the whole series of interchanges of formal thanks, requests, offers or announcements which occur in almost every recognized relationship . . . In all kinds of transactions, whether those to do with farm work, dances, political or judicial proceedings, initiations, ceremonies or negotiations for marriage, formal "speaking" is an essential part of the proceedings.   (Finnegan, 1988, p. 53)

The ethnographic evidence presented thus far provides ample ammunition to debunk the claims of those, such as Olson or Goody and Watt, who would view nonliterates as incapable of abstract thought, or incapable of a detached view of language; who see "the primitive as unreflective and unselfconscious" (p. 50). On Finnegan's account, the Limba philosophy of language is the embodiment of a clearly articulated abstract understanding of what language is (language as entity), and what can be done with it (its instrumental uses). The Limba are well aware of how their language unites them as a people and of how it distinguishes them from others.

At this juncture, however, one might ask: "What does all of this have to do with literacy?" We would suggest that it is relevant because assumptions about literacy inform social judgments and vice versa. As Finnegan notes, even a casual observer of social life would note significant differences between everyday life among the Limba and life in any contemporary industrial or postindustrial society – and such an observer might "put down many of such differences to the crucial distinction between literate and non-literate cultures" (p. 56). How-ever, it is not a question of "literate" and "nonliterate" but rather of attending closely to what a people actually know and the reasons they know what they do. As Finnegan argues, Limba "awareness of the relativity of their own lan-guage . . . seems to have little to do with the question of literacy or non-literacy. The crucial point, rather, seems to be their constant contact with speakers of other languages" (p. 56). In this regard, the Limba compare favorably with the "average Englishman who, notoriously, has little direct experience of lan-guage other than his own – and this *in spite of an educational system which stresses both literacy and instruction in or about a non-English language*" (p. 56, emphasis added). Thus, Finnegan concludes, even though the availabil-ity of written sources may aid the development of an abstract meta-awareness of language, "it is neither a sufficient nor a necessary condition" (p. 56).

But even if we grant this argument about the sources of metalinguistic aware-ness, what of the relation between literate traditions and the capacity for spec-ulative thought, for the development of a philosophy? Here the ethnographic evidence presented by Finnegan for the Limba leaves no doubt that tribal peo-ples have the capacity for philosophy and that literacy is not necessary for the development of philosophic thought.[9] One might further, however, take the po-sition that writing allows for certain *types* of speculative thought to appear and develop (Goody, 1982). Countering this argument, Finnegan points to ancient Greece as an epitome reminding us of

the fact that writing [there] was not universal, it was not the silent, remote communication that we now tend to regard it. The Greeks read aloud and much of their well-known philosophy was delivered in the form of lectures and discussions. The type of literacy was something very different from that of contemporary Europe and possibly not at all the same thing as that envisaged by modern writers who contrast the literacy of modern "developed" societies with the non-literacy of African cultures.
(pp. 56–57; see also Havelock [1982a] and Lloyd [1990] on this point)

Because the presence or absence of literacy seems an easily recognizable so-cietal trait, it is tempting to recruit it for the arsenal of causal factors used to explain social change. Finnegan's Limba example, however, demonstrates the dangers of employing literacy as a diagnostic category for making generaliza-tions about types of societies or, more perniciously, using it to rank them in some evolutionary schema.

In her effort to debunk literacy thesis arguments, Finnegan turns next to another controversial issue in the representation of traditional and nonliterate societies, viz., whether their oral epics, songs, prose narratives, and other artis-tic uses of language can be justifiably considered "literature." The concept of literature is now fiercely debated within literacy criticism (Guillory, 1993), so rather than try to assess whether Finnegan is right in arguing, contra Goody, that the Limba have "a literature," we want to follow the issues she raises, and the difficulties she encounters, in trying to characterize an oral literature and poetry. Finnegan is unequivocal in arguing that the oral form notwithstanding, the Limba have a literature, but what might distinguish oral poetry and oral literature from written poetry and literature? According to Finnegan, it is that they are *performed*. This, of course, begs the questions: what counts as performance? What is the nature of performance? And what difference(s) does it make that poetry and literature are performed rather than written? Finnegan's answers draw upon the classic work of Milman Parry and Albert Lord based on fieldwork with Yugoslav oral poets. She notes the importance of Lord's *The Singer of Tales* (1960) in an essay where she comments on the tricky question: what is oral literature anyway?: "From the standpoint of analyzing African oral literature, the two really salient points about oral literature that are made in *The Singer of Tales* are, first its variability: the absence of *the* single correct version; and second, the unique nature of *each* performance by the composer/performer: the poem or story as delivered, as a unique creation, on that particular occasion" (Finnegan, 1976, p. 128).

Finnegan starts here with what seems a clear-cut distinction between unique oral performances and invariant written texts. On this understanding, a written text is fixed, it can be referred to, and any variation from it can be easily verified. The entire enterprise of establishing the authoritative, definitive text of an author's work is intended to *fix* the text permanently. In theory this gives the reader the highest degree of certainty that what is on the page is what the author intended to write. In addition, the objectifying of verbal expression in writing, its permanence, makes possible communication over distances in *time* as well as in *space*; "[w]here[as] with oral (i.e. unwritten) literature, communication depends . . . on the *direct* personal interaction between author and public . . ." (1988, p. 18, original emphasis). However, while it may be conceded that the distance between author and reader creates a characteristically different relation between producer and consumer than between author and audience in face-to-face performance, an understanding of the implications of the distinction, especially for any claims pertaining to abstract mediation, will again depend on further clarifications of the terms such as "author," "text," and "performance."

Finnegan explores the nature of these terms by analyzing Limba storytelling performances. In such performances the Limba storyteller uses the techniques of dramatic or comedic narration to comment on the behaviors of characters or indirectly on aspects of social life. And this commentary creates a distance, now between author and "text," which the discerning audience must interpret. Finnegan adds that although much of this artist/performer commentary

fail[s] to come across in a written or translated version, away from the artistry of the actual narrator and from the situation and characters which he is portraying, . . . it is quite clear to an observer in the actual situation of story-telling that this kind of detached comment on reality is a central element in Limba literature. The composer/performer in story or poem exploits his medium whether humorously or tolerantly, maliciously or tenderly, to stand back from the world around him and express his detached reflections on it.

(p. 51)

What also fails to come across in written versions is how commentary, both serious and humorous, distances author from performance and subdivides audience. This is a point that has been repeatedly argued in anthropological studies of communicative events. For example, in a penetrating study of Wolof (Senegal) praise poems and ritual insults during weddings, Irvine (1996) has shown how, depending on event as well as participants, "author" can be broken down into information source, composer, and performer, while "audience" separates into direct addressee, addressee's family or lineage, wedding guests, and known but unacknowledged eavesdroppers. In a related vein, Bauman (1986) has shown how West Texas jokes are often told so that a member of the audience, but not the actual addressee, will be the object of the "barbed" wit. Similarly, Basso's (1990b) research on Western Apache narrative has analyzed how stories are told in various audiences, but often with a particular "overhearer," frequently a young person, as the specific target of the story's implied but unstated moral. The literature on African-American "signifying" and "marking" reports a related use of indirect, allusive reference to moral states through phrases and stories (Mitchell-Kernan, 1972; Morgan, 1998).

In short, what the analysis of "oral literature" shows is that there are degrees of distance and closeness between authors and texts, as there are between writers or performers and readers or audiences. It is not a simple contrast of the invariance and distance of written text versus the unique variability and immediacy of oral performance.

In thinking about the implications of Finnegan's analysis, what we come up against is the fundamental idea of structure or invariance versus that of event or variability. In the telling of stories there is always variability, but there is also a common belief among the audience that the story remains "the same" with each retelling. Something, the essence of the story, the thematic content, the moral lesson presented, is believed to be unchanged: the story remains the same, the performance changes. Indeed, the very idea of variation in performance seems to imply that there is a first, or pure, or "fixed" form from which variation is possible. It implies that there must be a first performance or text from which to establish the variation, from which to identify those elements which have changed, and those which remain unchanged, from one performance to another (Silverstein and Urban, 1996).[10] But this notion of variation in performances is derived most likely from comparing variation in written texts, or between performances and written texts (Bauman and Briggs, 1990). It is a literate notion, an intertwining of the written and the oral, as de Certeau would say, so that even when considering "oral" literature we tend to be burdened by the weight of the historical meanings associated with literature as a form of *writing*.

Finnegan tries to avoid some of this conceptual baggage by examining a genre more traditionally associated with performance than literature, that of poetry. However, since scholastic interest in poetry most often focuses on poetry as a form of writing, Finnegan still must add the qualifier "oral." This in turn makes it necessary, in order to be clear about the nature of oral poetry, to determine the reference of "oral." Finnegan's definition seems straightforward enough: "Briefly, oral poetry is *unwritten* poetry. It very often takes the form of song, or of verse in some way musically accompanied, and ranges from brief couplets like the 'miniature' Somali *balwo* lyrics or the 'songs of protest' of American or English coal-miners, to elaborate epic poems many of thousands of lines long" (Finnegan, 1978, p. 1, emphasis in original). Finnegan rejects, however, a "romantic" notion of a nonliterate primitive in some far-off locale performing traditional verse. The reality, Finnegan informs us, is more complicated *and* more interesting: "Most oral poetry in this century is likely to be produced by people who have at least some contact, however indirect, with the wider world in general – and with writing and its products in particular. The result is a *continual and fruitful interplay between oral and written forms of literary expression*" (1978, p. 2, emphasis added).

We have now reached a point familiar to de Certeau and Derrida, acknowledging "a continual . . . interplay between oral and written forms." And we face new questions, such as "Does this contact with writing contaminate the 'pure' oral nature of poetry?" "Can we justifiably speak of an oral poetry existing in a context where contact with writing is suspected or apparent?" In order for the category of oral poetry to remain useful it would seem necessary to determine to what extent contact with writing has affected the process of composition and performance. However, as Finnegan recognizes, no absolute distinction will hold up. Further, and this is of great significance: "the common criteria for 'orality' too – those of oral composition, transmission, and performance – are relative and elusive ones which may well conflict with each other, for a poem may be orally composed then later transmitted in writing, or perhaps written initially but then performed and circulated by oral means" (p. 2). This, in turn, leaves us in uncertain terrain: "it is in practice impossible to draw up a precise and indisputable definition of 'oral', one which would make the delimitation of 'oral' from written poetry a clear-cut matter" (p. 2).

The virtue of Finnegan's work is that in relentlessly pushing against received categories she shows their untenability. The use of "oral" and "written" literatures as mutually exclusive categories in distinguishing between literate and nonliterate societies is unsupportable once one attends to the ways in which literature is used, in this case among the Limba. Ample evidence exists that Finnegan's observations on the Limba are not unique and that "mixed forms" of the oral/written are found in aesthetic forms in societies throughout the world (Bauman, 1996; Herzfeld, 1996).

Finnegan's challenge to the "great divide" theorists is strongest where she has complicated the categories employed to uphold what she claims are spurious distinctions: oral versus literate, composition versus performance, abstract versus concrete. Her arguments for the aesthetic and intellectual depth of oral literature, oral poetry, and "primitive philosophy" are persuasive. They stand as pointed and detailed rebukes to the habit of literacy thesis proponents to assume rather than carefully study the characteristics of "oral" peoples, practices, or traditions. However, in order to make her arguments Finnegan has had to employ – and become entangled within – the very distinctions she wished to undermine. Perhaps this was impossible to avoid. Recent work in anthropology on the nature of text has argued that rather than analyzing text-artifacts we need to attend to *entextualizing*, that is, to the process whereby stretches of language, whether spoken or written, acquire their apparent fixity, authority, and artfulness. Such processualist accounts of textuality (Collins, 1996; Hanks, 1996a; Irvine, 1996; Mertz, 1996; Silverstein, 1996; Urban, 1996) are congruent with de Certeau's emphasis on situated practices, discursive forms, and power asymmetries. Attempting to move beyond the dichotomies of oral and literate, utterance and text, requires, however, an investigation of the intellectual legacies and social forces which create and support these distinctions, an examination of how power is implicated in the use of such categories, and a theory which explains both. In the field of literacy studies, the work of Brian Street moves us in that direction.

Street

The most comprehensive and sustained critique of the literacy thesis has been that provided by Brian Street in his *Literacy in Theory and Practice* (1984) and continued in *Cross-Cultural Approaches to Literacy* (1993). Street contends that the particular practices of reading and writing and their associated meanings in society – their uses, functions, and meanings – can only be determined adequately if they are studied in context. The nature of reading and writing are dependent on the contexts in which they are embedded. The sociocultural contexts of literate practices are also ideological contexts. To argue for the "neutrality" of literacy or to focus solely on its technical aspects leads to the creation of an "autonomous" model of literacy, one in which literacy, as a congeries of practices of reading and writing, is separable from the contexts in which it is found.

Street identifies the autonomous model with the work of Goody and with Olson. Already discussed at some length in chapter 2, it is unnecessary for us to rehearse the characteristics of the autonomous model here. Let us instead devote our attention to Street as he outlines an "ideological model" of literacy and provides an ethnographic example in support of such a model, an example from his own fieldwork in Iran undertaken between 1970 and 1977. Counterpoised to the autonomous model and a challenge to it, Street's ideological model has the following characteristics:

1. It assumes that the meaning of literacy depends upon the social institutions in which it is embedded [as in Heath's school and community literacies];
2. literacy can only be known to us in forms which already have political and ideological significance and it cannot, therefore, be helpfully separated from that significance and

treated as though it were an "autonomous" thing [as Finnegan argues of the very notion of literacy-as-technology; and as Bloch (1998) argues at length];

3. the particular practices of reading and writing that are taught in any context depend upon such aspects of social structure as stratification (such as where certain social groups may be taught only to read), and the role of educational institutions [such as in Graff's (1979) example from nineteenth-century Canada, Prinsloo and Breier's (1996) work from South Africa, and Sarris' (1993) case of a Native American reservation];

4. the processes whereby reading and writing are learnt are what construct the meaning of it for particular practitioners [cf. Heath's Maintown, Roadville, and Trackton; Finnegan's Limba poets; also Howe (1993), Camitta (1993)];

5. we would probably more appropriately refer to "literacies" than to any single "literacy" [Heath's strongest message];

6. researchers who tend towards this model and away from the "autonomous" model recognize as problematic the relationship between the analysis of any "autonomous," isolable qualities of literacy and the analysis of the ideological and political nature of literacy practice.   (Street, 1984, p. 8)

Street's ideological model has received considerable attention (Brody, 1996; Fabian, 1993; Prinsloo and Breier, 1996), but less attention has been given to his original ethnographic work in support of the model. We now turn to this in order to see how certain of the features listed above are exemplified in concrete description and analysis.

In the 1970s Street did field research in the fruit-growing villages "around Mashad, the holy city and capital of Khorosan province in North East Iran on the border of Afghanistan" (1984, p. 11), especially the village of Cheshmeh, a fruit-growing village which he compared with nearby grain-producing villages and with the central city of Mashad. Although by 1970, when Street arrived in the village, modern schooling had reached Cheshmeh, those who dominated religious and social life were not those who had acquired school literacy, but those who had attended the "maktab," a Koranic religious school. Street argues that "maktab" literacy contributed not just to a general social standing, of those with "good values" we might say, it contributed also to the commercial success of an emerging class of entrepreneurs – the very social group who would ostensibly benefit most from a formal, Western-style education.

In the "maktab" students learned the Koran, primarily by rote, "although in some cases, as in Cheshmeh, mullahs may add knowledge of commentaries and also teach vernacular literacy and numeracy" (p. 133). Although memorizing passages from the Koran did not lead to reading in the sense that students would be able to decode text phonemically, they were not without literate knowledge. They knew, for example, that meaning was not embedded entirely in the words on the page, but was dependent to some extent on the layout of the printed text. This prior experience with one form of literacy provided a context through which new forms were perceived: "when Cheshmehi entrepreneurs adapt their 'maktab' literacy to commercial purposes they are helped by the fact that fellow villagers are familiar with the uses of pieces of paper to signify lists, contracts, etc. and so are able to participate in their use in such ways as 'signing' with their thumbs papers of which they cannot read the verbal content" (p. 133).

Some students in the "maktab" did acquire an indigenous literacy by extension from Arabic to Farsi, "since the Arabic alphabet is largely the same as the Persian" (p. 134). Street makes a subtle point regarding this acquisition of vernacular or indigenous literacy. He notes that the mullah (or religious leader) in the "maktab" used commentaries on the Koran written in Farsi (rather than Classical Arabic) and even had Farsi versions of the Koran. In turn, what the students "derived from such commentaries was both facility in reading the script of their own alphabet and *an intellectual framework and ideology* which gave meaning to their particular literacy and . . . facilitated the adaptation of it to new purposes and a different ideology" (p. 134, emphasis added).

(After September 11, 2001, mention of Afghanistan, Iran, and schools led by mullahs have an unavoidably militarized connotation. We ask our readers to hold such images at bay and listen instead to our account of Street's analysis. Usefully, he portrays an Islamic tradition which is not a monolithic dogma, but rather interwoven in the give-and-take, the exchanges and disagreements, of daily life. Perhaps it is the historical period, prerevolutionary Iran, or perhaps it is an aspect of life that our media reports, filled with the certainties of a "war on terror," do not allow us to see, but for the people of Cheshmeh, "maktab" literacy contributed not to jihad but to the solution of prosaic commercial problems: how to distribute fruit to an expanding market. Let us now return to Street's account.)

As we saw with Heath and with Finnegan, in order to understand the particular literacy acquired in the "maktab," it was necessary to describe the contexts in which it is acquired and used. Of special contextual relevance was "the particular variety of the 'Islamic tradition' to be found in Iranian mountain villages in the 1970s" (p. 134), for, as Street was to discover, the Islamic tradition is not monolithic, indeed, it is characterized more by variability than by fixity. This may surprise some because a common expectation is that for "religions of the book" varying interpretations, when they arise, are due to textual variants and rival claims to establish authority for one version over others, but not to disputes over the meaning of the text once a variant is established. Street reminds us that "As Muslims would themselves say, the Koran is the Word of God and so there is no need for interpretations" (p. 135).

Nevertheless, despite this ideology of textual invariance, interpretations abounded. Street attributes this to the very "fixity" of the text itself, which involves an apparent paradox. The authority of the written text, in this case the holy word of God, rests in the fact that it is written. This allows for interpretations of the text to flourish – because of the acceptance by believers and nonbelievers, literate and nonliterate alike, that writing fixes a text. Once the word is written, its meaning is fixed, and thus the changeability believed characteristic of "mere speech" is avoided. Interpreters can point to the written text as grounds for universalizing what are, in effect, individual interpretations.

Like the Christian tradition, the Islamic tradition being taught in the "mak-tabs" studied by Street was not a singular or monolithic affair transmitted un-changed from one generation to the next. Rather, there was a rich intertextuality in play. The Koran, although never displaced from the center of Islam, was not the only "holy" book available for study. There was also "the 'Hadith', which transmitted the 'sunna', the body of reported actions and sayings of the Prophet and his companions" (p. 136). From this corpus teachers might select those "sunna" which provided an opportunity to comment on contemporary affairs. As Street reports: "In that variety of the Islamic tradition which I experienced in Cheshmeh and similar mountain villages in North East Iran, such stories were regularly adapted to contemporary issues and problems, notably the impact of western science and ideas" (p. 136). The number and variety of texts makes the process of selection important: The mullah could "select according to his own interests and belief" (p. 137). Even if the texts were fixed in the sense that they are authoritatively established and thus accepted as the word of God (or, in the case of "Hadith," of holy men), this, nonetheless, did not insure that interpretations would be uniform.

One must turn to how the texts were actually used, whether in religious wor-ship or as guides to behavior, in order to understand literacy practices. The mullahs, although they had memorized Koranic passages and sayings from the Prophet recorded in the "Hadith," did not usually rely on verbatim expressions of these texts when faced with the need to apply their knowledge to contem-porary issues. The potential and acknowledged variations in meanings of the sacred texts provided the flexibility observed by Street. The lesson he drew from this state of affairs was that: "the acquisition of literacy in the Koranic school does not simply 'fix' forever sacred rules and beliefs, but provides a particular development of the malleability that Goody would associate only with an oral tradition. The scholars of the 'maktab' exemplify a 'mix' of oral and literate modes of communication in which malleability and fixity are likewise 'fixed' " (p. 138, see also J. Boyarin (1993b) for a similar argument regarding Judaic "tradition").

What skills, then, were learned by those who attended the "maktabs"? For one, students could use "variability" in the texts to find meanings relevant to today; that is, to adapt to the demands of late twentieth-century life, the in-fluences of Western science, its methods and findings. They then could claim that the founders of Islam were, in effect, prescient, and therefore their teach-ings carried great weight when applied to contemporary moral issues. Likewise the many stories learned in the "maktabs" introduced story themes and formu-laic structures which could be employed in variable interpretations of Islamic history and tradition. Criteria of selection of particular interpretations, by the mullah or by students, were contingent on social and political factors. The col-lection of literate practices engaged in by students of the "maktab" surely was no simple, monolithic, mode of communication divorced from other available modes: "[It] interacted in complex ways with oral modes of communication, with folk traditions of story-telling . . . and more peculiarly Iranian versions and interpretations of Islamic tradition. It was within this context that the learning of certain literacy practices by these Iranian villages acquired meaning" (p. 144).

In order to analyze literacy practices more closely, Street adopted a framework developed by the Adult Literacy and Basic Skills Unit of the United Kingdom to delineate the various forms of "social knowledge" involved in literacy acquisition and use. Beginning with a basic understanding of the "links between speech and print" (p. 152), that is, that "sounds are represented by letters or combinations of letters," Street notes of his Cheshmesh novitiates that "even those who got little beyond rote learning had also to learn some further complexities to be found in Arabic script" (pp. 152–153). For example, because in Arabic there are "different forms for the same letter" depending on where that letter appears in a word, students had to learn to recognize them in order to mark word boundaries, and, because punctuation is not used, in order to recognize sentence beginnings and endings. In addition, Arabic script, unlike languages based on the Latin alphabet, is read from right to left. This, of course, is a learned convention. But Street informs us that the presentation of texts used in the "maktab" was of a particularly complex nature with text "broken up in various ways: blocks of words may be set at different angles, they may be placed in the margins or across corners of the page, and different kinds of print and lettering may be used for different purposes" (p. 153). What students learned from this was that the meaning of a text is not exhausted by decoding the script, but is partially contained in the form (format) of the printed page.

Although such "skills" may seem to amount to little when placed against what is traditionally viewed as school literacy, these are abilities acquired in contexts in which the comprehension or manipulation of scripts in some sense is central. Further, they have been acquired not as a result of direct instruction, but as a by-product of the culturally valued study of religious texts. Although learned in specific contexts, many of these "skills" were cognitive habits transferable by adaptation to new contexts and purposes, to new needs and interests:

> The [Adult Literacy Basic Skills Unit] type skills . . . "understanding the specific links between speech and print"; the significance of format, layout and conventions of presentation for meaning; and the skill of "non-sequential reading" – are all related directly to the purposes for which students came together in "maktabs" and in reading sessions at village dinner parties. The "skills" only acquired meaning for their exponents in these contexts – those of the Islamic tradition and of Iranian village values and "ideology."
> (pp. 155–156)

Street uses his analysis of "maktab" literacy – of the interpretive dispositions, the literary tropes, and the knowledge of print conventions – to frame his discussion of "commercial literacy" in Cheshmeh in the 1970s. Commercial literacy was situated within and developed as a response to a particular set of

social and political circumstances in Iran in the 1970s resulting from an economic boom related to rising oil prices. With an increase in money came an
increase in demand for food. Fruit-growing villages were able to respond to
this demand more easily and more quickly than grain-growing areas because
the changes in production processes necessary to meet the demand did not fundamentally disrupt the traditional means of production and system of exchange
and distribution.

The economic success of the fruit-growing villages, Street contends, was also
due to the ability of villagers to adapt a previously acquired set of literacy skills,
that of the "maktab," to the new demands of commerce. Key here is the notion of
"enabling." Street is careful not to claim that literacy causes economic growth:
" 'Maktab' literacy in Cheshmeh facilitated the development of 'commercial'
literacy and 'commercial' literacy 'enabled' economic growth. The fact that
literacy 'in itself' was not the *cause* of this growth is apparent from comparison
of the structural features of the two kinds of village" (p. 159, emphasis in
original).

Because Street's ideological model is not a simple causal model in which
schooled literacy drives economic development, he must demonstrate a more
complex interconnectedness. He must show that social structures, means of
production, and systems of distribution interact with a particular set of literacy
practices and uses and *together* provide factors to explain economic growth.
As he notes: "In Cheshmeh such growth required also the mediating skills
associated with 'commercial' literacy and they, in turn, rested on the prior
development of 'maktab' literacy" (p. 159). How practices of "commercial"
literacy reflected practices learned in the "maktab" can be seen by examining
its development in this one village.

Cheshmeh is situated in a deep valley with houses on one hillside and orchards
on the other, and communal, not private, control of the water supply was crucial
to sustained fruit production. Patterns of work in the orchards are dictated by
changes in the seasons intensifying as the various fruits ripen, are picked, and
transported to market or stored for later shipment, and labor might be exchanged
or sold. Since the fruit growers of Cheshmeh were not using land to produce
subsistence crops, once the fruit had ripened and was picked it must be brought
to market and sold or exchanged for subsistence goods. This was all part of
a traditional pattern of village-based production and distribution. During the
1970s, however, an increased demand for fruit created the conditions necessary
for one significant alteration in the traditional system. They needed an economic
middleman to coordinate village production and the enlarged external exchange,
so a class of village "tajers" arose:

The "tajer" bought fruit at an agreed rate from fellow villagers, who then took it to his
stores as it was picked. Then it was weighed and accounts were drawn up: the parties
would negotiate whether the producer would be paid when his whole harvest or all of a
particular fruit was in the store, or after the "tajer" had himself been paid by city dealers.

The "tajer" whose stores in summer would be bulging with the produce of various villagers and, more recently, also with fruit bought from other villages too, would take bulk loads to town where he had arrangements with wholesalers to whom he sold at considerable profit.   (p. 166)

As urban demand for fruit increased, the "tajer" organization allowed individual growers to meet it, while suffering little change in labor allocation and leisure patterns. (As Street notes, even during the busiest work periods men had time each week to sit and talk.)

Observing commercial transactions in the villages, what uses of literacy did Street find? As might be expected, writing was evident in the labeling of boxes and fruit crates, in the making out of bills, and in the signing of checks. Interestingly, school exercise books were used to keep accounts and "the layout of these was often precise and conventional: a page might be allotted to each separate deal; columns would be neatly lined down the page for sections of the accounts, with indications for weights, money etc.; space would be designated for signatures" (p. 172).

While a discussion of literacy delineating such "accounting measures" risks a descent into the mundane, it is the very practicality of the means of keeping accounts that causes them to be overlooked as significant in conventional investigations into the nature and application of literacy skills. Street argues that in the transactions being recorded in the account books use was being made of "hidden" literacy skills first learned in the "maktabs" and now being adapted to novel situations. Thus, students at the "maktab" had learned to attend not only to the words or groups of words on the page but to their placement on the page as well. Textual meaning was not exclusively the content of the words, the content of the form and format also must be included. As previously noted, the ability to attend to format was easily adapted from "maktab" to "commercial" literacy where "the layout and presentation of lists, tables, columns etc. were the crucial indicators of meaning as in 'maktab' literacy and information was retrieved in similar ways through the separation of categories and the associated use of headings, page numbers etc." (p. 173).

"Maktab" literacy and "commercial" literacy also differed in interesting ways. In the "maktab" the authority of writing was a given; it came from outside the village as part of a tradition interpreted by the mullahs. In "commercial" literacy, however, the "tajers" had to create the authority for the written forms they themselves were using. Street provides a brief example: "The concept of 'signature' . . . as indicating agreement to a transaction rests upon an institutional framework that specifies, whether implicitly or explicitly, formal relations between commercial and legal processes . . . [T]hose who could not write their names simply impressed inky thumbprints on appropriate pieces of paper, indicating participation in and agreement to this institutional framework and its new status" (p. 174). The affixing of a signature helps to render a transaction recorded on paper legitimate; it is a performative act of authorization.

The growers and "tajers" involved in legal or business transactions would use ordinary paper sheets, from school exercise books, for example, and transform them into an official document by affixing stamps and signatures. These were not government documents whose form and purpose had been determined elsewhere and put into use in the village, rather they were newly created by fruit growers and "tajers" as needed within the system of exchange and distribution.

Those able to adapt their knowledge and skills gained in the "maktab" to the needs of commerce could gain positions of economic and social power within the village. Street explains:

> The present generation of "tajers" had all been educated at the "maktab," often in the same period and even in the same class as each other. The hidden literacy skills which they had acquired there thus contributed to their ability to establish positions in the new village power structure which rested on command of both the expanded distribution and exchange systems and of the new "commercial" literacy. These "skills" in isolation held no significance. But, in relation to their development by specific groups of people in a context where they facilitated commercial expansion and economic growth, they were a crucial component of the power structure.   (p. 175)

The power of the "tajers," however, did not rest on their having exclusive possession of the skills derived from the "maktab" and adapted to commerce. The system of writing, if not the practice of writing, was shared. Those with whom "tajers" interacted had to have some knowledge of literacy, had to accept the legitimacy of certain types of writing, of signatures, etc., in order for the authority of the written forms to carry weight. They had to know, in short, the meanings of specific literacy practices even if they did not control them. In this sense, those who affixed their thumbprints on documents were writers, and those who recognized the names of producers on fruit crates were readers.

There are numerous ways in which Street's Cheshmeh studies challenge the literacy thesis and the "autonomous model" of literacy. In particular, the assumptions about the fixity of written meaning and the context-free nature of technical literacy skills are called into question, as is the idea that literacy has power separable from the social positions and practices of a given society's "literates." More broadly, Street's "ideological model" emphasizes that the meanings of literacy depend on social institutions, such as religious schools and market networks. The particular practices of reading and writing that are taught depend on aspects of the social order, such as religious institutions and "tajer" entrepreneurship. In short, we must conceptualize literacy as *literacies*, that is, as embedded in a multiplicity of social practices, rather than as a monolithic technology or tradition.

As we have noted, and will soon discuss further, there has been considerable uptake of Street's ideas in subsequent historical and anthropological research on literacy. There have, however, also been criticisms raised. Although Street mitigates the judgments of the literacy thesis, calling for attention to the complexities of oral traditions and documenting the dynamics of apparently "restricted" practices such as "maktab" literacy, he nonetheless remains stuck with the oral/written binary as analytic categories through which to organize descriptions of highly complex discursive events – as Fabian (1993) has shown in a close analysis of the processes whereby anthropologists generate texts from fieldwork encounters. In addition, as Probst (1993) has noted, in a penetrating discussion of literacy in the context of an anti-colonial religious movement, Street's argument for oral/written "mixing" fails to capture the specific forms of the power of writing in colonial settings.

This points to a more general problem with Street's approach. Through numerous arguments and cases, Street rightly shows that claims for the cognitive superiority or greater rationality of the written over the oral often depend on the unacknowledged institutional, political, or military power of those advancing literate accounts. A good example is Street's adaptation of Clanchy's (1979) historical findings regarding Norman versus Anglo-Saxon land registration (1984, pp. 110–121). After the Normans conquered medieval England, they instituted a system of "modern" land registration using written titles and deeds, and this replaced the "oral" Anglo-Saxon tradition, in which seals, carved knives, and other artifacts, plus the testimony of "12 honest men" secured claim to real property. In this case, however, the superiority of Norman land registration was more due to the success of their swords than the accuracy of their pens. The aptness of such analyses notwithstanding, problems remain. Although the concept of power in *Literacy in Theory and Practice* is often used to criticize claims for the intrinsic superiority of literacy, power itself is not sufficiently theorized. More precisely, although Street is often a sensitive analyst of macro-power, in the sense in which we have previously discussed it regarding Heath, his framework does not attend to micro-power. As we will see in following chapters, understanding micro-power is essential to understanding the myriad ways in which writing is both an effect and a form of power.

Influences of situated approaches

The import of the work of Heath, Finnegan, and Street is easily stated: any understanding of literacy and literate practices allowing cross-cultural comparisons calls for ethnographic descriptions of those practices in their cultural contexts. The positive aspects of their work are contained in their thorough descriptions of the intertwining of talk and text and the *uses* of print in the everyday communicative activities of the peoples they studied. Key for Heath, for example, were the various uses of language in the social environments of child and adult, not literacy *per se*. She began with language in action and described the contexts of language use because the communicative contexts in which literacy events and socialization to literacy occur are contexts in which the oral uses of language are inextricably interwoven. To separate the "oral" from the "literate" *a priori* would be an imposition of the researcher, not a judgment necessarily recognized nor acknowledged by the participants in the communicative events under study.

The work of all three has had considerable influence within and beyond anthropology, notably in culture history and in education. A spate of studies of preschool and in-school language socialization appeared immediately upon the heels of Heath's *Ways with Words* seeing it as both model and inspiration (Schieffelin and Gilmore, 1986) or as "baseline" from which to assess new findings.

Miller, Nemoianu, and DeJong (1986) studied how the preschool socialization of three two-year-old working-class children in South Baltimore prepared them for reading at school. They found that much interaction between mother (or other caregiver) and child involved "direct instruction as a way of entertaining the child or redirecting her activity" (p. 5) and that "the largest category of direct instruction involved naming people and things, including pictures in books. That is, direct instruction formed the child's first experience of reading" (p. 5). Adopting the definition of reading from Anderson et al. (1980), Miller et al. present the structure of reading events at home: the nonverbal activities (e.g. holding and opening a book, pointing to pictures) and the verbal activities (e.g. labeling, offering positive feedback).

Granting that it might be a later development, they found that the least frequent type of verbal activity that occurred in relation to books was storytelling: "storytelling at two tended to involve the verbal and non-verbal re-creation of an experienced or witnessed event, without accompanying text" (1986:10). Alternately, on occasion connections were made between storybook content and "real-life events or characteristics of the child." This leads to an important observation regarding schooling:

We suspect from our observations of reading in first-grade classrooms in South Baltimore that a later development involves the elaborations of these real-life connections into narratives of experienced or witnessed events. In other words, the printed story eventually becomes an occasion for relating a personal story. (This contrasts with the Maintown practice described by Heath, 1982, in which the child's personal experience becomes an occasion for referring back to a printed story.) If this finding is borne out in subsequent observations, it provides a unique opportunity for classroom teachers to make reading meaningful to children like Amy, Wendy, and Beth by building on the child's spontaneous tendency to relate the printed to the personal.   (p. 10)

The contrast with Heath's work points to a strength of ethnographic accounts – their description of actual practices allows for comparison and the generating of questions as to the significance of any similarity or difference in those practices. As well, such accounts call for an assessment of the importance of such (reading) practices to ultimate success at school. In a little-heeded warning, Miller et al. caution against inflating the importance of early reading at home, with its concomitant emphasis on individual achievement, to the neglect of those factors, such as educational resources and community beliefs about education, which together comprise the social and cultural contexts for academic achievement (see Bialostok [1999] and Rogers [2000] for an appreciation of the pertinence of this warning).

Zinsser (1986) extends the Heath-inspired study of socialization to literacy beyond home and public school settings by describing literacy events in "pre-primary classes of four- and five-year old children . . . who had not yet been 'officially' taught to read and write" (1986, p. 56) in a fundamentalist Sunday school and vacation Bible school. The Bible was the only text present, and its centrality to literacy acquisition and in the (spiritual) life of each child was unquestioned: "The function of the text, as taught in these settings, was to provide divine inspiration as a guide to daily behavior and as a means to personal salvation. Pre-primary children were considered old enough for the experience of being 'born again,' a most valued consequence of learning text" (p. 56).

The discourse structure within which Bible literacy was acquired, was, interestingly, primarily oral. Teachers told stories from the Bible in their own words and children were exhorted to listen. Indeed, since the Bible texts were accepted literally, children were instructed to "listen" as "God speaks" (p. 60). Children memorized Bible verses through repetition and song, and parents were encouraged to assist their children through practice worksheets at home. Question and answer patterns were tied exclusively to the text in ways contrary to what is expected in school settings. Children were *not* rewarded for imaginative answers and were discouraged from speculating about the Bible stories (p. 63). Formulaic answers were expected and children learned to respond correctly to teacher's cues (see Heath, 1983).

Reading and writing as traditionally understood (i.e. school literacy) was neither taught nor practiced in the Sunday school or Bible school. Bible texts were considered too difficult for children this young to decode. But in a finding that echoes Street's account of "maktab" literacy, Zinsser concludes that "[t]hese nonreading and nonwriting children nevertheless assumed the roles of literate people. They were surrounded by printed messages on walls and on hand-out materials. They could memorize and repeat textual material. They were practiced in listening to text read aloud. They carried their Bibles with them and sometimes opened them into reading position" (1986, p. 66). They learned as well that textual authority was to be differentiated from speaker authority. There were, then, some continuities and some discontinuities between home, Bible school, and public school literacy practices for these children. How they fared in the public schools may very well have depended on the degree of discontinuity and its significance. What should be noted is that such discontinuities exist in a group not ordinarily singled out as linguistically or economically different. As Zinsser notes, significant differences occur within groups comprising the dominant culture (p. 69). These two studies and other works by educational anthropologists and others influenced by Heath (Brandau and Collins, 1994;

Duranti and Ochs, 1986; Lofty, 1992; Reder, 1993) demonstrate the richness of ethnographic perspectives on literacy. They support the underlying assumption of such studies "that an understanding of literacy requires detailed, in-depth accounts of actual practice in different cultural settings" (Street, 1993, p. 1). Recent work in history has also taken an "ethnographic approach" drawing especially on the work of Finnegan and Street. Coleman (1996), in her *Public Reading and the Reading Public in Late Medieval England and France*, laments the influence that Ong's strict dichotomizing in *Orality and Literacy* (1982) has had on medieval historians, who either simply discount the presence of oral traits in the production and reception of written texts, or treat them as a "residue" in a process of transition from orality to literacy (for early modern Europe see Chartier, 1989b, c). In her investigation of aurality, i.e. "the reading aloud of a written text to one or a group of listeners" (1996, p. 1) we hear echos of Street and Finnegan as she demonstrates that aurality was "a vital, functioning, accepted part of a mixed oral-literate literary tradition," for readers from kings to commoners.

Lepore (1998), in her award-winning *The Name of War*, a study of King Philip's War, cites both Street and Finnegan to counter Goody's and Ong's "consequences argument" and the myth/history dichotomy. She argues that historians make myths and oral peoples preserve history systematically. She argues, further, that to give priority to literacy as a means of preserving history is a culturally acquired value and a historically situated possibility. She notes that for Indians of New England to become literate was part of an assimilationist process requiring the learning of English, conversion to Christianity, abandoning villages to live in towns, in short, adopting English ways, not to preserving an indigenous past or an especially accurate account of that past. The result was that Indians were placed in "a particularly perilous, if at the same time, a powerful position, caught between two worlds, but fully accepted by either" (1998, p. 27; see also Monaghan, 1990).

When considering "the predicament of literate Algonquians in seventeenth-century New England," Lepore exposes consequences unacknowledged or unforseen by literacy thesis adherents. She asks a radical question that resonates with Street's claim that "literacy can only be known to us in forms which already have political and ideological significance":

If literacy is employed as an agent of assimilation, can one of its uses be the devastation of a society's political autonomy and the loss of its native language and culture? Can literacy destroy? And, in the context of a broader cultural conflict, can one of the consequences of literacy be the death of those who acquire it? Can literacy kill? Perhaps most important, if literacy can be wielded as a weapon of conquest and can effectively compromise a native culture, what then of that culture's history and who is left to tell it? If the very people most likely to record their story, those who are so assimilated as to have become literate, are also the most vulnerable, does it then make sense to explain that culture's lack of written history by simply pointing to its attachment to mythical thinking?

(1998, p. 27–28)

This question, motivated in part by the achievement of situated approaches, registers a number of complex issues involving writing, history, forms of belonging, and effects of power. Nonetheless, its anti-modern query – "Can literacy kill?" – points beyond the horizon of most ethnographies of literacy.

Conclusion: implications of situated approaches

The accounts of literate practices provided by Heath, Finnegan, and Street, and those who follow them, teach us much about the flawed assumptions of the literacy thesis. More specifically, the study of literate practices situated within specific cultural contexts demonstrates that "the generally assumed functions and uses of literacy which underlie [the literacy thesis] *do not correspond to the social meanings of reading and writing across either time periods, cultures, or contexts of use"* (Heath, 1986, pp. 15–16, emphasis added).

In rejecting the rigid dichotomies of the Goody–Olson thesis – oral/literate; abstract/concrete; history/myth – Heath, Finnegan, and Street have supplied alternative, flexible means for understanding literate practices and literacies in traditional and complex societies. Literacy by itself is not determining or causal. Some literate practices in one domain, as Street demonstrated for the "maktab," are enabling when employed in another domain, that of the "commercial." Other practices might be "disabling," as Heath demonstrated for Trackton and Roadville children facing alternative literacies in school classrooms. These children brought literate-and-linguistic abilities, dispositions, and values which differed from schooled literacy. Whether particular practices are enabling or disabling depends upon both the processes of socialization in which they were acquired and the sociocultural contexts in which they are employed. Literate practices are not merely technical means transportable unchanged across sociocultural contexts. They are specific practices manifested in different ways in differing contexts, whose meanings are more dependent on the processes by which they were acquired than on the specific skills applied.

However, although we have gained insights from the richness of particular cases concerning domains of literacy and literate practices, it remains difficult to find within the work of Goody's most tenacious challengers a carefully worked out account of why literacy matters in the way that it does in the modern West. We suggest that key to such an account will be the question of power in literacy and that the ethnographic tradition falls short on just this question.

In Heath's work, as well as in Finnegan's, we find no exploration of power relations, nor of how power is implicated in the construction of literate selves. This is not to say that Heath and Finnegan do not recognize power in its manifestations in language and literacy, it is simply not their focus. In Heath power relations as such are implied, but not addressed. Schools, government organizations, and bureaucratic institutions have power over and through folks in Roadville, Trackton, and Maintown. To take a common line of argument, schools have the power to set standard uses of language in the classrooms, which, once the standard is set, creates the disjunction between home and school for Trackton and Roadville kids. But as we have previously argued, there is more at issue than power as an external imposition, there is also the question of an internal power at once intimate and historical.

In Street's descriptions of "maktab" literacy and "commercial" literacy we are presented with a solid alternative to the autonomous model. And Street himself has recognized the next step: "we also need bold theoretical models that recognize the central role of power relations in literacy practices" (1993). Street's delineation of the ideological model prevents issues of power from being denied – as he argues, literacy is not neutral, and viewing it as such is an ideological stance. However, we still lack an account of power-in-literacy which captures the intricate ways in which power, knowledge, and forms of subjectivity are interconnected with "uses of literacy" in modern national, colonial, and postcolonial settings. This issue is the substance of the next three chapters.

4
LITERACIES AND POWER IN
MODERN NATION STATES:
EURO-AMERICAN LESSONS

At the base of the modern social order stands not the executioner but the professor. Not the guillotine, but the (aptly named) *doctorat d'état* is the main tool and symbol of state power. The monopoly of legitimate education is now more important, more central than is the monopoly of legitimate violence. When this is understood, then the imperative of nationalism, its roots, not in human nature as such, but in a certain kind of now pervasive social order, can also be understood.   (Gellner, 1983, p. 34)

Introduction

We have argued in the preceding chapters that the "literacy thesis" attributing extensive sociocultural and cognitive change to a general literacy was untenable, but also that the situated, ethnographic approach – notwithstanding the contributions of studies within this tradition – has failed to confront the intellectual, cultural, and political significance of the dichotomy oral/written. We are going to suggest a way out of this impasse by drawing upon and presenting historical accounts. Historical studies of the "uses of literacy" during different phases of modern Western culture portray a complex interplay of text-and-talk which was part of the emergence of new forms of identity, power, and communication. Such historical research supports the emphasis on a "bottom-up" view of literacy taken by ethnographers of literacy, but it also suggests specific connections between changing literacy practices and political and economic conditions in Europe and North America. (These connections between language and political economy have been explored in work by linguistic anthropologists analyzing language ideologies, but the focus has not been on literacy [Hill, 2000; Silverstein, 2000] or else not on Europe or North America [Blommaert, 1999; Schieffelin, 2000].)

In this chapter we begin with early modern case studies. These suggest familiar links between political, economic and religious power and the desire to regulate literacy as a means of regulating conduct more generally. They also reveal pervasive counter-tendencies: secrecies and transgressions and a complex interplay between senses of public and private. The tension between regulation and transgression of literacy practices will be important throughout our account. In developing a historical case study of literacy in America, we begin with arguments about print cultures and nationalism. These allow us to explore the complicated dialectic between textual processes and new political subjectivities in early and mature American nationalism. Although the relation between literacy, public education, and nationalism changes considerably as we examine early and later national periods, it is possible throughout to register the exclusions built into a scriptural economy of schooling, literacy, and citizenship. It is possible also to discern the new techniques of power and subjectivity that underlay a progressively modern concern with education, letters, and persons.

The interplay of text and talk in early modern Europe

In order to develop our argument, let us first look briefly at two historical studies of literacy in sixteenth- and seventeenth-century European contexts. They argue for significant roles for reading, writing, and print technologies in social and cultural orders, and they also provide useful information about the contexts which shaped and were shaped by those literate practices and technologies.

Burke's (1988) "The Uses of Literacy in Early Modern Italy" focuses, as the title suggests, on the contextualized uses of reading and writing. It gives us a picture of literacy practices in a flourishing mercantile city state. The analysis is organized into an unsurprising set of social domains: business, family, church, and state. We learn, also not surprisingly, that in the sixteenth-century city state of Florence there was a flourishing "notarial culture": merchants kept extensive accounts and engaged in a voluminous correspondence, tracking expenditures and profits over far-flung trade networks. Perhaps as important as the correspondence were the numbers. As Crosby's (1997) history of quantification shows, the sixteenth century was an explosive time in many European cities and states for extending means of measurement, calculation, and visualization. As Burke reminds us, the merchants of early modern Italy invented double-entry bookkeeping.

However, in addition to these familiar utilitarian uses of writing and reading, there were also more ritualistic uses of script, by institutions and individuals, to summon powers, regulate behavior, and escape scrutiny. From Burke we learn that the Counter-Reformation Church in sixteenth- and seventeenth-century Italy was troubled both by literacy and *il*literacy. Literates were problematic because they might read heretical works – the Counter-Reformation had after all emerged in reaction to Martin Luther's Protestant revolt and its print-disseminated views. Illiterates were problematic because they were fond of and susceptible to superstition and magic (Ginzburg, 1982). But this was not just a case of the dark arts for dark minds. Instead, like the twentieth-century Mende of Sierra Leone (Bledsoe and Robey, 1993), the "illiterate majority" of early modern Florence had access to a *written* magic – spells, incantations, and medical cures that used alphabetic sequences (such as *abracadabra*) on cards, amulets, and other objects in order to evoke and control the supernatural. This reminds us that the distinction literate/illiterate is always relative to time and place. Unschooled Florentines took part in practices that sought to harness certain dimly perceived powers associated with manipulating representations, hardly a novel idea in our own age of computer-driven "virtual" realities, fortunes, and crimes. As we will subsequently see, such efforts at unlicensed appropriation are not unusual plebian responses to official institutions and their inscription practices.

The church's concern in sixteenth-century Florence with surveillance and regulation was shared by the state.[1] Whereas the church issued tickets which were collected at communion, a record book that registered attendance and nonattendance, the Florentine state pioneered the use of passes in order to regulate subjects' travel. It also conducted an ambitious series of censuses in the fourteenth and fifteenth centuries, and published numerous proclamations, edicts, and sets of regulations. The state also shared the church's concern for unlicensed or transgressive literacy, pioneering the use of ciphers for encrypting correspondence in order to ensure that literate access was restricted to approved eyes. This is an unsurprising development, given the politics of intrigue that characterized the princely dynasties of the Italian Renaissance (Tuchman, 1984), but it testifies also to the pervasive desire of political regimes for classifying information and "official secrets." And it reminds us as well, in our self-proclaimed age of "the information super-highway," of the ongoing efforts by governments and corporations to protect their electronic inscriptions by hacker-proof encryptions. The Florentine ciphers also present an interesting inversion of the "magic" abhorred by church authorities: whereas the practitioner of magic uses arcane, hermetic script to reveal hidden truths and summon supernatural powers, the cipher-encoder uses arcane, hermetic script to hide official truths and mask secular powers.

The concern with regulating access to literacy extended from spiritual and secular to sexual power. Literate Florentine males proposed what Burke calls a "rule of female illiteracy" (p. 38). Simply put, many men argued that women should not learn to read or write because if they could read and write they might transgress the sexual code by trafficking in love letters and love acts. Despite this norm, some women could read and write. Burke's discussion of family literacy mentions women sending and receiving letters, though their numbers were probably small. A census of schooling in 1587 reveals that out of 4,481 schoolchildren only 28 were female. Although these figures do not preclude girls learning to read in family and workplace settings, they do attest to the power of public exclusion.

What should be borne in mind is the presumption that women were to be illiterate, at a time when it seems a majority of men were also unlettered. This suggests that despite the many uses of written texts in business, familial, church, and state affairs, and despite the "invasion of printed matter" (p. 39) in the sixteenth and seventeenth centuries, early modern Florentine culture would have required a range of oral/literate intermediaries, perhaps of the sort described by Clanchy (1979) and Marvin (1984) for medieval England and Europe: public readers of religious texts and government proclamations, special castes of scribes and clerks. In addition, as the worries of church and state attest, the entire social system was pervaded with entextualized secrecy – traffickers in magic and love letters; devisers of ciphers. All this represents a decidedly unmodern denial of the ostensible nature of Western reading and writing – which is that texts are to be explicit (Olson) and widely disseminated (Goody and Watt), with social progress following from maximum access to written meaning.

Such a modern vision of accessible literacy informs Eisenstein's (1968) "Some Conjectures about the Impact of Printing on Western Culture and Thought." It is a seminal essay – later developed into a full-length study (Eisenstein, 1980) – exploring the consequences of the far-flung distribution and progressive standardization of book-commodities in modern Europe but especially the mid-sixteenth to mid-seventeenth centuries. Like Goody and Olson, Eisenstein is also given to a style of thinking in which the literate means cause cultural or intellectual outcomes. However, because she is work-ing within a narrower historical compass, has a more precise focus (print rather than literacy in general), and is usually more sensitive to text/talk interactions, she is less prone to their style of unidirectional explanation.[2]

In an interesting discussion of "the uneven rise of reading publics," Eisenstein argues for relations between print, literacy practices, and new forms of symbolic collectivity. In particular, she argues that more lives became more procedure-bound when individuals and groups began "going by the book" (1968, p. 39, passim). Such "going by the book" was a textual ethos and practice character-izing a " 'middle-class' secular puritan" ethos, found in Protestant Europe and North America, in which domestic handbooks, marriage guides, and etiquette rule-books were paramount in the conduct and judgment of lives. Relevant to our argument to follow, as well as to Heath's findings about differences in Main-town, Roadville, and Trackton, such book-following also informs shifts in fam-ily life, in particular, the emergence of modern childhood, in which "learning by reading" replaced "learning by doing," and schooled routines replaced earlier responsibilities and freedoms visited upon the young (Luke, 1989). Eisenstein argues that the appearance of stricter domestic disciplines, in the preceding developments, were part of a sharper marking of boundaries between the pri-vate and the public. This had an apparently paradoxical result, noticed by other scholars of modernity: the privacy of solitary reading made it easier to identify with the new totalizing projects of class, race, and nation.

The historical development of what we understand as "public" and "private" zones of behavior and of rights and responsibilities is a topic of enduring inter-est and conflict – consider, for example, the current arguments about privacy and the Internet. The public/private dichotomy has also been the subject of much philosophical, political, and anthropological inquiry. The nature of the public/private distinction has figured in many debates about gender, for it appears that in most human societies, women are expected to be more oriented to the domestic or private, because of child-rearing responsibilities, while men more oriented to the nondomestic or public (Rosaldo and Lamphere, 1974). In an influential work on political spheres in modern nations, Habermas (1989) has argued that the communicative underpinnings of public opinion and civil society in constitution-based nation states (we would now say "democracies") lay in the spread of the publishing of journals and newspapers and of sites for debate, such as coffee houses and discussion societies, which were public and nongovernmental. (This is the Kantian *Leserwelt*. See chapter 7, note 7, below.) Counterpoised in his analysis was a complementary private sphere, an increasingly domestic family site, from which market-productive activities were removed, and in which feminine virtues of sentiment and care were increasingly valorized (see also Barker-Benfield, 1993). In this emerging zone of the middle-class nuclear family, an increasing number of novels were consumed by an interiorized subjectivity, which was encouraged via print, and especially the novel, to imaginary participation in larger collectivities of class and nation.

This line of argument – about the literate practices underlying a middle-class public and private sphere – was developed in more anthropological terms by Anderson's (1991) *Imagined Communities*, an influential comparative study of nationalism. Briefly, Anderson argues that the social origins of nationalism lie in a set of changes in which language figured prominently. In particular, an older European cultural model of belonging or "community" declined as the power of religious belief and explanation deteriorated, divinely justified dynastic regimes were overthrown, and the influence of Latin as a pan-European *lingua franca* waned. The new cultural model, which has comprised the dominant form of political organization in the nineteenth and twentieth centuries, involved the imagining of "nation." The growth and spread of this new system of representations of political belonging were promoted by the ascendance of new secular temporalities, cosmologies, and spatializations (e.g. the time of Darwin, the space of Copernicus and the Mercator projection map), and the emergence and spread of print vernaculars allowing a common language of books and newspapers. The re-ordering of concepts of time and space found political expression in the rise of nationalist regimes claiming primordial origins and citizens' "equality and common belonging." The imagining of primordial origins and common belonging was underwritten, so to speak, by standardized language and print production and consumption.

The analysis of print capitalism is central to Anderson's argument. If the new national consciousness could find evidence of folkish origins in the fixity of print vernaculars, it was because the print vernacular was not just archived for official record and scholarship but also widely available in the form of print-commodities, accessible to emerging middle-class and bourgeois reading publics.[3] If the new consciousness could imaginatively participate in the collectivity of nation by consuming novels and newspapers, and thus entering into landscapes, temporalities, and daily rituals of a given nation, this was because printed books and newspapers emerged in complex symbiosis with the market economies of the given nation. Printed books were an early, archetypal commodity; they were unique yet mechanically produced, widely available yet relatively expensive. Newspapers were primary purveyors of commercial news, notice, and advertisement, and they were very important in republican-constitutionalist ideas about political discourse.

In retrospect, Burke's and Eisenstein's discussions of literacy and print remind us of several things. First, historical studies of literacy show that ambiguities and exclusions in "modern" uses of literacy are fundamental, not accidental, a lesson that needs to be remembered, given our current tendency to simply equate literacy with social progress. Second, the apparently technical consequences of a representational means often result from analytic procedures that collapse complex histories into simple dichotomies, such as in Eisenstein's counterposing print versus manual inscription.[4] Third, and related to the preceding, it is essential to contextualize and historicize, if we are to appreciate the intertwining of literacy practices with other social-semiotic processes – e.g. the dynamics of money and measurement in the early mercantile capitalism that preceded print standardization (Crosby, 1997) or the concern of churches and states with regulation as well as knowledge, with secrecy as well as utilitarian order.

What Anderson clearly shows is that in order to understand "the consequences of print," we cannot treat print as a technical isolate. He rightfully emphasized the importance of print-and-capitalism in North American and European nationalisms, which, with their ideology of national belonging seem to override the divisions of class, race, or gender. However, as Warner (1990) has noted, Anderson does not analyze specific cases of national print capitalism in any detail. As Warner and others have argued, we need to analyze the cultural mediation of the print medium, and of writing more generally, in particular national political economies and cultures, analyzing racial and gender dichotomies and contradictions, as well as their symbolic resolution in an imaginary community of nationality (Pratt, 1987; Silverstein, 2000).

Interlude: practice theory and modernity

Arguments about print capitalism and the cultural mediation of print primarily address the period from the late eighteenth to late twentieth centuries, the era of modern liberal nation states, citizens, and (re)publics, with the ideal of equality twinned to enduring inequality. Understanding this era is also the concern of recent French social theory, in particular works by de Certeau, Bourdieu, and

Foucault, each of whom direct their attention to the symbolic dynamics of belonging and the changing modes of domination in contemporary state-based social orders, but do so while grappling with the problem of practice – how to understand intentional, strategic yet everyday behavior as both conditioned and creative. Their emphasis on practice is grounded in a deep skepticism about Enlightenment legacies and an interest in how rationalized procedures are intertwined with domination, that is, how knowledge and power are linked. Their emphasis on practices has also provided new insights into the role of symbolic processes in the political and economic dynamics of contemporary societies.

De Certeau (1984) perceptively addresses the modern constitution of writing by focusing on ordinary language use, everyday routine, and broadly conceived literacy practices. As we have discussed in chapter 2, his conception of a "scriptural economy" is based on a double separation, one, of a polarizing class structure, separating the people from the bourgeois, the other, a polarizing conceptual structure, separating the oral from the written. In this chapter we will be particularly interested in how schooling in modern nations contributes to this double separation and in using his analyses of oral/written complementarity to understand the culturally shaped exclusions which underlay the emergence in the United States of a common schooling, a national identity, and a "universal" literacy. Bourdieu, especially in his analysis of education systems (Bourdieu, Boltanski, Passeron, and Martin, 1993; Bourdieu and Passeron, 1977), has put forth concepts of cultural and linguistic capital, that is, officially recognized and school-approved symbolic wherewithal – what we might roughly think of as literary heritage and national standard language – in order to explain how schooling functions to perpetuate class privilege and class division, even as the relations change between culture and the economy under capitalism. The capital concept, together with the concept of *habitus* – a socially inculcated disposition to perceive, judge, speak, or act – inform a number of his analyses of symbolic power, the noncoercive yet pervasive power of legitimate language, authorized procedure, and prestigious position (Bourdieu, 1977; Bourdieu, 1991). Overall, Bourdieu's work provides a distinctive and useful emphasis on (1) the increasing centrality of schooling systems in modern social formations and (2) the role of knowledge and culture in strategies of symbolic domination.

In his influential *Discipline and Punish*, Foucault (1975) analyzes the school as one in a set of institutions which regulate ordinary people, a site for the practice of a new kind of power, in which establishing groups, precise measuring and recording, and the careful scheduling of bodily action are micro-techniques of a "disciplinary power" (pp. 170–228). This is a power which is neither centralized nor repressive in the usual sense; it is unlike the raw coercion of dynastic monarchies, of the lord's bailiff or the king's army. Instead it is pervasive and complex, insinuating itself into modern subjectivity, bringing the identities and physical characteristics of ordinary populations within the purview of bureaucratic procedure. In the case we will develop below, as in Foucault's analysis, bureaucratic procedures expand in response to the disorder wrought by the massive population movement and growth of economic forces that characterized the nineteenth and twentieth centuries. In Foucault's account, disciplinary power comprises one of the darker legacies of the Enlightenment as "really existing" in modern nation states, for knowledge techniques are used not to increase freedom and well-being, as our ideals would have it, but rather to adjust ordinary people to a bourgeois domination that presents its rule as justified on universal principles, even while it subjugates others on the basis of their class, race, and gender.

In much of what follows, we confirm this bleak assessment, arguing, in particular, that schooling has been more about discipline than enlightenment, that literacy has been more about difference and hierarchy than about universal inclusion. Nonetheless, we also emphasize that literacy and schooling have been means of struggle for belonging, i.e. for "being American," by groups treated as inherently different and subordinate. We will endeavor to represent this complex historical dialectic – of ideal promise and actual constraint, of intertwined power and resistance-to-power – by means of a historical sketch of the United States, its schooling, and its evolving literacy practices.

Literacy, nationalism, and education in the United States: the early national phase

In the cases that follow we will be concerned with two broad periods of American history, an early national (1780s–1880s) and mature national (1880s–1960s) phase. As periodizations, they are not controversial, they roughly parallel, for example, Cremin's (1976) "national" and "metropolitan" phases of American educational history. They are bounded by severe political and military crises: initiated by the political ferment and seven years' war achieving the American colonies' break with the British empire; punctuated by the American Civil War and the aborted Reconstruction; closed by America's imperial war in Vietnam and the domestic political and cultural upheaval that accompanied that war's latter years, the famous "sixties." Although these two phases do not present unitary periods in terms of dominant literacy practices or educational philosophies – Myers (1996), for example, presents a more fine-grained periodization – they will enable us to examine significant historical eras which reveal changing interactions between politics, economics, and schooling.

The early national phase spans the 1780s–1880s. It is a period in which colonial conceptions of citizenship and print-based public spheres give way to Jeffersonian republicanism, which emphasizes the equality of small producers as the bedrock of a literate, civic virtue. The agrarian-craft ideal of society gives way, in turn, to an expansive society with an industrial economy and increased acceptance of class division and hierarchy. The early national phase begins with a close association between what we would now call "literacy practices" and political subjectivities. In the colonial and early national periods, newspaper publishing, writing, and readership were viewed as essential to the ferment and debate of self-government, to the formation of civic ideals, civic responsibilities, citizen-subjects. This was one strand of a pluralistic culture of literacy of the early nineteenth century, which associated diverse literacy practices with personal and political development.

Many have commented on the role of printer-publishers in the American colonies' break with Britain, including Anderson (1991), in remarks distinguishing North American from European nationalisms. But it is Warner's (1990) *The Letters of the Republic* that develops a full-fledged case study of the cultural mediation of print: the role of publicity and norms of public access in republican ideas about citizenship and government. Prior to this republican constellation of print, publicity, and citizenship were early eighteenth-century literacy regimes emblematized by puritan and planter-aristocratic intellectuals, each dependent upon private libraries and presuming a link between "letters" and "voice" while exemplifying a life of public writing and speaking. As we will see more fully below, there were significant exclusions and hierarchies in these formations: blacks were presumed illiterate; women might read and were expected to do so, especially in puritan New England, but they were not to write – the pen was unwomanly (Monaghan, 1989).

The crystalizing of "republican print ideologies" did not occur until the middle of the eighteenth century. Henceforth, emerging norms of public access to information about the conduct of those governing and of the preferred anonymity of those reporting attest to a further separation of print from particular voices (Warner, 1990) – as well as to the familiar interplay between knowledge and secrecy in literacy practices. For the early American republicans, publicity and public discussion was a North American variant of what Habermas (1989) calls "the bourgeois public sphere," that zone of civil society in which norms of rational discourse – arguments and evidence – ideally hold sway over any other considerations; a discursive sphere in which by participating in public debate, citizens shape the general will while holding those who rule accountable (Cmiel, 1990).

This discursive process is embodied, or better yet, entextualized, in the career of Benjamin Franklin, a printer, publicist, statesman, inventor and land speculator, who wrote prolifically about rights, rationality, and making a modern living as well as a modern political order. Franklin wrote often under pseudonyms, as in his *Autobiography* (Franklin, 1964), or using other ventriloquisms. For example, in the introduction to *Poor Richard's Almanac*, the fictional "Richard" describes overhearing his maxims from an equally fictional "Father Abraham"; then the studiously unidentified author/printer (Poor Richard? Ben Franklin?) complains at length about not being credited with the wisdom of the maxims. In addition to negating the author's voice, Franklin typically represents rational thinking as a manipulation of objects, akin to a printer/editor's manipulation of text. In this way Franklin promoted a view of rationality stripped of authority except for that of logical force or arrangement (Warner, 1990, pp. 88–90). The anonymity of print and the depersonalization of reason were centerpieces of Franklin's view of what the new Republic's political discourse must be like, that is, his view of how the American political subject must enunciate itself. His republican "print ideology" draws upon the Enlightenment assumption that humans are defined essentially by, that their subjectivities are best based upon, their capacity to reason. And writing, as with Hume or Kant (Gates, 1986), or print, as with Franklin, was the means and signifier of such "reason."

The republican ideals of a nation of self-reliant small producers, actively assuming the rights and responsibilities of self-government, powerfully impressed foreign observers, such as Alexis de Tocqueville (1969), who nonetheless noted the exclusions on which such democracy was based: only freeholders, that is, property-owners, were citizens and entitled participants; wage-workers, women, and nonwhites were presumed by early American intellectual elites and the main Enlightenment philosophers to lack the resources and the rationality necessary for political participation (Gates, 1986; Macpherson, 1962; Pateman, 1988). Basic literacy, as opposed to print-mediated political discourse, was less constrained, although it was also shaped by region and category of person.

It is against a backdrop of differentiated but robust literacy practices, together with republican commitments to informal and participating citizenry that we must assess the early American concerns with common or public schooling. What is striking from the beginning is how deeply intertwined are enlightened and democratic impulses with elite fears of common people and strategies of control. The first *public* schools, launched at the end of the eighteenth and beginning of the nineteenth centuries, were a system of charity schools. These were organized and subsidized by business and political elites in response to what they saw as the undisciplined nature of the working classes (Katz, 1969; Nasaw, 1979). Modeled on the Lancaster "factory" system of education, charity schools used strict physical regimentation, rigid hierarchy, surveillance, and precise scheduling. In the words of one historian of education, students were punished for:

talking, playing, inattention, out of seats; being disobedient or saucy to a monitor; snatching books, slates, etc., from each other; moving after the bell rings for silence; stopping to play or making a noise in the street on going home from school; staring at persons who may come into the room; blotting or soiling books; having dirty face or hands; throwing stones; calling ill names; coming to school late; playing truant; fighting; making a noise before school hours; scratching or cutting the desks.

(Ravitch, cited in Nasaw, 1979, p. 20)

Such schools were supposed to discipline the poor, inculcating habits of obedience, punctuality, and thrift, as well as rudimentary literacy and numeracy. They present an austere and exemplary form of the "disciplinary power" Foucault has called to our attention. Conceived as a moral order, they were to transform the character of the working classes and the poor. As might be expected, they were popular with their moneyed patrons, but widely avoided by their intended clients.

In the 1820s a change in the United States' political institutions resulted in increased attention to the question of common education. Suffrage was granted to all white males, regardless of property rights, and this change in political constituency greatly increased the concern of the elite classes about the discipline, character, and morality of the working and pauper classes. In order to address the defects in the embryonic public schools, while capitalizing on elite fears of the enfranchised "King Mob," Horace Mann and allied reformers proposed the common school. These were to be modeled on New England's local or district schools, paid for by compulsory taxes, and staffed by officially selected men of exemplary character. Although the common schools kept much of the disciplinary apparatus of the charity schools, the advocates of the new system aspired to a watered-down version of earlier ideals of literate political participation and civic virtue. Common schools were to strike at the evil of social inequality by enrolling the prosperous as well as the poor, the child of the middle as well as working classes. Compared to charity schools, there was to be less regimentation, more space; less monitorial supervision and more emphasis on the exemplary characters of gentleman/woman teachers. As with the charity school, but now spread across a wider social compass, the common school was to replace the family, workplace, or community in the formation of character and literacy (Lasch, 1996; Ryan, 1981; Zboray, 1993).

This was a significant break with republican belief that participating in the world of work and politics shaped civic character. In the common school two mainstays of early American civic life – political partisanship and denominational rivalry – were forbidden. Politics was to enter the life of youth through the school, and to enter the school only through approved textbooks; so also religion: only if approved and Protestant. Although the new system fit well with precocious middle classes, such as Ryan (1981) describes for Oneida County, New York, what the common school offered and expected as political order and citizen-subjectivity was, in the words of one historian, a "whiggish republicanism" which "emphasized the need for public obedience rather than public participation" (Nasaw, 1979, p. 41).

In studies of literature and histories of reading for this period we can discern a similar cultural shift. Ideals and direct participation in public life are replaced by a more capacious, symbolic form of nation and belonging, which is enacted through the production and consumption of literature. According to Warner's (1990) analysis of literature and political identity, republican print ideologies and conceptions of civic participation give way, early in the nineteenth century, to novelistic fantasies of a publicity and a public life. In the reading of such novels, women as well as men were able to imaginatively participate in the nation, and in the early decades of the nineteenth century, women were given some of the symbolic attributes of citizenship – not suffrage, to be sure, but a place as guardians of the American home in an emerging discourse of domesticity. Zboray, in his study of readership in the antebellum United States (1820s–1850s), shows that the discipline of the charity and common schools coincided with the growth of a discourse of women's domestic sphere, conceived of as morally essential yet counterpoised to public life (Zboray, 1993; Ryan, 1981). This discourse of male public and female domestic spheres emerged in symbiosis with the separation of family from school and school from community. It coincided with technological changes, such as the railroad-based movements of both print commodities and human populations, which contributed to a burgeoning production and consumption of novels and how-to manuals. This was a literature of national lore and self-improvement. It enabled Americans, increasingly dislocated from knowable small towns and rural settings, to construe themselves as and through "a fictive people." Living increasingly "by the book," literate antebellum Americans were able to imagine themselves as a nation, as a people sharing an origin. This occurred at a time when the American state was continually expanding, and when industry and immigration fueled the growth of an evermore complex population differentiated by region, class, national origin, and racial assignment.

What we find in the early national period are different literacy configurations. One, dominated by upper- and middle-class reading publics, was formed in private schooling, family instruction, and church schools, as well as associations and institutions such as lyceums, maternal associations, and libraries. In this configuration there is a shift during the first half of the nineteenth century. As republican print ideologies and political ideals gave way before the press of capitalist development – the widening gap between rich and poor, the forming of large cities, the ongoing westward dispersal of families and individuals – literate Americans increasingly produced, consumed, and defined themselves through a symbolic nation, a literature of a "fictive, ever-shifting and elusive, largely imaginary community" (Zboray, 1993, p. 178). Another configuration, characteristic of the working classes and the poor, had throughout the period shown surprisingly high rates of newspaper readership (Hall, 1993, 1996), less, though still robust consumption of Bibles and psalm books, as well as almanacs and "wonder stories." Formed initially in unpaid family instruction, workplace encounters, diverse church provision, and nascent labor institutions such as the Mechanics Institutes, this plebian literacy was progressively remade by formal schooling, initially the charity and later the common schools (Graff, 1981b; Hall, 1993; Kaestle, Stedman, Tinsley, and Trollinger, 1991; Zboray, 1993).

The brief history of nation, school and text just sketched raises questions about race and gender hierarchies, institutional response to class division, as well as the development of unified fields of symbolic value (Bourdieu, 1991). As significant as the class differences in literacy and schooling appear to be, more profound were the ways gender and race interacted with literacy practices and ideologies, justifying differential access to literacy education and materials, defining legitimate and illegitimate subjects of reading and writing. We can understand this in de Certeau's framework: the separation of writing from orality in the late colonial and early national periods was articulated in terms of *complementarities* of gender and race. As noted, in colonial intellectual formations, including the vaunted literacy of New England, women were not to "take up the pen" in public matters (Monaghan, 1989). Women were more likely to fall prey to what Cremin calls "inert literacy" (1976, pp. 32–33), a "read-only" capacity formed in authoritarian institutions such as churches, with recitation the dominant literacy practice for the dominated. Women in this period rarely received external tuition, having to rely instead on domestic settings and the church (Monaghan, 1989).[5] Even the grim charity schools of the early nineteenth century were for poor male children only (Nasaw, 1979, p. 22). Women might read, listen, be lectured to, but were not to participate in public in speech or print. White American women did subsequently pursue education and employment through the common schools; they showed relatively high rates of signature literacy and of book readership during the early national period, at least in the Northeast (Hall, 1993); and they were avid correspondents with westward moving family and friends (Ryan, 1981). Although assumptions about a "woman's sphere" did not strictly determine antebellum reading materials (Zboray, 1993), they do seem to have been an ideological barrier preventing all but the most determined women from pursuing journalism or other public professions "of letters."

For nonwhites, the situation was different and more dire. As noted earlier, African Americans were deemed "naturally" unfit for literacy by colonial era intellectuals and Enlightenment philosophers more generally. In particular, the argument was that African Americans were inherently inferior to Europeans because they lacked the capacity for reason, and the sign of their lack of reason was their presumed inability to read or write (Gates, 1986; Warner, 1990). Although Native Americans and, later, Mexican populations in the Southwest would be denied access to public schooling and officially sanctioned literacies (Babb, 1993; Foley, 1990; Green, 1994; Walker, 1981), African Americans faced the most fundamental oppression and the sharpest form of exclusion. When postrevolutionary liberalism and the growing abolitionist movement threw the ideology of race-and-writing into doubt, individual states defended and strengthened racial barriers to literacy (Salvino, 1989). In reaction to the movement for common schooling, a number of Southern states passed legislation in the 1830s imposing jail terms and serious fines for anyone caught teaching blacks – whether free or slave – to read or write (Cremin, 1976; Nasaw, 1979). Even under such adversity, African Americans strove to educate themselves, in slave quarters and under various strategems of individual tutelage, for they often equated literacy with liberation from servitude and economic dependency (Salvino, 1989). This liberationist account of literacy has a paradigmatic figure in the life and career of Frederick Douglass, who went from being an illiterate slave to a nationally known man of letters.

A tireless writer, speaker, and publisher for the cause of abolition and the defense of African Americans, Douglass' literacy efforts began under prohibition and in secrecy. He learned to read and write while enslaved, although it was legally forbidden for slaves to do so. Douglass had come to believe early and passionately that in the forbidden scriptal practices of reading and writing were powers of expression and forms of knowledge that would aid his struggles for freedom. In his famous *Narrative of the Life of Frederick Douglass: An American Slave*, Douglass describes how he was initially taught the rudiments of reading by the wife of his owner. When that was forbidden, and the mistress turned against him, he used a subterfuge of ignorance and error to trick white children and workmates in the city of Baltimore into providing lessons in reading or writing:

She [the owner's wife] was an apt woman; and a little experience soon demonstrated, to her satisfaction, that education and slavery were incompatible with each other... From this time I was most narrowly watched. If I was in a separate room any considerable length of time, I was sure to be suspected of having a book, and was at once called upon to give an account of myself. All this, however, was too late. The first step had been taken. Mistress, in teaching me the alphabet, had given me the *inch*, and no precaution could prevent me from taking the *ell*. The plan which I adopted, and the one by which I was most successful, was that of making friends of all the little white boys whom I met in the street...   (Douglass, 1995, p. 48)

There are several things to be noted in this account. First, it begins in violation and transgression of the social and political order imagined by Benjamin Franklin and his Enlightenment forebears. As a slave, that is, a category of person defined in the US Constitution not as a citizen or potential citizen but as property, Douglass acquires initial instruction in the forbidden secrets of literacy from his slave-owning mistress. Acquisition of literacy requires not only secrecy but strategy and determination. When the mistress is forbade teaching by her husband, and comes to see that "education and slavery were incompatible," she and the master mount a vigilance against the forbidden effort by Douglass who was "most narrowly watched." This surveillance, however, is to no avail, for "the first step had been taken." Besides, Douglass was not bound to the domestic realm but employed for wages in the wider city, where workmen and "all the little white boys" could be persuaded or tricked into providing literacy lessons.

In Douglass' life and career, we find an early, defining example of the trope of literacy and liberation – of the perceived link between literacy, freedom, and financial independence. The liberationist motif captures a powerful historical impulse, whatever the complex realities. It is reflected today in African Americans' ongoing if conflicted faith in education and social mobility (Mickelson,

1990; Ogbu, 1988). However, it is important to note also the partial nature of this account, for, as Bassard (1992) reminds us, the ideology of African-American writing and liberation was, in important ways, a masculine story. Freed women slaves published their accounts usually without achieving economic self-sufficiency, and careers in the church, such as other literate former slaves undertook, were closed to women because of their sex. Literate and economically successful African Americans of the antebellum era, such as the free-born abolitionist and journalist Mary Shadd Carey, are usually ignored in such accounts (Rhodes, 1998) because they were not slave, illiterate, or male.

In the emerging American nation state, nonwhites and women occupied subordinate political, social, and cultural positions. Unlike the theoretically "free and equal" citizen-subjects, they were deemed as *by their nature* unfit for full citizenship or full literacy. Hence the ongoing need to struggle, for human recognition, political rights, and educational opportunities. In the case of Euro-American males, however, both working and middle class, we find a more complicated picture. Ostensibly at the center of the developing literacy order, they were more directly implicated in and shaped by the new forms of power associated with literacy and schooling. The older practices of patriarchal and master/slave regulation of access to reading and writing would have involved domestic and community surveillance – husbands and clergy discouraging overly literate wives or daughters; masters and mistresses "narrowly watch[ing]" their inquisitive slaves. But with the emergence of public schooling we confront a "literacy institution" that is a puzzling mix of surveillance, regulation, and freedom.

As we have noted, public schooling embodied conflicting beliefs and practices regarding education and literacy. On the one hand, it drew upon Enlightenment ideals about education, autonomy, personal development and social justice (Cook-Gumperz, 1986; Cremin, 1976). On the other, it was powerfully shaped by elite desires to discipline the sprawling lower orders – to prepare the children of failed farmers and artisans as well as incoming immigrants for work as factory operatives or clerks; literate yes, but compliant also (Graff, 1981b; Nasaw, 1979). Early American educational reformers, such as Horace Mann, sought a system of schooling for all, in which the children of the poor as well as the prosperous would be given the tools for life and citizenship through education. But early American economic and political elites had endorsed and supported the procedures of the charity schools. They had abandoned (if they had ever held) republican ideals of virtue and responsibility, formed through economic self-reliance and self-government, and had opted instead for institutions of discipline and moral order for the children of the laboring poor. They brought this vision of regulation to the implementation of the common schools, in which possibilities for literate self-determination and an enlightened social participation were always secondary to order, that is, an obedience achieved through barracks-like regimentation, supervision, and hierarchy (Salvino, 1989). With

the common schools, the disorder of partisan conflict or denominational passion
was excluded from public education. A scheduled knowledge of wholesome
patriotism and liberal piety would henceforth be the content of a primary literacy, officially recognized and shaped in standard English. Such literacy would
become the norm, the normal literacy against which all other scriptal practices, all other blendings of text and talk, would become not just different but
abnormal, an *il*literacy.

In a provocative early analysis of the changing relations between schooling
and literacy, Cook-Gumperz (1986) has argued that "schooled literacy" emerged
by displacing earlier forms of literacy and education. Recall that colonial
America and England (Cremin, 1976) had quite high literacy rates, based on
task-specific learning in households, workshops, churches, and other sites of
gathering and endeavor, and all of this occurred prior to the providing of universal, compulsory education. Indeed, in the early decades of the nineteenth
century, European visitors to America, such as de Tocqueville (1969), frequently commented on the fervor with which Americans built schools, even
though they were highly variable "dame schools" and community schools with
religious affiliations.[6] What the common school movement did was usher in,
roughly from the period 1820–1870, a system of universal schooling, in which
family, community, and church were pushed further from the educative process,
and in which literacy, formerly a multiplicity of practices and aspirations –
for civic participation, religious piety, workplace advantage – became increasingly a unified system; measured, assessed, and ranked; acquired and expressed
through officially approved texts.

What we have in the early national period is an historical process in which
an intimate, pervasive disciplinary power emerges along with Enlightenment-
inspired political processes and institutions, such as expanding suffrage and
public education. Expressing a liberal optimism about modern institutions and
liberty, Cremin has said the following about literacy in this era: "If nothing else,
the intellectual and social literacy fostered by churches and schools (by which
I mean the near-universal ability to read, write and interact with individuals
who were not kin) afforded people the possibility of release from geographical and social place, and in so doing augmented personal liberty" (Cremin,
1976, pp. 85–86). Expressing a sharp pessimism about modern institutions and
freedom, Foucault has argued that modern schooling is a prominent site of disciplinary power, a "power-knowledge" that remakes morality through relentless
observation, measurement, hierarchy, distribution into groups, and scheduling.
Disciplinary power is the "other face" of Enlightenment universalism, creating
subjects who may live in a world of universal rights but are inured to economic,
political, and cultural domination (Foucault, 1975). It is pertinent in this regard
to note that immediately after his praise for education and liberty, Cremin notes:
"the vernaculars [literacies] did not necessarily augment liberty for the slaves,
or for the Indians, or for the voluntarily or involuntary segregated, or for those

who failed to perceive the opportunities or who were prevented from taking advantage of them" (p. 86).

Literacy, nationalism, and education in the United States: the mature national phase

During the subsequent historical period, the mature national phase, the United States emerged as a major industrial economy. The school system greatly expanded, refining the nature and scope of a schooled literacy which, despite its universalizing idioms, retained the familiar hierarchies of race, gender, and class. The normative literate subject of this later period continued the earlier emphasis on an American cultural–national identity, but now as part of explicitly hierarchical, meritocratic social order. This phase spans the 1880s–1960s. It is a period initiated by the closing of the Western frontier, a period in which there is a dominant corporatizing of many aspects of American life, and a period in which technical efficiency, quantification, and rational planning emerge as dominant values. It is also a time of standardization – in language, in markets and taste, and in the scale and organization of schooling.

During this second phase, the nineteenth-century ideal of common schooling gave way to a twentieth-century emphasis on individualized, ability-ranked, and curriculum-tracked schooling. The emphasis on the promotion of individual talent required, in turn, the separation and ranking of individuals in new ways. This seriating and stratifying was aided by greater technical sophistication in teaching and learning and, in particular, by the emergence of a testing paradigm that assumes differences on tests are due to differences in individual ability. As testing became pervasive, and twentieth-century schooling practices such as ability grouping and curriculum tracking became common, literacy shifted from being conceived as a civic–moral virtue to being conceived as an economic–technical skill.

In this period a familiar, contemporary conception of literacy emerges: literacy is an "autonomous skill," a set of socially neutral and context-independent aptitudes with the standard language, which underpins the entire project of education and of political and economic participation. Writing generally of industrial economies and modern nations, Gellner (1983) provides a useful characterization of the relations presumed to hold between modern industrial economies, literacy, and categories of belonging, such as "employability" and "citizenship":

a society has emerged based on a high-powered technology and the expectancy of sustained growth, which requires both a mobile division of labor, and sustained, frequent, and precise communication between strangers involving a sharing of explicit meaning, transmitted in standard idiom and in writing when required. . . . [In such a society,] [t]he level of literacy and technical competence, in a standardized medium, a common conceptual currency, which is required of all members of this society if they are to be properly employable and enjoy full and effective moral citizenship, is so high that it simply *cannot* be provided by the kin or local units, such as they are.

(pp. 34–35 emphasis in original)

In light of this familiar, recurring but still interesting claim about "level[s] of literacy... required of all members of society," let us now briefly sketch the changes in the economy, the official language, and the organization of schooling which brought about the conditions for this ostensible "common conceptual currency." As we will see, there is much to debate about its commonality, and a tale to be told about power in the construction of a "conceptual currency."

The period under review is one in which the large-scale organization of the system of production became a dominant feature of US social life (Bowles and Gintis, 1976; Lasch, 1991). The mature national period is when the great American monopolies emerged in transportation, agriculture, banking and finance, and food processing (Zinn, 1980). It is the age of the corporation, understood as a centrally sited, bureaucratically organized business concern in which rationalization, compartmentalization, and hierarchical command are taken as given (Spring, 1972). This brought in its train the dominance of corporate models and the pervasive standardizing of key areas of social life. This occurred in education from the 1880s to the 1910s as a number of states enacted compulsory attendance laws, and a new system of public secondary education emerged (Cazden and Dickinson, 1981; Nasaw, 1979).

The standardizing of language also proceeded along several fronts. First, in reaction to the great labor migrations of the turn of the century, which had enriched, diversified, and complicated the American social order, a number of laws were passed from the 1880s to the 1920s, at the state and federal level, enforcing a policy of monolingual English use in education and official business (Heath, 1981; Urciuoli, 1996). Second, in the 1890s, in anticipation of the great expansion of secondary education then underway, the discipline and subject matter of English was organized. English received a particular curricular and textual-linguistic specification when the Committee of Ten, an elite planning group, devised "School English," a general set of principles and maxims for appropriate language use in the secondary curriculum (Wright, 1981). Lastly, a broad-based concern with the relation between standard language and education was articulated in the post-World War II period. The great rural-to-urban internal migrations in the United States, from the 1910s to the 1950s, had brought millions of rural migrant children into urban school systems, where they disproportionately failed (Nasaw, 1979); in this period the numerous regional varieties of English spoken by those migrants became thematized as "Nonstandard English" and hence as part of the educational "problem" (Shopen and Williams, 1982).

Perhaps the greatest change in schooling during the mature national period was the development of public high schools, a system of universal secondary

education, in the period 1895–1915 (Cremin, 1976; Nasaw, 1979). This expansion of the schooling system led to a series of technical–organizational
changes which have characterized American public education through much
of the twentieth century, and these changes give specific content to the notion
of a stratified, hierarchical literacy. The transformation from an elite system of
classical education into a public secondary system had created a pedagogical
and organizational crisis. What were the new kinds of student – female and
working-class – to be taught? Elite reformers judged the new entrants as unprepared and perhaps congenitally unfit for classical education (Nasaw, 1979) –
the rigors of algebra, geometry, and Latin.[7] The problem of what to teach was
dealt with by providing for a tracked curriculum, one track "academic" and
the other "vocational," the former for the sons of the middle classes, the latter
for the sons and daughters of factory operatives, small farmers, and unskilled
laborers.[8]

Curriculum tracking in high school is a primary aspect of educational grouping, but the practice of grouping also spread downward into the earliest primary
years, where it more finely differentiated and segregated the student population. Grouping in the elementary school was based on putative ability, and such
groups were formed within individual classrooms. As with tracking, the ratio-
nale for ability grouping was that it provided greater efficiency: such grouping
would enable teachers to tailor instruction to the needs of small, relatively ho-
mogenous sets of students. The slow-learning or underprepared would not be
baffled by lessons appropriate to the advanced classmate; similarly, the quick
and clever student would not be held back or bored by slower-paced lessons.
(So also in the counterpart tracked curriculum, the daughter of a laborer would
not be frustrated by her inability to master algebra if she never took algebra
[but learned typing instead], and the son of a store owner, en route to becoming an engineer, could be given and learn his algebra more quickly.) In this
way and under this justification, equal opportunity – to learn according to one's
aptitudes and prospects – could be wed to unequal outcomes. For along with
a meritocractic ideology, an avowed purpose of the school was to prepare its
student population for different positions in a highly stratified workforce, and
the preparation began early and continued throughout the schooling process
(Collins, 1988; Eder, 1986; Oakes, 1985; Rosenbaum, 1981).

This significant increase in the differentiation and stratification of students
and knowledge could not have been achieved without the spread of testing.
By quantifying selected aspects of educational or psychological performance,
testing turned heterogeneous multitudes into discrete series (Gould, 1981). Once
it is accepted that differences on tests are differences in individual aptitude, it
is possible to group and stratify neutrally, that is, on apparent ability and not on
overtly social criteria such as prosperity or poverty, dialect or language spoken,
skin color, or gender. Tests thus work toward a new, individualized subjectivity,
dissolving and reconstructing individuals and groups into discrete traits which

can be organized along unilinear scales – say, IQ or Reading Readiness. We do not here want to enter into the ongoing debates about "standardized testing" in American life, but do want to point out that testing procedures comprise a new kind of impersonal power involving "the management of persons through the subjection of individual actions to an imposed analytic framework and cumulative measures of performance. The quantitative comparison and evaluation of these evoked individual performances leads to an ordering of individuals under statistical norms" (Danziger, 1990, p. 70).

Writing on the politics of educational remediation, Rose (1985) has described the drive to quantify aspects of literacy in the early decades of this century. Quantifying literacy was integral to the rise of testing and, in Rose's view, is part of a quintessentially American desire to provide technical descriptions and solutions to complex social problems. In the case Rose discusses, quantifying approaches to literacy arose from the desire to turn the analysis of reading and writing problems – which were encountered on a greatly increased scale as the schooling system expanded – into apparently precise, technical procedures. In this effort, aspects of the form of language (words known; knowledge of parts of speech) are taken as diagnostic of literacy more generally. They may be indicators of reading problems or writing quality, but on their own they are too often a superficial diagnostic. There is also, as Rose notes, a distinctly Foucauldian aspect to these developments. In the testing-and-quantifying approach, which employs a "normalizing" practice as just described in the preceding quote, problems with reading or writing standard English texts are interpreted in a medical framework. In this framework, rates of individual errors become evidence of so-called deficiencies and disabilities, that is, of *ab*normalities. These, in turn, require a special class of medical–educative intervention – remediation – which emerges as a construct early in the century and now pervades our thinking about literacy and schooling (Rogers, 2000; Spear-Swerling and Sternberg, 1996).

Here, in a nutshell, we have the main features of attempted technical resolutions to the social, educational, and literacy problems brought forth at the turn of the century and continuing through much of the next half-century. As Lasch (1996) has argued, with the closing of the American frontier in the 1880s, and the flowering of an industrial capitalist social order, republican conceptions of democracy were largely abandoned. From the 1880s onward, an elite discourse of social mobility and meritocracy became dominant. In this elite view, society would be hierarchical rather than democratic, and headed by an "aristocracy of talent." This "talent" would be the apex of a greatly expanded education system, which must more assiduously perform its role of rationing class privilege by normalizing, differentiating, and ranking an increasingly schooled and literate population. As schooling was transformed during this period, literacy was increasingly conceived of in terms of autonomous skills, measured by tests, conceived of as foundational to all education and necessary for participation in the industrial economy. In this process, the dominant conception of literacy shifts from that of a moral–civic virtue to that of a basic technical skill, differentially distributed across populations which are constructed quantitatively, that is, as aggregates of trait-bearing individuals. Schooled literacy becomes part of a technical economy of literacy, presuming an individualized literate subjectivity defined within an increasingly stratified educational system.

The preceding summary is necessarily a simplification of a vast and complex history in which there were numerous countercurrents. To take but one example, progressive era educators, such as John Dewey, argued for civic-minded conceptions of education and literacy. However, we think that our account is basically accurate: as Dewey's admirers as well as critics admit, his efforts to ground knowledge in experience was over-ridden by business-led efforts to regulate job training through narrow vocational education (Aronowitz and Giroux, 1985); and his vision of learner-centered literacy was always overshadowed by the testing paradigm (de Castell and Luke, 1983). The overall significance of the developments we have described is that the school became a central institution through which the conditions of appropriate belonging were defined for the polyglot, racialized, and working-class multitudes of the US nation state. Literacy, in turn, became the basic criteria for educability and, hence, for what Gellner describes as "full employab[ility]" and "full and effective moral citizenship."

What we know now, however, and it is a lesson registered in many other advanced industrial societies, is that key organizational and social assumptions about meritocratic equal opportunity have proven untenable (Bourdieu and Passeron, 1977; Jencks, 1972). Furthermore, if we acknowledge legacies of racism in the formation of the US, meritocratic ideology is put yet more sharply into question. If the perpetuation of class division was one outcome of grouped, stratified schooling during the mature national period, racial division and hierarchy were reinforced throughout the period by having a so-called "separate but equal" educational system. (In sketching the relations between racialized political domination, education, and literacy, we will again focus on the African-American experience. Different though commensurable accounts of "separate and unequal" education could be provided for the boarding school system which Native Americans were subjected to (e.g. Ellis [1996] or the racially segregated schooling fought by Chicanos in the American Southwest; Foley [1990]; Ogbu [1979]).)

Long-lasting educational apartheid had significant consequences for language-and-literacy attitudes as well as literacy achievements. Surveys of literacy from the 1870s onwards consistently report lower literacy rates among nonwhite populations. In 1900, for example, on a national survey of literacy, 4.6% of native whites, 12.9% of white immigrants, and 44.5% of nonwhites reported themselves as illiterate (Kaestle, 1991, p. 25). Although African-American literacy rates improved significantly over the next thirty years, African Americans have never achieved parity in literacy rates with

Euro-Americans.[9] If we ask why this is so, that African Americans predominantly resided in the South is part of the reason, for this region had lower literacy rates than the rest of the country from the antebellum period through the 1970s (Kaestle, 1991; Zboray, 1993, Appendix). But lesser literacy achievement also reflects the specific effects of post-Civil War white supremacy, in particular, the drastically underfunded system of "Negro education" that held throughout the Jim Crow South, from Reconstruction to the 1960s (Ogbu, 1979). Notwithstanding the achievements of African-American writers and intellectuals in the first half of the twentieth century – W. E. B. DuBois, Zora Neale Hurston, and Langston Hughes spring to mind – for the majority of African Americans, the Jim Crow system of *de jure* segregation and the urban North system of *de facto* segregation (Lowi, 1969) created a parallel, inferior system within the public schooling system.

One aspect of the Jim Crow mentality was a customary Euro-American hostility to African Americans being educated "above their station." This last is well captured in Richard Wright's *Black Boy*, an autobiographical account of growing up in Mississippi and Tennessee in the early decades of this century. In a famous passage, he describes the subterfuge employed to obtain books from the public library in the city of Memphis, Tennessee, where he was living as a young man. In order to obtain books from the public library – an institution from which African Americans were refused admission, let alone book-borrowing privileges – Wright must use the library card of a sympathetic Euro-American co-worker. He carries a note to the library as if he is merely a Negro fetching books for a white man. Although sharply questioned by the librarian, his deception works, and he returns home with a stack of novels. These simultaneously whet his appetite for more books and feed his desperation to leave the South (Miller, 1997).[10]

Wright's story of literacy, secrecy, and the desire for freedom reminds us, of course, of Douglass' account. There are shifting alliances with whites, and various subterfuges, necessary to circumvent a racial system of power by becoming literate, and there is the promise that through becoming educated one is able to speak more directly against that system and to one's individual and collective place in the world. This account reminds us, anew, that the legacies of literacy are complex; they involve exclusions and shifting boundaries as well as technical measurement and the promise of social progress (Graff, 1988).

Striving for literacy and the full citizenship education seems to promise, African Americans have been nonetheless associated with orality, in popular imagination, academic analysis, and intellectual self-definition (Baker, 1988; Jordan, 1988; Salvino, 1989). There is much to commend in this emphasis on the human voice. The blues, a great twentieth-century musical form, emerged from vernacular story-and-song traditions (Baker, 1984; Erickson, 1984; Jones, 1963). African-American narratives, from the street corner anecdote to the preacher's sermon to the rapper's ballad, are seen as deeply rooted in speech traditions, traditions that contrast, where they do not conflict, with the language of schooling (Gee, 1996; Gilmore, 1986; Gilyard, 1991; Labov, 1995; Morgan, 1998). We must, however, also realize that "black orality" emerges in relation to ideologies of "white literacy" (Salvino, 1989). Indeed, in the modern era there is a negative sense in which "orality" equates with "illiteracy." Despite the many contributions of African Americans to twentieth-century arts and letters (Baker, 1988; Gates, 1990) and the post-Reconstruction commitments to education and literacy, culminating in the civil rights movement (Babb, 1993; Marable, 1984; Ogbu, 1979), a popular perception by many Euro-Americans and some African Americans is that speaking "dialect" means "ignorant and uneducated" (Jordan, 1988; Mitchell-Kernan, 1970; O'Neil, 1998; Perry, 1998). The polarizing of "black voice" and "written language" is a gross stereotype, but we would suggest that it points to a historical relation holding between African Americans, public schooling, and officially recognized literacy. As Salvino (1989) has argued for the nineteenth century, "black orality" emerges in relation to dominant ideologies of "white literacy." We continue to live with that legacy: as we discuss more fully in the next chapter, it is a distinctive feature of the post-civil rights era that the question of vernacular speech versus officially recognized school language has periodically erupted into the public arena (Baugh, 1999; Morgan, 1994). The late recent Ebonics controversy, over the use of African-American Vernacular English in public schools, attests to the continuing volatility of speech, literacy, and racial identity (Collins, 1999; Delpit and Perry, 1998; Long, 2003).[11]

Along with class and race, another major axis of inequality in the mature national period was gender. In the struggles against slavery and Jim Crow segregation, African Americans and their historical allies have challenged Enlightenment-inspired nationalism, showing that it involved racism and racial exclusion along with the ideal universality of enfranchised citizens. In a similar vein, the struggles of successive women's movements have questioned fundamental assumptions about public and private, in particular, that the former is a realm of "fraternal" equality, the latter a domain of "natural" difference (Pateman, 1988). Instead, feminists have persistently argued that sexism, not nature or free choice, accounts for their subordinate place in family settings, educational contexts, legal arenas, and job markets. But the relations of gender to literacy do not replicate those of race. If African Americans as a group are historically associated with *il*-literacy, women as a group are associated with *different* literacies. Rather than residential segregation, women have faced domestic sequestration.

The cultural ideal for women in the mature national period assigned them to a special "woman's sphere." Largely domestic, but in the case of middle-class women extending outwards to charity and good works, the woman's sphere idealized female roles in the family and community but also allowed them to appropriate responsibility for portions of the education system. For example, although women were not initially intended as common school teachers, within a few decades they had achieved a rough parity with men (Zboray, 1993; Ryan, 1981), and in the great school expansion of the 1880s–1910s women became the overwhelming majority of primary school teachers. The reasons for this workplace success lay in teachers' organizations as well as cultural assumptions and economic calculations. The cultural assumption was that women's nurturing domesticity made them natural teachers of young children, an idea prevalent today (Luttrell, 1996; Mickelson, 1992). The economic calculation was simply that women could be paid less than men for equivalent work, including the work of teaching (Apple, 1987; Pollit, 1993).

The separation of spheres, as gender norms and lived realities, shaped women's work opportunities in the expanding school system as well as the knowledge female students were prepared for and allowed access to. In the public high schools that emerged from 1895 to 1915, the new-coming girls as well as working-class boys were shunted into vocational tracks and discouraged from traditional academic pursuits (Nasaw, 1979). Women's access to high school teaching was greatly restricted throughout much of the mature national period, and even more so their access to professional training (Apple, 1987). The separation was reflected also in the emergence of gender-specific advertising and mass-circulation magazines early in the mature period. The *Ladies Home Journal* was established in 1883, quickly reached a readership of over a million, and, as its name suggests, was targeted at women and their normative spheres of concern and consumption.[12] As a recent historical study of magazine publishing and readership has reported, the gender dichotomy has continued throughout this century: "pervasive differences in reading material aimed at women and at men continue. This is one dimension on which popular reading material has not drawn American readers together to promote common aspirations, interests, and expectations. . . . popular magazines reflect and reinforce a culture divided by gender" (Damon-Moore and Kaestle, 1991, pp. 270–271).

Numerous women, however, worked against the cultural, political and economic constraints of a patriarchal social order. While the magazine as mass cultural form reified domesticity and the household as woman's natural social sphere, it also opened a venue for the presentation and discussion of the aspirations toward freedom of the New Woman (Ohmann, 1996, pp. 266–272). Building upon earlier abolitionist–feminist arguments, suffragettes of the 1910s and 1920s challenged their constitutional exclusion from the political sphere, organizing, agitating for, and winning political suffrage in 1922 (Zinn, 1980). Activated during the general social mobilizations of the civil rights and anti-war movements, feminists of the 1960s and 1970s demanded and gained legislative and jural redress for unequal treatment in the workplace and educational system (Pollit, 1993). As might be expected, oftentimes literacy and education were sought as a means of individual autonomy in defiance of family patriarchy. In Tinsley and Kaestle's (1991) study of reading practices in the first decades of this century, we find that for women from prosperous "native-born" families, as well as those from struggling immigrant families, extensive reading was often a way of exploring alternatives to the traditional domestic roles of wife and mother. The life of Emma Goldman, a turn-of-the-century immigrant from Russia who became a well-known writer, political activist, and cultural and sexual iconoclast, exemplifies a radical version of this challenge. Her autobiographical descriptions of reading, studying, and defying her father's commands that she marry early provide a striking example of a woman drawing upon print to find resources for pushing against the traditional gender identities of the period, for defining an alternative feminine subjectivity (Goldman, 1970).

At other times the challenge to patriarchal assumption about gender identities and literacy practices was less radical. Sicherman (1989) provides a case study of the reading practices of the prosperous Hamilton family, who lived in Fort Wayne, Indiana, in the latter decades of the nineteenth century. We are told that three generations of women in this "self-consciously literary family" (p. 202) read widely and often, constituting themselves into "a sort of reading club" (p. 206). In their reading, talk about reading, and writing and exchange of letters, Hamilton women liberally interspersed references to works read, appropriated characters, and discussed plot lines, and proclaimed and apparently lived lives of independence and achievement quite at odds with the ideal of domestic, submissive femininity characteristic of the era. It is notable that there was an unusually large number of careers among the women of this family, and an equally notable antipathy to marriage: eleven out of twelve third-generation women chose not to marry. This suggests something of the intertwining of normative assumptions about women's place, women's knowledge, and women's literacy. The assumptions could be challenged, but not separately.

If the experiences and struggles of African Americans for equality have confirmed DuBois' observation about the centrality of the "color line" in the twentieth century, American women's struggles for equality during the mature national phase have shown the "woman's sphere" to be a site of struggle as well as sequestration. However, as with African Americans, the legacies of literacy are more complex than a simple matter of gaining greater access and equality. Though that has been undeniably important, also significant are enduring puzzles which show that literacy practices are deeply entangled with forms of identity and structures of privilege and disprivilege. Mickelson (1992), in an essay entitled "Why Does Jane Read and Write So Well: the Anomaly of Women's Achievement," discusses how girls and young women currently outperform their male counterparts but do not fare as well in later stages of schooling, nor in the job market. The possible reasons for this differential "payoff" for schooled literacy are maturational issues (young girls identify keenly with school; young women do not) as well as sex-segregated job markets. Several ethnographic studies of working-class women's experiences of adult literacy and education have suggested that, in the words of Kate Rockhill, "literacy is women's work but not women's right" (Rockhill, 1993). What this refers to is that women bear a culturally defined responsibility for literacy, sharply expressed in the 1990s explosion of interest in "family literacy" (Rogers, 2000), but they often do not feel entitled "by right" to education or schooled literacy (Luttrell, 1996; Puckett, 1992).

The practice/post-structuralist approaches can provide new perspectives on these familiar paradoxes and anomalies, for they also question Enlightenment assumptions about the relation between political rights and social identity. Otherwise put, and paraphrasing an old slogan, they enable us to crosscut the personal and the political, analyzing how definitions of literacy create new understandings of personal adequacy and inadequacy and how school procedures adjust individuals to structural inequality.

Let us take first de Certeau's concern with the *complementarity* of writing and orality. We have previously discussed the association of African Americans with lesser rates of literacy and noted that the concern with the "spoken" versus the "written" is part of the ongoing debate about African Americans, their cultural practices, and social justice in the American state. In thinking about the mature national period, we may profitably focus on the contrast literate versus illiterate, viewing it as a reformulation of the writing/orality dichotomy, and bearing in mind de Certeau's reminder that the writing/orality contrast is not an analytic constant but an historically variable relationship. Germane to this matter is an essay by Donald (1983) "How Illiteracy Became a Problem (and Literacy Stopped Being One)." Using English historical materials pertinent to our prior discussion, Donald shows that in the nineteenth century, literacy was often seen as a problem: how to prevent seditious or "unwholesome" texts from being consumed; more generally, how to regulate the literacies of the working masses. By the twentieth century, however, the problem has become one of "insufficient" literacy, or *il*literacy.

The issue of illiteracy, in the guise of recurring "literacy crises," has occupied public attention at various times in the twentieth century, and now occupies the US political establishment in the twenty-first (Coles, 1998; Ohmann, 1987; Rose, 1989). In thinking about this issue, we should begin by noting that current debates about illiteracy usually have little to do with the basic ability to decode or encode text – those capabilities, which we might consider literacy, are near-universal in the United States. A National Assessment of Education Progress (NAEP) survey from the mid-1980s reported that 95 percent of young American adults, excluding those who did not speak English, had basic literacy skills: they could write a simple description, locate a single piece of information in a newspaper article, match grocery store coupons, and fill in personal information in a job application (Kirsch and Jungeblut, 1986). Nonetheless, we have frequent media alarms about a literacy crisis complete with national campaigns to "combat illiteracy," such as the national volunteers program America Reads, which was launched as a national presidential initiative in 1996 (Edmondson,

2000). In light of such contrary facts and tendencies, we are understandably puzzled. What is going on here?

One thing to bear in mind is that in debates about "illiteracy," the definitions are typically cast in terms of years of schooling, not literacy *per se*. More significantly, the number of years of schooling used as diagnostic of literacy has steadily increased throughout this century. As Rose has observed:

> In the 1930s "functional literacy" was defined by the Civilian Conservation Corps as a state of having three or more years of schooling; during the Second World War the Army set the fourth grade as a standard; in 1947 the Census Bureau defined functional illiterates as those having fewer than five years of schooling; in 1952 the bureau raised the criterion to the sixth grade; by 1960 the Office of Education was setting the eighth grade as a benchmark; and by the late 1970s some authorities were suggesting that the completion of high school should be the defining criterion of functional literacy.
>
> (Rose, 1989, p. 6)[13]

What we have in such a chronology is a conflation of years of schooling and literacy, in which the lack of a certain number of years of formal education is taken as *prima facie* evidence of *il*literacy. This is relevant to an old theme in the literacy debate: that claims about the social or cognitive "consequences of literacy" – or in this case, illiteracy – often confound the effects of institutional practices and the results of literacy practices. In this case, as Gee (1996) has cogently argued, the discourse about "literacy" often expresses a thinly veiled fear about the school abilities of a younger and increasingly nonwhite US population.

Pertinent also to our thinking about the changing quantitative criteria of literacy are the *values* which adhere to either side of the modern literacy divide, for these also vary historically. According to historians of education, many elites in nineteenth-century Europe and England saw literacy for the common people as an evil that would promote subversion and disorder. The idea of universal education was at that time associated with the French Revolution and the American national experiment, both of which were viewed with distaste by traditional conservatives (de Tocqueville, 1969; Graff, 1988; Resnick and Resnick, 1988). A similar but racialized reaction was evident in the acts of the Southern elites who outlawed schooling for African Americans in the 1840s. However, as noted, in the United States, from the earliest years of the republic, widespread *white* literacy was promoted as necessary to secure social order and prevent disorder. This viewpoint, with or without the racial exclusiveness, spread throughout much of the world in the latter nineteenth and early twentieth centuries. As we noted above, throughout the twentieth century it has been *il*literacy which has been the object of official concern. If we view literacy/illiteracy as complementary terms, in de Certeau's sense, then literacy has been equated with order, progress, and social potential, and *il*literacy with disorder, backwardness, and futility; literacy has been specified in terms of years of education or specific test scores, *il*literacy has been everything else, and rarely studied in its own right.

Challenging such inherited stereotypes has been difficult because we do not know very much about the "practical lives" of nonliterates in the contemporary US. As Rockhill (1993) has argued, large-scale literacy surveys ignore peoples' everyday literacy practices, and the official discussions of "illiteracy" are particularly prejudicial against the mundane literacy practices of working-class women. Although the number of descriptive studies is small, where nonliterates have been studied, a varied picture emerges. In contrast to the media and governmental presentations, in which illiteracy is a dangerous and crippling incapacity, nonliterate adults usually have what anthropologists call "coping strategies." In particular, they have social networks through which they can turn to others for help with the reading or writing tasks they have to accomplish (Fingaret, 1983). It also appears that the meaning of illiteracy is strongly influenced by one's social position and gender.

An interesting case is provided by Soltow and Stevens (1981), who conducted extended interviews with three adult nonliterates – a miner, a pipe-fitter, and an electrician – as part of their study of literacy and the economy. Each interviewee was quite aware of literacy, and engaged in literate communication through intermediaries. The miner's wife, for example, read his mail and transcribed his dictated responses. Each also had job-specific adaptations. The electrician, for example, had learned to read blueprints, though he did not read alphabetic text of the usual sort. Most striking, however, given the low evaluation of their abilities reported by many poorly schooled people (Luttrell, 1997; Rogers, 2000), these adult, male nonliterates argued that *literacy* hinders thinking, that the unlettered are more creative and independent in their thought (see Lee, 1976; Soltow and Stevens, 1981, pp. 8–9).

This reversal of usual expectations about literacy recalls Eisenstein's distinction between populations that learn by doing and those that "live by the book." But in this case it is living by the book that is viewed with skepticism, a minority viewpoint in contemporary America, but not without precedent. There is evidence of a class-based distrust of people who live by manipulating symbols, of "pencil pushers" as they used to be called, and in working-class communities in the US and abroad there are reports of profound, if conflicted, feelings about the value of "working with your hands" (Bourdieu, 1984; Brandau and Collins, 1994; Hoggart, 1957; Lamont, 1998; Sennett and Cobb, 1972; Willis, 1981). In this case, it is surely also significant that the men espousing such skeptical views were employed in skilled jobs which allowed them to provide a secure living for their families.

A different picture is formed when we turn to a recent study of a young, nonliterate woman. *Other People's Words* (Purcell-Gates, 1995) is a study of an urban Appalachian family in which parents and children have very minimal abilities with conventionally recognized reading or writing. The author argues that the partially literate young mother, Jenny, lives under numerous profound constraints because of her lack of reading and writing skills. Although it is debatable just how constrained Jenny is, and just what her "nonliteracy" consists of, what is undeniable is that she feels deeply shamed by her experiences of schooling and her lack of formal education. Further, she sees her lack of literacy preparation as a sort of disease that she may pass on to her children. What is interesting, and sufficient to our purposes here, is that neither her husband, who is also apparently nonliterate but also usually employed as a roofer, nor her son, who is low-achieving in school literacy, but otherwise an intelligent and quick-witted child, share the mother's high valuation of school literacy nor her sense of stigma at being "illiterate." These gendered attitudes about literacy seem to have deep cultural roots (Puckett, 1992).

We have suggested that so-called illiterates often have more resources and resourcefulness than official representations suggest, but also that the experience and expression of nonliteracy may be strongly influenced by gender. These findings are relevant for de Certeau's general argument that the "oral" (or illiterate) and "written" (or literate) are not fixed entities with some transhistorical inherent content, rather they are intertwined categories suffused with the intentions of modern power and progress. In terms of de Certeau's model of writing (chapter 2 and de Certeau, 1984, pp. 134–135), we may consider *il*literacy as the "blank page" against which literacy, the ability to read and write in officially approved ways, works a transformation, providing the conditions and occasions for meritocracy to unfold and be understood. Acceptable education and literacy are always defined against an "other" with an insufficient or *il*literacy. Literacy tests specified the inadequacies of World War I army recruits, of millions of immigrants and their children, of the "remedial" reading and writing of new arrivals to the expanded high school. Testable literacy helped delineate a new subjectivity: quantitatively ranked populations of educable (or ineducable) individuals stripped of class, race, or gender, and of the experiences of language and literacy that go with those social positions, and so equally ready for reward or failure. In this sense, the literacy/illiteracy dichotomy marks a crucial social boundary in the mature national era and, as a categorizing of knowledge and identity, helps consolidate schooled literacy.

There is also, as noted earlier, a Foucauldian aspect to the development of schooled literacy. The advent of universal schooling did not simply replace prior nonliteracy with literacy. Instead, schooled literacy emerged out of and in response to a complex, multifaceted commonplace literacy – of workplace, church, family, and politics. But schooling and school literacy became the norm, against which all other practices and capacities are either invisible or seen and judged deficient (Cook-Gumperz, 1986; Rockhill, 1993). In this way, disciplinary power transforms a multiplicity of practices into a graded series. In this new system of power, normalization is a key tactic: to fall outside the norm is to be deviant, not different, incapable, not otherwise endowed. To read a blueprint is not literacy, though to read a prose passage is. In this normalizing practice, functional illiteracy is not the inability to read or write but the inability to read or write at certain levels within a prescribed domain. One can be "illiterate" by reading or writing at fourth-grade levels when fifth is the criterion, at ninth-grade levels when tenth grade is the benchmark.

Foucault argued that "disciplinary power" formed subjects adjusted to inequality, disposed in the depths of their being to accept hierarchy, discrimination, and domination, despite their living in nation states committed to formal legal–jural equality. Grouping practices, which are endemic in US public schooling and a primary feature of school literacy (Collins, 1986; Eder, 1986), are a form of such power. Grouping entails the careful monitoring and recording of performance, rigid categories of legitimate knowledge, the pervasive ranking of ability, and concomitant segregation. Grouping practices have been a primary pedagogical and organizational practice for "managing diversity" in American schools for most of the twentieth century (Oakes, 1985; Rosenbaum, 1981). They have helped construct and reinforce a modern literacy, and literacy inequality, through fine differentiations of standard language, school literacy, and school knowledge (Collins, 1989; 1996).

Conclusion

In this chapter we have argued that literacy has been fundamentally shaped by the emergence of modern forms of power and, further, that education and literacy have been fundamental aspects of this "new power." As Gellner argued in his study of nationalism, "The monopoly of legitimate education is now more important, more central than is the monopoly of legitimate violence" (1983, p. 34). As we saw in our discussion of early modern literacy practices, the power of fathers, churches, and princes was greatly concerned with regulating literacy and education, for literacy practices always went beyond paternal, religious or political control, "aiding and abetting" heresy, sexual transgression, or political intrigue. The early modern synergy of print technologies and capitalism gave the possibility of new ways of belonging, beyond the familiar institutions of family, church, and kingdom.

The truly modern political entity, emerging throughout the world in the nineteenth and twentieth centuries, was the nation state. A major challenge facing modern states has been how to form a nation from a state, that is, how to form a cultural–ideological identity from among the diverse populations administered and regulated by a given state. The historical question may be posed as follows: given the ongoing divisions and conflicts between the rich and the poor, women and men, the European-descended and other "races," how is a unity such as "The People" to be created? The historical pathways are diverse, but seem to involve three general processes or features: (1) careful definition and extension of citizenship; (2) extension of a system of social welfare; and, less often noted, (3) racism (Asad, 1990; Wallerstein, 1995).

The delimitations of US citizenry, both actual and symbolic, are important to recall. Republican virtue of the Jeffersonian type, with its commitments to participation, debate, and local self-governance, was only for freeholders, that is, property owners. As the extensions of "universal" suffrage to a white male electorate occurred in the 1820s, the creation of common schooling – a classic social welfare provision – became a pressing concern of American elites as well as nascent middle classes, and a now-familiar American equation of literacy and prosperity emerges. Women are often potent symbols of nation, those who protect the home and must be protected from foreign violators. In the US one thinks of Betsy Ross and the flag, as well as the heroines of pioneer novels. But in the US women were not granted suffrage until 1922 and then only after a long, protracted struggle, and they were consistently provided second-class educational opportunities (Cott, 2000). Nonwhites in many respects faced a more extreme exclusion from the citadel of citizenship. Except under the de-tribalizing requirements of the Allotment Acts of the 1880s, Native Americans were not granted citizenship until 1924. African Americans were legally sub-human prior to the Civil War and the Emancipation Proclamation. Although adult men were given the vote in 1865, white reactionary violence, as well as stratagems such as manipulating voting rolls and literacy tests (Marable, 1984; Zinn, 1980), kept the majority of African Americans residing in the South effectively disenfranchised until the 1960s.

Although not directly concerned with nationalism, practice/post-structuralist theorists nonetheless provide us with concepts for integrating analysis of language and literacy with such general social and historical analysis. De Certeau's conception of a scriptural economy alerts us to cultural links between social categories – male and female, white and black – and historically situated practices of reading and writing. It reminds us of the active influence of received categories, which lead us to equate illiteracy with passivity and ignorance, literacy with mental development and social equity; which lead us to take literacy and illiteracy as self-evident things in the world rather than as historically changing and mutually defining categories of understanding through which we value and devalue groups, individuals, and practices.

Foucault's analyses of disciplinary power allow us to appreciate the fundamental ambivalence of modern social welfare. In the case at hand, universal education is both the bedrock of modern nations, the incubator of a basically literate and generally skilled population their economies require (Farkas, 1996; Gellner, 1983), and a new form of power. This new power generates subjectivities for a social order in which impersonal procedures of knowledge – Foucault's power-truth – often enter into the most intimate sense of self. Practices of reading and writing often become acts of self-making: identifications made and potentials sensed through books, whether antebellum readers imagining a nation through literature or the Hamilton sisters glimpsing other ways of being women; transgressions and transformations achieved through writing, whether the deceptive notes which aided Douglass in his flight to free-dom or Wright in his search for books, or the self-articulating autobiographies that Douglass, Wright, and Emma Goldman would subsequently write. At its best, schooled literacy provides the skills and inclinations toward such readings and writings, but it also exemplifies – is based upon – the rise of an impersonal power in which people are managed by subjecting "individual actions to an im-posed analytic framework and cumulative measures of performance" followed by "an ordering of individuals under statistical norms" (Danziger, 1990, p. 70). Such power is not simply exercised from above. It represents the limit of our technical conception of rational procedure and theoretical fair play, despite the often inegalitarian outcomes of test-driven literacy education (Coles, 1998; Johnston, 1997).

In presenting an account of the intertwining of literacy, the formation of nation states and the emergence of new forms of power, we have emphasized the increasing centrality of schooling in the history of the United States and in the construction of official or legitimate literacy. At different historical points, the working classes, the racially oppressed, and women have had to struggle in a political system in which their ascribed inequality has denied them the rights and status, the social being, of the "free and equal" citizens. Literacy and education have been important tools in those struggles, and, as with dominated groups in many parts of the world (Scott, 1990), subterfuge and informal challenges were necessary along with the more familiar open struggles for access to political enfranchisement and social welfare provision. We would be foolhardy to deny the benefits of literacy and education in a social order in which literacy and education are increasingly seem as essential to "proper employab[ility] and full and effective moral citizenship" (Gellner, 1983, p. 35). Nonetheless, schooling is also where lessons are learned about class, gender, and race, where one's self or one's literacy are deemed adequate or inadequate. Put otherwise, school-related categories are available as categories of identity, that is, as forms of self-definition. Such categories presume a "progressive" modernity, long taken for granted as the context and horizon of literacy and education, but this modernity seems to be giving way to a postmodern era of distinctly different features, in which inequality is more frankly acknowledged, and in which the question of identity has emerged as a dominant topic of popular and social science discussion (Jenkins, 1996).

5

LITERACIES AND IDENTITY
FORMATION: AMERICAN CASES

Beyond the *origins* that have assigned to us biological identity papers and a linguistic, religious, social, political, historical place, the freedom of contemporary individuals may be gauged according to their ability to *choose* their membership, while the democratic capability of a nation and social group is revealed by the right it affords individuals to exercise that choice.
(Kristeva, 1993, p. 16)

A dominant culture does not define itself in the first place by what it renounces, whereas the dominated are always concerned with what the dominant refuses them, whatever is their attitude: resignation, denial, contestation, imitation, or repression.
(Jean-Claude Passeron, cited in Chartier, 1995, p. 96)

Introduction

What we have called the mature national period ends in the 1960s and 1970s in the context of cultural and political upheavals and the onset of a substantial reworking of economic institutions and practices. A lively critique of schooling and literacy also emerged during this period of transition, and it can be understood as part of the "legacy of the sixties." That is, it was part of the political and intellectual upheaval that called into question American imperial power, the meritocractic vision of the nation state, and core features of the national culture, including the pervasiveness of standardized consumer culture and large-scale bureaucracy. The cultural and political revolts of the sixties were not simply national but international in scope, occurring in Paris and Prague as well as Chicago, in Mexico City and Tokyo as well as San Francisco. This suggests that we should see the 1960s and the decades since as an American manifestation of a more general change in the organization of contemporary societies. This change, variously called "postindustrial," "postmodern," or "late modern" society, has been analyzed by social theorists. In characterizing the current era, they point to the declining power of the nation state and widespread deregulatory dynamics, which has significant implications for the social welfare functions of the state (including education), as well as a generally heightened reflexivity, which includes the efflorescence of identity politics in recent decades (Bauman, 1992; 1997; Castells, 1996; Giddens, 1984; 1991). The relevance of such a general level of analysis for historical argument and, more pointedly, for contextualized discussion of literacy practices, is that it helps to show that the problematic of language, literacy, and identity has its basis in fundamental social dynamics.

Before further discussing features of the postmodern era, it would be helpful to briefly review characteristics of "modern" nations, their economies, educational requirements, and cultural expectations. Useful in this regard is Gellner's (1983) summary account of self-confident nation states. Analyzing the economic-and-information basis of modern nations he argued that "a society has emerged based on a high-powered technology and the expectancy of sustained growth, which requires both a mobile division of labor, and sustained, frequent, and precise communication between strangers involving a sharing of explicit meaning, transmitted in standard idiom and in writing when required" (p. 34). As we may recall from our previous chapter, such a political economy required a certain kind of culture: "The level of literacy and technical competence, in a standardized medium, a common conceptual currency, which is required of all members of this society if they are to be properly employable and enjoy full and effective moral citizenship, is so high that it simply *cannot* be provided by the kin or local units, such as they are" (pp. 34–35, emphasis in original). In a word, for Gellner modern industrial economies required the regulating institutions of the nation state, or "Nationalism, the organization of human groups into large, centrally educated, culturally homogeneous units" (p. 35).

What is striking is how much Gellner's summary, published in 1983, seems to characterize a previous era. The industrial economies he describes now seem transnational, rather than national, in their organization of production and distribution (Castells, 1996). They also as frequently pursue a low-wage, undereducated workforce as they seek a highly educated and high-wage workforce (Singer, 1999). In addition, the hierarchical, centrally controlled institutions of economy and state which Gellner presupposes have mutated in recent decades. In the economic realm, "decentralization," "flexibility," and "creative destruction" are the watchwords of a new economy in which short-term intensities are valued, life-long routines or commitments are out, and "risk" is a pervasive part of the landscape (Sennett, 1998).

What is notable in retrospect, however, are the cultural ambitions of nations during the modern era. Their effort to organize "human groups into large, centrally educated, culturally homogeneous units" is a legacy that continues to haunt as well as inspire. A notable characteristic of nation states until quite recently has been their ruthless determination to bring the culturally "backward" into the culturally modern mainstream. Whether the Soviet Union handling its ethnic diversity via a project of "Russification"; Britain dismissing the linguacultural legacies of Ireland, Scotland, or Wales; France ignoring those of Corsica or Brittany; or the US confidently "Americanizing" Poles, Hungarians, Russian Jews, Lakhotas and Cherokees, Puerto Ricans and Mexican Americans – in all cases the superiority of a modern, schooled national identity was assumed.

The right and responsibility of a state to transform its diverse peoples into a single national culture was strongly expressed in the United States. It is a nation founded on Enlightenment assumptions about liberal individualism and citizens' equality but facing the historical legacies of wars of conquest of indigenous peoples, African-American slavery, and successive mass immigrations. In addition, as we have previously argued, the school was a central institution for achieving the desired cultural transformation, and schooled literacy became a central linguistic means for crafting a monolingual American identity. Until the social upheavals of "the sixties," the right and ability of state institutions to assimilate the socially distinct populations to the conditions of national identity went largely unquestioned. Since the 1960s challenges to the project of enforced assimilation have produced a multitude of contending identity claims, a hallmark of the late or postmodern era we now inhabit.

In developing this chapter, we will briefly consider sociological and anthropological arguments about the current prominence of issues of identity in politics, social analysis, and personal life. We will then focus upon the relation between language, literacy, and identity, first by reviewing arguments about the relation between language variation, social dynamics, and group membership. What the concept or "problem" of identity forces us to acknowledge is that discovery of self through alignment with others is more a choice than a given fate, especially in the contemporary era. Further, the language signifying such choice is diversified (hybrid or polyglot) rather than uniform, and it is performative (creating effects in the world) rather than just descriptive or indicative. However, literacy in the West has long been associated with social transformation (Graff, 1981b), often state-led transformation, as well as with the crafting of individual identities. In order to examine this modern narrative of literacy, at once social and individual, and also to understand the reasons for the fracturing of this narrative in the contemporary era, we take up basic arguments about identity, language, and literacy through a series of cases studies. These illustrate the complex ways in which literacy and identity are bound up with the dynamics of class, ethnorace, and gender. We thus continue a major theme of the previous chapter, the interplay of literacy and the historical dynamics of social division, but now with primary attention given to questions of identity rather than the analysis of power.

Basic arguments

The salience of identity in the current era

Concern with and awareness of identity as a social phenomenon is relatively recent. Up through the 1950s and early 1960s the term was understood primarily as referring to individuals and thus as the province of academic psychology, as indicated by Erikson's (1959) influential work on adolescence and identity crises. However, the late 1960s and subsequent decades saw a series of developments in the United States, and elsewhere in the world, which brought questions of group identity to the fore, along with political claims based upon those identities. In a brief and general fashion these developments may be described as the decentralization of production and consumption within an overall global capitalist system, and, linked to this, movements – of youth, women, anti-colonial and civil rights forces – which questioned both traditional and modern forms of authority.

As examples of the overall pattern, consider the following: as part of a worldwide neoliberal agenda, the legitimacy of nation states and their regulatory efforts has been attacked, as has the efficacy of fiscal–industrial planning or social welfare provision (Singer, 1999). The system of public education has been continuously questioned regarding its goals of cultural assimilation, its ability to produce a skilled workforce, and its reliability as a vehicle of social mobility (Apple, 1996; Bernstein, 1996; Lasch, 1996). The revival of religious fundamentalisms that so bedazzles many observers, and now haunts many as a source of "terrorism," has nonetheless occurred against the backdrop of a general postwar decline in participation in organized religion in the US as well as Europe (Hobsbawm, 1996). Finally, in much of Europe, North America, and the Middle East, male familial authority has been extensively criticized and often substantially weakened, parental authority in general has been curtailed, and heterosexuality is less taken as the touchstone of normality (Coontz, 1992; Hobsbawm, 1996; Moghadam, 1993; Nicholson, 1986; Weis, 1990).

In a series of provocative essays, the anthropologist Jonathan Friedman (1994) has analyzed the recent efflorescence of cultural identities – e.g. Fourth World/indigenous peoples in formerly colonized regions of the world, ethnic minorities within long-standing nation states, and the social movements for gender and sexual rights. He argues that the various collective actors differ in significant respects. They differ in whether they are asserting cultural rights or calling for more basic political and economic autonomy; whether they make appeal to nongeographic and nonethnic identities (as in gender-based identity politics); and how they call upon and rework premodern traditions and customs. What they all share, however, is a heightened sense of both freedom and insecurity.

With the nation and its state institutions in question, minorities feel more empowered to assert alternative political projects, but their capacity to marshal resources may be lessened in an environment of economic deregulation and social welfare cutbacks. With schooled assimilation in question, linguistic and cultural minorities are able to assert the educational rights of alternative identities; but with schooled outcomes in doubt, goals of social mobility through decent education are thrown into question (Aronowitz and Giroux, 1985). With organized religion in decline, many feel released from the moral constraints of sacred text, pastor or congregation, but the source of shared or secure values grows evermore problematic (Lasch, 1991). With domestic patriarchy in disarray, there are new rights for women and children, for gays and lesbians, within and outside changing family structures, but there are also the specters of increasing poverty in female-headed households and of fundamentalist and homophobic backlashes (Coontz, 1992; Moghadam, 1993). Put most generally, the multifaceted decline in traditional sources and mechanisms of normative control, an increase in freedom, has increased the need for self-monitoring and self-constitution (Giddens, 1991).

In place of the order wrought by sovereign states and their regulating institutions in the modern era, our late or postmodern era reveals a need for self-constitutive capacities in the face of social fluidity and potential disorder (Bauman, 1997). As we might expect, in a time of substantial social, economic, and cultural change, the projects of identity associated with literacy and schooling have been rendered problematic. As the legacies of class rendered problematic a shared national identity, so also ethnorace reveals further fault lines in a common class or national identity, providing alternative grounds for constructing a sense of group and self (Patterson, 1997). Gender, in turn, interacts with national, class, and ethnoracial identity, providing yet another difference for identity. In the context of movements for civil rights, identities and needs based on ethnicity, gender, sexual orientation, and (dis)ability have been articulated and put forth as part of a "politics of recognition" (Fraser, 1989; Taylor, 1992).

This politics moves beyond our familiar, Enlightenment-derived categories of "citizens" and principles of "equal treatment under the law." It argues instead for political recognition of an identity-based *difference* within the citizenry, requiring special provisions for its distinct needs – whether it be, for example, women's need for domestic violence legislation, the disabled persons' needs for access to public facilities, or disprivileged ethnic minorities' need for affirmative action measures. A problem now widely recognized is how to reconcile acutely differentiated identities and needs with a project of social justice and social welfare that has some common claim, once ostensibly general categories such as "citizen" have been called into question. There is a cultural and discursive dimension to this political question.

In a recent study of debates about culture within anthropology, the field of cultural studies, and the broader public arena, Kuper (1999) has noted that claims about culture quickly mutate into claims about identity. In an era which celebrates diversity – an era which appears to repudiate Gellner's "centrally educated, culturally homogeneous units" – the cultural actor often eclipses the citizen or worker as the agent of politics. But there's a wrinkle: the right of cultural actors to act depends on who they would presume to act for – that is, on questions of rightful belonging and identity. In discussions of cultural pluralism it is typically presumed that the most legitimate voice will come from an authentic member of the given group, but questions of "voice" and "authenticity" themselves raise more questions than they answer (Guillory, 1993). Identity, while central to discourses of culture and diversity, is difficult to pin down. It hinges on, and does not resolve, troublesome polarities: between essential versus constructed traditions and group-bound versus voluntarily chosen affiliations. Such dichotomies also inform the dynamics of language, literacy, and identity, which we now take up.

Language, literacy, and identity

A basic finding of sociolinguistic research is that language variation is pervasive in modern societies and, further, that this variation marks social background and signals social activity (Gumperz, 1982; Labov, 1972). In an influential work advocating a situated approach to literacy, Gee (1996) has provided a clear account of how language variation figures in processes of identity construction. He starts with a familiar example, that different socioeconomic classes vary in the extent to which they use standard or colloquial forms of pronunciation, as in the contrast in English between *-ing* and *-in'* suffixes in verbs such as *talking/talkin', singing/singin'*, or *sleeping/sleepin'*. All social classes use the formal *(-ing)* and informal *(-in')* variants, but they differ in how frequently they do so. In addition, Gee emphasizes, the selection of one or another alternate is used to signal status and solidarity. The use of a standard variant like *-ing* has more status than a colloquial form like *-in'*, that is, *-ing* marks hierarchy. Conversely, a colloquial *-in'* has less status but more "sociability." It is used when speakers are showing fellow-feeling, that is, solidarity or belonging (Trudgill, 1974).

Thus far we have the beginnings of a rudimentary account of language variation and identity. Speakers may choose alternates to signal solidarity – co-membership in a group, presumed or imaginable, and the fellow-feeling that follows therefrom. Conversely, they may choose alternates to mark status – position in a larger social hierarchy that distinguishes oneself and one's group from one's interlocutors and their group(s). As Gee notes, the rudimentary interchange of identification and differentiation is quite complex in actual practice, for languages don't vary on just a few features, instead there are hundreds (if not thousands) of points of contrast and variation in pronunciation, word choice, and syntactic alternates (Biber, 1995; Gumperz and Cook-Gumperz, 1982; Labov, 1972; Romaine, 1994). Speakers use these contrasts in signaling and assessing fluid social identities as well as strategically shifting communicative intentions (Gumperz, 1982; Heller, 1988; Rampton, 1995).

The lesson we may draw, along with Gee, is that speakers do not assume simple, singular identities, rather they inhabit multiple identities (as, say, Chicana, mother, and factory worker), and this multiplicity highlights the constructed nature of society. Groups don't simply exist, they must be mobilized or otherwise "called into being." Face-to-face groups, neighborhoods, institutions, and social classes emerge out of dense, overlaid networks of real and potential association, on the basis of shared "objective characteristics" (co-residence;

years of education; occupation; skin color; gender or sexual orientation) but also on the basis of shared representations and undertakings. Since language provides representations (images, discourses), the means of coordinating undertakings, and sensitive indices of social background, language has come to be seen as integral to "the constitution of society" (Bourdieu, 1991; Giddens, 1984; Kontopoulos, 1993; Sapir, 1949, pp. 7–32, 357–364).

Much of the investigation of the place of language in the constitution of society has been conducted under the rubric of "discourse." Discourse analysts, among whom there is overlap with practice theorists, have emphasized the constructed, nonessential nature of social groups and identities. They argue that discourses, conceptualized as coherent ensembles of language and action, do not just enable subjects to express themselves; instead, they select or create subjects, binding speakers/interlocutors to positions within discourses (Fairclough, 1992; LaClau and Mouffe, 1985). These positions may be defined in formal institutions, as doctor or patient, teacher or pupil, employer or employee, or they may be positions articulated in the everyday lifeworld, as father or daughter, joketeller and audience, fellow consumers of book or television programs ("Have you read...?" "Did you see...?"), but as discourse positions they combine practices, values, and forms of language into recognizable "ways of being" in the world (Crappanzano, 1996; Foucault, 1975; Gee, 1996; Hanks, 1996b).

So far we have two related ideas – (1) that selections from a multiplicity of language variants enable people to inhabit a multiplicity of overlapping identities, and (2) that discourses provide subject positions, enabling some identities and opposing or disabling others. Both contribute to a now-familiar view that identities are constructed, rather than given by primordial criteria of race, language, place of origin, etc. (Friedman, 1994). However, many sociological and anthropological theorists do not accept a strong constructivism, that is, the idea that discourses create the social world out of an endless mosaic of differences. They insist instead on an interaction between discursive positioning and the space of possible positions (Asad, 1993; Bourdieu et al., 1993). They argue that there is a relation, albeit "semi-determined," between agents' intentions and the pre-givens of organizational and institutional structure (Kontopoulos, 1993; Rabinow, 1986). They study the interplay between local action and translocal ecological structures, considering a neighborhood or urban sprawl, as well as nation states and empires, as constraints on "ways of being" (Comaroff and Comaroff, 1992; Giddens, 1984; Kuper, 1999).

Concern with the tension between social constraint and construction has been a central preoccupation of practice theory – indeed, thinkers cited above, such as Bourdieu, Giddens, and Kontopoulos, may rightly be considered theorists of practice, that is, of an action/structure dialectic. Foucault is well known as a theorist of the subject, an analyst of what we could call the "conditions of identity." Thus, in his major work on disciplinary power (Foucault, 1975), forms of self and self-understanding are shaped by the procedures and judgments of power–knowledge, a "network of writing" (p. 189) in which examinations, records, and archives are central features.[1] More prosaically, we may say that school shapes identity by accepting, promoting, rejecting, and transforming the senses of self and social belonging that children bring to and take from this institutional encounter. De Certeau (1984), with his emphasis on a "bottom-up" view of everyday life, reminds us that practice is not simply determined by institutional or other technical-knowledge regulation. Rather, there are zones of everyday life in which approximations are more important than standards, in which vernacular blendings of word and deed predominate, in which people fashion senses of self and group through tactics of transgressing rather than "measuring up" to official expectations (for a comparative analysis of "practical knowledge" see Scott [1998, pp. 309–341], and Brandau and Collins [1994] for an ethnographic case).

The debate between those who emphasize discourse and fluid identity construction versus those who emphasize society and constraints on identity need not be polarized. A characteristic of most social thinking in the contemporary era is that it grapples with problems of language as well as society, of identity practices as well as social structuring. The relevance of this debate for our thinking about literacy and identity is that it reminds us, yet again, of some basic tensions – between fixity and fluidity, authenticity and hybridity, constraint and choice – in the claims about identity found in work on literacy, schooling, and senses of self.

Literacy and identity projects: cases

In order to attach specifics to such general arguments, let us now delve into some sustained accounts of literacy in peoples' lives and schooling. Our order of presentation begins with straightforward cases – clear boundaries, simple beginnings, obvious preferred endings – and ends with more complex accounts of identity and literacy. We begin with a work that argues clearly for the need to transform identities in the direction Gellner presumed, with the local and subordinate changing toward the "middle class" and presumably universal. We follow with two works that closely probe the costs of such transformation; they explore the identity conflicts which follow upon embracing schooled literacy. We then briefly take up the question of gender-and-class, an intersection of identifications which fruitfully complicates our account of schooling, literacy, and self.

Heath

The first study, Shirley Heath's (1983) *Ways with Words*, has already been discussed at some length in chapter 3. As previously noted, *Ways* describes and analyzes language use and child socialization in three separate groups: a white working-class group residing in a neighborhood called "Roadville"; an African-American working-class group residing in a neighborhood called "Trackton";

and a middle-class group, both white and African American, referred to as "Townspeople," who live in various neighborhoods and suburbs of a nearby city (called "Gateway").

Heath's discussion of language and social life is of singular ethnographic detail and depth. It uses the concept of "literacy event" to push at the limits of the oral/literate dichotomy (pp. 196–201), and it argues forcefully and extensively that values and recurring practices contextualize and shape the meanings of encounters with text. It shows how fundamental assumptions about the nature of persons and of learning interact with church attendance and work-day lives to influence how children are "brought up" or "come up" (pp. 144–145) to participate through speech and writing in their homes and with neighbors and peers. What Heath also analyzes, and this is why *Ways* has become an educational classic, are the many assumptions and practices concerning language use, literacy, and learning in schools. These include ideas about the sequencing of knowledge – for example, that children should know the names for things and be proficient labelers before they practice analogistic or causal reasoning. They include assumptions about the uses and meanings of questions. Many queries in school are rhetorical or indirect: rhetorical in that teachers are not genuinely seeking the information they ask children about; indirect in that a question is about something other than its strict form suggests. "Do I hear talking?" uttered by a first-grade teacher, is not really a question about what the teacher is hearing. Finally, they include assumptions about and practices requiring prior experiences with print stories (as opposed, say, to spoken narratives).

What the reader of *Ways* discovers is that the language practices and literacy events characteristic of Roadville and Trackton form coherent ensembles, they "make sense" in terms of mill-based, working-class lives, shaped by the strong religions of the American South, with distinctive ways of speaking to babies, disciplining a child, and relating to books. Growing up in these communities apparently leaves children underprepared for school. The disjuncture between the discourses of home and community and those of the school is present at the very outset for Trackton children, rendering them "unready" for schooled reading:

> No one lifts labels and features out of their contexts for explication; no one requests repetitions from Trackton children. Thus their entry into a classroom which depends on responses based on lifting items and events out of context is a shock. Their abilities to contextualize, to remember what may seem to the teacher to be an unrelated event as similar to another, to link seemingly disparate factors in their explanations, and to create highly imaginative stories are suppressed in the classroom. The school's approach to reading and learning establishes decontextualized skills as foundational in the hierarchy of academic skills . . . Trackton children receive little encouragement [from this approach].   (p. 353)

The home/school disjunction occurs a few years later for Roadville children, when their avidity for labels, truthful language, and getting the facts "right" is no longer sufficient for school tasks involving synthesis, contextualization, or extended accounts. Heath puts the matter this way:

> The social activities in which they [Roadville children] participate are constructed to make them focus for the most part on labels and features, and they are given few occasions for extended narratives, imaginative flights of establishing new contexts, or manipulating features of an event or item. Thus their readiness for school is a limited readiness – and not a preparedness for the types of task necessary for higher-level school work.
>
> (p. 352)

"Townspeople" children are, conversely, well matched with the school. The ritual of bedtime story is firmly entrenched in their lives, as it is in the lives of many middle-class populations (Bialostok, 1999; Cochran-Smith, 1986; Taylor, 1983), and from it they learn to look, name, and classify. They also practice relating texts read to the real world, quoting from and referring to children's stories in the flow of everyday life. They learn schoolish lessons even from out-of-school activities: they lead highly scheduled lives in which much of their leisure is organized by adults who will call them to order ("stand in line, please") and evaluate their individual performances ("good swing, Johnny"). Perhaps most important, they are socialized by observing myriad ways in which the literacy practices of schooling carry over into the work their parents do.

Heath does not directly address the issue of language, literacy, and identity till the very end of *Ways*, but what she then writes is worth repeating in full:

> The school is not a neutral objective arena; it is an institution which has the goal of changing people's values, skills, and knowledge bases. Yet some portions of the population, such as the townspeople, bring with them to school linguistic and cultural capital accumulated through hundreds of thousands of occasions for practicing the skills and espousing the values the schools transmit. Long before reaching school, children of the townspeople have made the transition from home to the larger societal institutions which share the values, skills, and knowledge bases of the school. Their eventual positions of power in the school and the workplace are foredestined in the conceptual structures which they have learned at home and which are reinforced in school and numerous other associations. Long before school, their language and culture at home has structured for them the meanings which will give shape to their experiences in classrooms and beyond. Their families have embedded them in contexts that reflected the systemic relationships between education and [their future place in] production. From their baby books to their guide books for participation in league soccer, the townspeople's children have been motivated towards seeing their current activities as relating to their future achievements. *Their socially determined habits and values have created for them an ideology in which all that they do makes sense to their current identity and their preparation for the achievements which will frame their future.* (pp. 367–368, emphasis added)

What this passage strikingly condenses is a leifmotif of the entire book: how the wherewithal of everyday practice – habits and identities, values and meanings, inculcated senses of power or powerlessness – interact with schooled expectations to promote one social class and demote others.

Heath's findings, if not her terminology, are strongly reminiscent of Bourdieu and collaborators' (Bourdieu and Passeron, 1977) arguments about schooling and social reproduction. They argued that the interaction of *habitus* and cultural–linguistic capital are much more important than a supposedly natural "aptitude" or "intelligence" in influencing school outcomes and subsequent employment. In their account, the *habitus* (i.e. dispositions to act and react rooted in socially inculcated senses of self), along with the abundance or scarcity of cultural–linguistic capital (in this case, school-valued linguistic practices), strongly influences the likelihood of success or failure in school and subsequent achievements in the job market (Bourdieu, 1984). We should note in this regard the congruence for "Townspeople" between "current identity" and "socially determined habits and values," between "meanings [that] give shape to their experiences in classrooms" and their "eventual positions of power in the school and the workplace." Such are the promises offered by the school, "an institution which has the goal of changing people's values, skills, and knowledge bases," to those who can identity with – whose subjectivities are evoked by, whose practices are confirmed by – what the school presumes about language, literacy, and learning.

One of the many merits of *Ways With Words* is that it presents a strong argument for "multiple literacies," for the realization that communities produce distinct ways of being, shaping distinct social identities by drawing on uses of spoken and written language in the course of everyday life. In her description of Roadville and Trackton uses of literacy in religious practices, child-rearing, problem-solving, and everyday socializing, Heath describes a dense intertwining of text and talk in ways that are often passionate, principled, and playful, and sometimes all at once. The harsh reality, however, underneath the sympathetic ethnographic account, is that Roadville and Trackton "ways with words" produce identities and verbal proclivities that clash with what the school expects. *Their* socially determined habits and values interact with the school in ways that do not "make[] sense to their current identity." In a word, they are torn by the encounter with schooling; their school lessons and life lessons prepare them for different, dominated places in "education and production."

Rose

That "[t]he school is not a neutral objective arena" is a persistent theme in our second case, Mike Rose's (1989) *Lives on the Boundary*. Indeed, the very title, with its "boundary," evokes the acts of inclusion and exclusion. *Lives* is a hybrid work, part educational memoir, part teacher's story, part extended essay on the challenges facing American education. Beginning from a bleak youth of family misfortune, poverty, and educational mishandling, the autobiographical Rose yearns for and eventually achieves that literate, schooled identity that Heath writes about as the unperturbed cultural inheritance of "Townspeople." Because this educated self is achieved from the outside, rather than assumed

from the inside, Rose remains acutely sensitive to the obstacles faced and efforts
made by the educationally underprepared.

He also is acutely sensitive to social class. As he says in the book's first
chapter, as part of a justification for drawing on his own experiences in thinking
about education more generally:

> there are some things about my early life, I see now, that are reflected in other working-
> class lives I've encountered: the isolation of neighborhoods, information poverty, the
> limited means of protecting children from family disaster, the predominance of such dis-
> aster, the resilience of imagination, the intellectual curiosity and literate enticements that
> remain hidden from the schools, the feelings of scholastic inadequacy, the dislocations
> that come from crossing educational boundaries.   (p. 9)

Rose presents rich portraits of the people behind educational "problems" when
describing the students he has encountered, who are struggling and underprepared, as he himself once was. Through evocative vignettes and short cases he
suggests how identities are shaped by neighborhood, family, and social suffering, by feelings of scholastic inadequacy, but also by intellectual curiosity and
literate stirrings.

The image of literate selves is complex in Rose's account of his life and that
of others. There are styles of reading, from the bored or frightened glance to vo-
racious and indiscriminate immersion to fine-grained textual interpretation; and
diverse sets of texts are encountered, from adolescent science fiction to avant
garde literature, film, and art, to the texts of science, literature, and philosophy
which formed a good liberal arts education in the 1950s and 1960s. There are
also many ways of writing: children's drawing plus "invented spelling"; a college freshman's awkward mix of demotic and learned voices; a veteran's prison
journals; and the academic mainstay, the compare-and-contrast essay. There is
also a consistent emphasis on "educational dislocation," prominent in Rose's
own life, and pervading his accounts of diverse working-class, immigrant, and
minority students, who range from very young children to middle-aged adults.
It reminds us both of the fate awaiting Trackton and Roadville children and of
de Certeau's more general argument: that the scriptural economy of the modern West originates in and rests upon a division of classes in which only one,
the settled and privileged, are truly educated and literate (de Certeau, 1984,
pp. 131–132 and 139).[2] Both emphases – the crafting of literate selves and the
inherent disjunctions of working-class identities and educated lives – contribute
to what we will call Rose's trope of literate salvation.

At various points in *Lives*, Rose describes how senses of real and potential
selves are brought into being through the reading, inscribing, and imagining of
worlds suggested by texts of diverse sorts. In his early, pre-adolescent years,
school did not figure importantly: teacher[s] recalled are "faceless and . . . very
far away"; he "defended [him]self against the lessons [he] couldn't understand
and . . . got very good at watching a blackboard with minimal awareness . . .
drift[ing] more and more into a variety of protective fantasies" (p. 19). One

fantasy was of being a boy space explorer, for which he read voraciously. Rose describes his solitary pleasures in terms that suggest de Certeau's argument (1984, pp. 173–174) that reading is poaching and idling, rather than sober processing of information: "I would check out my books two at a time and take them home to curl up with a blanket on my chaise longue, reading, sometimes, through the weekend, my back aching, my thoughts lost between the galaxies. I became the hero of a thousand adventures..." (pp. 20–21).[3]

Reading did not just fuel his fantasies, it also provided a vehicle for interacting with peers. During an early summer job picking strawberries, he learns he can entertain his fellow child-workers by "fill[ing] up...time with stories." And the stories which "fill[ed] time" were literate/oral blends. In ways recognizable by de Certeau, Heath, or Havelock, texts read were drawn upon and recast to meet the exigencies of telling in the course of travel to and from work:

Reading opened up the world. There I was, a skinny bookworm drawing the attention of street kids who, in any other circumstances, would have had me for breakfast. Like an epic tale-teller, I developed the stories as I went along, relying on a flexible plot line and a repository of heroic events... I sketched out trajectories with my finger on Frank's dusty truck. And I stretched out each story's climax, creating cliffhangers like the ones I saw in the Saturday serials. These stories created for me a temporary community.

(pp. 21–22)

Later, in junior high school, Rose would be misassigned to a vocational curriculum track. From this error and the experiences which follow, he provides a first-person account of Foucauldian power-knowledge: how a system of depersonalized measurement, normalized distribution, and consequent segregation has profound consequences for possible identities. He spends several years in "Voc Ed" learning about educational dead-ends, about using cynicism, boredom, and rage to protect oneself against the degradations of institutional stigma, thuggish or disaffected teachers, and empty lesson drills. As he writes later, he experienced directly how the school's tracking decisions contribute to the class-differentiated identities and aspirations so widely reported in the education research literature (Oakes, 1985). In discussing tracking decisions, how they are internalized, and so regulate subsequent behavior, Rose sounds a Bourdieuian note about schooling, social-and-self understanding, and educational outcomes: "children gradually internalize the definition the school delivers to them, incorporate a stratifying regulator as powerful as the overt institutional gatekeepers that, in other societies, determine who goes where in the educational system" (Rose, 1989, p. 128).

When Rose's misassignment to "Voc Ed" was subsequently discovered, and he was reassigned to an academic track, he was desperately underprepared and floundering. It was an unusually understanding and supportive teacher, a Jack McFarland, who interceded on his behalf, coaching him through his English classes and finagling admission and a scholarship to Loyola College in Los Angeles. With a peer group centered around McFarland, Rose embraces a "bohemian demi-monde" of books, music, and movies. In MacFarland's book- and magazine-strewn living room, Rose acquired the names of and initial familiarity with a wide range of texts, the "linguistic capital" (Bourdieu and Passeron, 1977) of the soon-to-be educated:

I had never seen anything like it: a great flophouse of language furnished by City Lights and Café le Metro. I read every title. I flipped through paperbacks and scanned jackets and memorized names: Gogol, *Finnegan's Wake*, Djuna Barnes, Jackson Pollock, *A Coney Island of the Mind*, F. O. Matthiessen's *American Renaissance*, all sorts of Freud, *Troubled Sleep*, Man Ray, *The Education of Henry Adams*, Richard Wright, *Film as Art*, William Butler Yeats, Marguerite Duras, *Redburn, A Season in Hell, Kapital.* (p. 36)

Of this period, the avant garde texts and the bohemian talk, Rose writes: "Knowledge was becoming a bonding agent... It provided a critical perspective on society, and it allowed me to act as though I were living beyond the limiting boundaries of South Vermont [Street]" (p. 37).

Escaping the boundaries of home and neighborhood becomes a persistent theme in Rose's account, but it contributes to a troubling inconsistency in *Lives*. Rose is relentlessly empathetic about the circumstances, efforts, and failures of others. Whether he is describing refugee children from war-torn Central America, struggling Vietnam Vets, college freshman placed in "remedial" composition classes, or mature women of color attending adult education classes at an Oakland community college, Rose insightfully explores the logic underlying peoples' efforts and errors in schoolwork. He connects people's fears, hopes and literate aspirations to their homes and neighborhoods. Rose is at once detailed and schematic, however, about his own life and "the limiting boundaries of South Vermont." He is careful and evocative when he describes his early life in South Los Angeles – the disappointments in his parent's life; the look of his living room; the feel of the streets, with the comings and goings of people and storefront businesses, and the presence of petty criminals and cops. But he also polarizes family and neighborhood versus the promise of education.

This is graphically portrayed in a scene where he decides to leave home in his freshman year at college after a family friend and lodger has committed suicide:

Lou's suicide came to represent the sadness and dead time I had protected myself against, the personal as well as public oppressiveness of life in South Los Angeles. I began to see that my escape to the trailer and my isolationist fantasies of the demi-monde would yield *another kind of death, a surrender to the culture's lost core.* An alternative was somehow starting to take shape around school and knowledge. Knowledge seemed... was it empowering?... I felt freed, as if I were untying fetters. There simply were times when the pain and confusion of that summer would give away to something I felt more than I knew: *a lightness to my body, an ease in breathing.* (p. 46; emphasis added)

The contrast is powerful – between "a kind of death," "the culture's lost core" and an "empowering" knowledge, "a lightness" and "an ease in breathing." But we should not be swept away by this dichotomy. It is part of a familiar, if poignant, modern narrative, a tale of backwardness transformed, fetters broken, in the light-and-might of knowledge and schooling; we should remain skeptical. As a way of gaining perspective, let us juxtapose this dichotomy to another. Let us contrast the working-class fate of dislocation and uncertainty, emblematized in Rose's account of the decision to leave home, with the settled identities and trajectories of Heath's "Townspeople." Of these children we may recall: "Their eventual positions of power in the school and the workplace are foredestined in the conceptual structures which they have learned at home and which are reinforced in school" (Heath, 1983, p. 368). In this contrast we have a dramatic rendering of the apparent determinism of class, literacy, and identity: security of "conceptual structures" which "foredestine" "eventual positions of power in the school and the workplace" is opposed to the "culture's lost core," "educational dislocation," and the institutional boundary which becomes deeply internalized.

Gilyard

Keith Gilyard's (1991) *Voices of the Self* is, like *Lives*, a composite work in which chapters of educational memoir alternate with discussions of research literature concerning language, identity, and schooling. In *Voices* Gilyard both presents and undermines images of educational salvation, questioning the terms of linguistic and cultural assimilation that schooling seems to require. It is not that he rejects education or educationally motivated linguistic change, for he himself eventually becomes a professor of English. Instead, he insists that his "broken" Harlem home nonetheless gave him the language skills and textual orientations that supported and enabled his early literacy endeavors. Arguing that a literacy orientation, a "literacy set" (Holdaway, 1979), requires emotional commitments, linguistic knowledge, predictive capabilities, and knowledge of print conventions, Gilyard analyzes how his early home life supported his early literacy. It did this by providing him with continual lessons in cross-dialect code-switching – an ongoing schooling in the relation between language and social identity – and with frequent examples of the importance of reading and writing in negotiating social relations. As he says of this period: "It is clear that my early reading skills, like my oral ones, developed largely within a family context. Familial relations dictated that these skills were to be regarded as cherished possessions" (p. 40).

Gilyard was educationally dislocated, but in a different sense from Rose. He was an African-American first-grader placed in an overwhelmingly Euro-American classroom in a Queen's public school in the late 1950s. He thrived academically and competed regularly in sports, playground rituals, and aca-demics with the Euro-American (largely Jewish) students. He dealt with the social chasm separating home and school by using two names: Keith is used at home and in his neighborhood; Raymond, his first name, previously unused, is now employed at school. Consistent with this Keith/Raymond split, Gilyard the author never reconciles home and school. Educational assimilation, in this case, success in the Euro-American milieu of teachers and fellow students, carried a psychic as well as social cost. Keith/Raymond became cunning, a juggler of impressions as well as varieties of English, a striker of deals, with teachers and principals as well as family members, neighborhood pals, and schoolmates.

Like Rose, Gilyard sees his life as representative, but he refuses to view his individual efforts and achievements as a template for group advancement:

> Looking back at the early years, I find it impossible to recommend that African-American students be asked to follow in my footsteps, to leave the onus almost entirely on them to fit in, to hope they can pull together a similar but just as improbable combination of pacts in order to accomplish the task of language learning in school . . . I learned a lot, but I had to foot the psychic bill for any success I managed to attain.   (p. 70)

Voices also questions the equation of school success with linguistic assimilation, that is, the argument, recently seen in the mainstream response to the Ebonics controversy (Collins, 1999; Delpit and Perry, 1998), that in order to succeed American-American youth must "lose the dialect," exchanging native voice for proficiency in Standard English. Instead, Gilyard argues that vernacular use is a way of belonging that cannot simply be stripped away from the individual. In his account, language and identity are inextricably bound together. In addition, it is unclear that having Standard English skills in itself protects African-American youth from racist judgments. On this point Gilyard cites the Southern-born and anti-racist dialectologist, James Sledd: "in job-hunting in America, pigmentation is more important than pronunciation" (Sledd, 1973, p. 212).

The gist of the argument in *Voices* is that the relation between schooling and a racially stratified society, between a speaker's *actual* and *potential* communities of identification, sets the framework against which formally defined linguistic differences may be significant or insignificant:

> Social relations are a far more vital factor for Black students in school than differences of language variety . . . If [Black children] were to perceive that the social dialectic were in their favor, learning another dialect could not be a major problem . . . For most Blacks in school such perception can form only within a setting in which teachers genuinely accept them as they come and respect them enough not to sell them myths of simple assimilation. The worst thing any of us can do, who have bought such a myth for however long, is to pretend the package was always an easy one to carry home.   (p. 74)

In presenting these arguments, and an account of the challenges and pitfalls that accompanied his progress through school, Gilyard presents a de Certeauian account of how social dialects are intermingled, orality and writing intertwined, in forming a strategic hybrid identity. He describes and analyzes numerous encounters between codes and discourses: between African-American Vernacular English and Standard English, but also between his childhood space hero poems and readings from Langston Hughes; between diligent readings of the sports section of the newspaper and of articles about the emerging civil rights movement, but also conversations overheard in a local barbershop – about sex, civil rights, white supremacy, and big league sports. These diverse sources in print and conversation, approved (Langston Hughes), tolerated (sports pages) or disapproved (barbershop talk) by the school, were all part of what Gilyard calls his "hybrid self" and his "advanced literacy set." This "set" combined emotional engagement, linguistic knowledge, and knowledge of print conventions in a mingling of sources that fed a protean sense of self:

> During the latter half of elementary school my writing ability came to the fore ... [but] writing only appeared significant to me when I could use it as a means of expressing myself ...
> Of course poetry wasn't all I read. There were science fiction books, the comic books, the child-detective and adventure books, the encyclopedia my mother insisted we have despite its cost ...
> My interest in sports made reading about sports necessary ...
> [But] my oral skills were an equally important source of funding for my developing writing. *It was largely through conversation that I was able to gauge how the self I expressed in writing was being received by others, thus enabling me to adjust my self concept in ways I deemed appropriate, in essence, to create the self I would express in subsequent writing.* (pp. 106–108 [emphasis added])

Although *Voices* may seem a straightforward account of educational confidence and success built from diverse literacy resources, the account grows more complex as Gilyard matures. Keith/Raymond shows increasing strain as he progresses through the racially stratified public schools of 1960s New York City.[4] Refusing to forsake the loyalties and enabling resources of home, neighborhood and street, Gilyard registers sharply the force of urban African-American youth rebellion against schools, police, family authority, and essentialized "Whites."[5] The constraints on identity, the difficulties of hybridity in a polarized social arena, are depicted in harsh detail. The promising middle-school student was also a bicycle thief; the student at one of the city's elite high schools an occasional strong-arm robber; the college-bound scholarship boy a careening junkie sent to NYC's infamous Riker's Island jail.

It is a testimony to Gilyard's gifts, his family support, and his "literacy set" that he pulled back from that abyss of jail and drug addiction. The epiphanous event for Gilyard, analogous to Lou Minton's suicide in *Lives*, which triggered Rose's decision to leave home and embrace school, is an act of political militance. The nationalist politics of the period – in particular, George Jackson's effort in the spring of 1970 to forcibly free his imprisoned Black Panther brother, in a famous court hostage-taking and subsequent fatal shootout with police – inspire Gilyard to change his life. In short order he "kicks" heroin while in jail, finishes high school, and attends college. A powerful Black Nationalist claim to identity stabilizes Gilyard's sense of self for the next phase of his life.

The strength of *Voices* as narrative and essay is that it portrays the psychic costs of educational success, as well as the mechanisms of that success, for one whose identity lies well outside the narrative of "Townspeople"; it complicates any salvific narrative of educational change. Congruent with sociolinguistic research and post-structuralist argument, *Voices* insists on full-throated language variety as a resource for a self formed in conflict as well as in collaboration with social others and the bureaucratic institutions of society.

Gender and identity: counter-cases

The agonistic social fate of working-class youth bound for higher education institutions is captured by the English term "scholarship boy," which was introduced in a classic study of literacy and ways of living in post-World War II working-class culture (Hoggart, 1957). The category speaks to Rose's and Gilyard's accounts of conflict, ambivalence, and effort; it speaks to the often pained transformations of the new arrival. Until recent decades, however, cross-class educational efforts have been predominantly a masculine enterprise. In America, for example, several generations of young working-class men received assistance from the GI Bill for their post-secondary educational pursuits (Nasaw, 1979), a route to higher education from which women were excluded (Wrigley, 1992). The central stories of *Lives* and *Voices* are masculine: being selected as "bright" and "promising" happened more often to disprivileged boys; the willingness or need to separate from home in acceptance of school (Rose), or due to the maelstrom of adolescence and school (Gilyard), seems to occur more "easily" for men, contributing to the accounts of selves relatively independent of natal family (Luttrell, 1997; Mickelson, 1992; Steedman, 1987).

What this means is that we should expect different themes to emerge when we examine accounts of education and literacy in the lives of working-class and minority women. In what follows we will briefly counterpose such accounts to the preceding cases, in order to add other dimensions to our arguments about literacy and identity, examining the effects of legacies, often intertwined, of gender as well as class and race. It should be emphasized at the outset, however, that our accounts are partial and one-sided. There is no single way in which a multifaceted phenomenon like gender interacts with a complex phenomenon like literacy. Consider, for example, the following contrary findings. In most historical cases of so-called restricted literacy, situations in which there are sharp social restrictions on who can learn and who can use literacy, it is women who are excluded or kept to a minimal form of literacy practice ((Besnier, 1995, pp. 170–172) and the Florentine and colonial New England cases in chapter 4). Conversely, however, in recent decades it has been documented that young girls, on average, outperform boys on reading and writing tasks in US schools (Mickelson, 1992); Chiseri-Strater's (1991) study of academic writing suggests that female undergraduates may find it easier to negotiate the identity demands made in initial college writing; and the case of the Hamilton sisters, discussed in chapter 4, indicates a strong and positive relation between reading, writing, and identity fashioning. We should note of these latter cases, however, that they either ignore class variations, as in the young girl studies, or they concern women from middle-class backgrounds, as with the college study and Hamilton sisters.

When we focus upon working-class women of color we find another situation. A theme of language stigma and female educational exclusion is prominent in Kay's (1998) study of "literacy shutdown" – the self-imposed exile from reading, writing, and education experienced by certain women. One of Kay's interviewees is Ella, a forty-year-old African-American woman who grew up in a supportive rural home and community but who had a very different experience from Gilyard of school desegregation, language variety, and sense of self. Unlike Gilyard, who experienced being the rare African American in a Euro-American school as a challenge, she experienced the desegregation of a 1960s Alabama high school as force-field of interracial avoidance and hostility: "The White kids would sit on one side of the classroom, and we'd sit on the other side. They didn't want anything to do with us. And when the bell rang, they went down one side of the hallway, and we went down the other. Teachers didn't want us in the classroom" (Kay, 1998, p. 35).

Once Ella left the protection of home, church, and early primary school, education became a series of challenges in which she was found wanting, improper, or "country."[6] In Kay's account, Ella has faced language prejudice much of her life, from teachers and schoolmates, but also from her own children, who correct her "country" way of speaking. Even her contemporary urban neighbors, who are African American, show an urban middle-class bias against her "Southern" (and "Black" / "country") ways of speaking (p. 29). Class and ethnoracial language stigma broadly affect Ella's literacy engagements. As Kay observes: "Her perception of her accent and grammar and its probable reception by people who speak "properly" carries over into her [dis]comfort with writing, reading, and public performance" (p. 33).[7] Consistent with the thesis that many women carry the burden of education, the responsibility but not the "rights," Kay argues that Ella understands school success and the things that influence it – "race, correct speech, dress, and literacy capital"(p. 37). She uses this knowledge "[i]n fighting for her children's right to an education" (p. 37), but not, significantly, in fighting for herself. Instead, "Ella's early lessons about herself and her background were so powerful that she has never learned to be totally comfortable about who she is and where she is from" (p. 37).

The sense of conflict with one's identity and one's social origins seems to be a legacy of working-class encounters with schooling (Sennett and Cobb, 1972; Williams, 1983), but it is often particularly intense for women. In Luttrell's (1997) recent study of working-class women's school experiences, aspirations, and identities, African-American women in North Carolina and Euro-American women in the city of Philadelphia chronicle the small indignities, lack of en- couragement, and conflicting demands, through which schools and mothers

are remembered as thwarting girls' educational possibilities and literate entice-
ments. A sense of responsibility without entitlement comes through powerfully,
as an obdurate legacy passed from mother to daughter. School is the place where
social class becomes personal. Says Joanne of Philadelphia: "What I remember
most about school was that if you were poor you got no respect and no encouragement" (p. 53); and concurs Cora of North Carolina: "when I was going to
school... if your parents wasn't a doctor, a lawyer, or a teacher, or someone,
you know, high, then the teachers would look down on you... they would class
you as a nobody" (p. 53).

Luttrell's respondents are adult, typically middle-aged women, and they are
pursuing adult education for high school diplomas never received. Their educational efforts are deeply intertwined with a sense of mothering, as are their
memories of their initial schooling.[8] Their aspirations are enmeshed in a pervasive sense of responsibility for their children's educational success, as if by
"setting a good example" they can ensure the next generation's educational
well-being, righting the wrong they perceive themselves as receiving. Hence
they typically view their own goals as "selfish," as says Dora of Philadelphia:
"I guess you could say my reasons are selfish – I have always wanted to get
my high school diploma. I just don't feel complete without it. You know, when
the girls were little, I put myself on the shelf. Now that they are old enough,
I can think about doing some things that I need to do for me. But mostly, it's
for them" (p. 112). In a separate essay focused specifically on literacy and gender, Luttrell (1996) draws upon Rockhill's aphorism that "Literacy is women's
work but not women's right"[9] to argue that an ideological framing of literacy as
"women's work" reflects and perpetuates this identity-in-obligation. Because
they take little heed of poor and working women's lived situations, as students
or as mothers, dominant social assumptions about women's responsibility for
school literacy undermine working-class women's identities.

A woman's educational disprivilege, combined with an aching sense of
responsibility for her children's educational success, is starkly portrayed in
Purcell-Gates' (1995) *Other People's Words*. Jenny, the urban Appalachian
woman who is the primary character in this study, is similar to the women in
Luttrell's study. Like them, her literacy aspirations are deeply intertwined with
fear for her children's lack of school success. She is also desperate to right the
wrong done to her in schooling – a result of which are her minimal skills at
deciphering or inscription[10] – and does so by trying to defend her sons' educational interests against an indifferent school system. As she says of her eldest,
Donny, a struggling second-grader in a local school: "They ain't gonna do my
kid like they done me and his dad!" (pp. 13–14).

As we commented earlier regarding this study, one theme that emerges clearly
from Purcell-Gates' account – though it is not her focus – is the gendered
nature of Jenny's *concern* with literacy and schooling. Unlike Jenny, neither
her husband nor her son are much bothered by their lack of schooled literacy.

Indeed the son, Donny, grows more resistant as he grows more familiar with the "meaningful literacy" Purcell-Gates is trying to inculcate (pp. 144–154). Jenny, however, is gripped by a conjoined sense of her inadequacies, in language and literacy, her responsibilities, and the transforming potential of schooled literacy.

Conclusion

Although the right to education is now held to be universal, somehow working-class feminine subjects are "made"[11] who occupy different positions in relation to family, schooling, and language than either their working-class male or middle-class female counterparts. Discomfort with self, who we are and where we are from, may be a common human predicament, but that should not blind us to variation in the severity and consequences of this self-estrangement, nor to the historical specificities contributed by one's class, gender, and race to the tribulations of the self. The circumstances of working-class and minority women discussed above remind us that modern formulations of universal rights had significant exclusions – of laboring classes, women, and the racially stigmatized.

Identities are built, constructed, with the discursive resources which are our birthright, our "mother tongues," but also with other, competing discourses of street, school, and workplace. These may call us to "eventual positions of power" (Heath, 1983, p. 368), sell us "myths of simple assimilation" (Gilyard, 1991, p. 74), or convince us our "words don't come out the way they're supposed to" (Purcell-Gates, 1995, p. 100). Rose's internalized "stratifying regulator" (p. 128) points to a process whereby the "objective" social position in hierarchies of class, race, and gender becomes "subjective"; a sense of self and self-as-literate emerges from experiences of historical exclusion and schooled judgments of class background, "country" dialect, appropriate femininity, and skin color.

A significant development in post-civil rights America – both the broad movements for social equality in the early decades and the reactive restoration of neoliberal orthodoxy in the 1980s and 1990s – has been a heightened sense of the question of identity. The contemporary period seems to spawn and require unprecedented levels of "self-awareness," whether we are tending to our physical health, ruminating on ourselves as men or women, plotting a career, or planning our children's "early literacy experiences." Such reflexive awareness can seem overwhelming, hence the appeal of pat solutions – a foolproof diet, nostrums about "family" or "Christian" values, or standardized literacy programs. But the recognition of difference, and the value placed on freely chosen identities, are prominent in our contemporary social order (Bauman, 1997; Kuper, 1999). Language and literacy are prominent aspects of difference; they shape and are shaped by class, gender, and ethnorace, the great "totalizing projects" of modern nation states (Kontopoulos, 1993).

Categories of class, gender, and race have, however, proven surprisingly unwieldy exports. Once we move beyond the affluent European and European-derived nation states of the "First World," assumptions about "post" or "late" modern social formations must be held in check, and we must be open-minded about the actual content and analytic relevance of class, gender, or racial categories. In the next chapter we will explore a long colonial effort to remake subjectivities through the power and practice of writing. Literacy was an integral part of colonizing efforts, and its legacies remain in postcolonial responses. But modern institutions such as schooling, both religious and secular, had differing purchase in different societies, and their ability to shape literacy and literate persons into recognizably Western forms varied accordingly. As we will see, textual practices implicate questions of power in colonial as well as national settings, and questions of identity are prominent in postcolonial resistance to domination, as they are in postmodern efforts at self-making.

6

LITERACY, POWER, AND IDENTITY: COLONIAL LEGACIES AND INDIGENOUS TRANSFORMATIONS

In addition to being a military and political invasion, the Spanish conquest of the New World also entailed a conquest *of* language and a conquest *by* language... Throughout the conquest, language became an instrument of domination, a means of coercing speakers of indigenous languages in order to mold their minds, expressions, and thoughts into the formulas, ritual phrases, and inflections of sixteenth-century Castilian culture. (Seed, 1990, p. 12, original emphasis)

The education of colonial subjects for proselytizing... suggests a form of violence perhaps even more insidious than the destruction and persecution of the exterior manifestations of belief. It is an epistemic violence that seeks to implant an institution of knowledge and European subjectivity. (Rabasa, 1993, p. 69)

Introduction

Recognizing the interrelatedness of text, power, and identity is unavoidable when one turns to investigate the relation of colonizer to colonized. Colonial encounters, from their inception, were marked by a clash of unequal powers engaged in struggle: on the one hand, by aboriginal peoples to resist the encroachment from without which threatens the very structure of their society and the culture which sustains it, and, on the other hand, by the colonizers to remake the subject populations into Christians, both politically subservient *and* literate. The colonizing effort was all too often written not as a history of capitalist expansion, but as a massive, entirely laudable, educational enterprise bringing enlightenment and religion to those left behind in the civilizational process. Such a view masks the actual history of political and economic domination, sanctioned by church and crown, which resulted in the destruction or radical transformation of indigenous cultures throughout the non-Western world. Although initial successes of the colonial effort often resulted in the decimation or enslavement of the conquered peoples, continued dominance rested on the establishment of a colonial administration capable of reading the culture of the indigenes and incorporating those cultural meanings and mechanisms which facilitated colonial administration. Thus, conquest was often accompanied by the schooling of select aboriginals in the cultural ways of the colonizer, such educated subjects then serving to administer the colony in response to the dictates of the imperial power.

Schooling for the subject population entails the acquisition of the language and literacy of the colonial power. This was no neutral undertaking. The language of the colonizer carried with it the ideological framework and ideological judgments which were part and parcel of the language itself and of its uses. The purposes and functions of literacy for the colonizer subsumed the uses of language (and in some venues, literacy) of the indigenous populations with little or no recognition of the power of the traditions inherent in the uses and functions of native modes of communication. Simply put, in the face of the imperial power, the language and literacy of the conquered peoples counted little, or not at all, save as obstacle to or means for the evangelizing and colonizing efforts of the conquerors.[1]

But in colonial projects to reeducate subject populations in ways of the colonizer the indigenes were never completely quiescent. Always and everywhere people have resisted and rebelled against the imposition of Western cultural forms, transforming them in ways congruent with their own culture (Guss, 1986). The process of creating, through schooling, a select class who would act to interpret dominant ways (religious, political, social) and bureaucratic directives of the colonizer also opened a space for the creation of a "counter-subject." In such spaces those selected for schooling might construct an identity which incorporated native meanings into the colonial discourse in ways *contra* the colonial order. It is here where the subalterns' struggle for voice is located. Thus, the "new" identity of the colonial subjects is no mere amalgam of indigenous ways and colonizer manners, but is a true hybrid, an identity born of struggle with and against imperial powers.

This forging of a hybrid identity has its provenance in the colonial encounter, yet continues even into today. From the colonial to the postcolonial world the struggle for identity is a struggle to write the lives of subject peoples, such writing being in the language of the victors (or in the language of the conquered *transformed* by the colonizer, as was the case with Sahagún's construction of precontact Nahua). The languages used and the literate means employed, the texts produced and read, tell us much of the construction and transformation of selves through literate practices. Such selves are not *formed* by literacy; but the forging, both social and personal, of a "new" hybrid identity occurs in the cauldron of culture clash where literacy is both weapon and shield. Literacy is neither cause nor consequence; the process of self-formation, self-fashioning is, rather, mediated by literacy. As Greenblatt (1980, p. 9), discussing sixteenth-century England, reminds us: "Self-fashioning is always, though not exclusively, in language." And, we should note, especially for post-Enlightenment political movements, "the importance of shared participation in literacy activities (like reading newspapers and popular novels) written in standardized, national languages, as a means of creating national identities" (Kroskrity, 1999, p. 111).

Although the social theories of Enlightenment thinkers linked the spread of literacy "to the democratization of power" (Warner, 1990, p. ix), this was more hope than reality. The compendium of useful knowledge gathered in the *philosophes'* Encyclopedia was of little use in the countryside as educating the peasantry proved near intractable (Chartier, 1988). But if literacy may be linked to the democratization of power in post-Enlightenment societies, the obverse is certainly true in the colonial enterprise, where the spread of literacy was a means to efficiently administer the colonies, not to facilitate the sharing of power with a subservient population. In attempting to spread literacy in Western languages, that is, alphabetic literacy, among their colonies, imperial powers were not faced with the task of educating freemen, citizens/subjects, but rather of creating docile, subservient subjects, subjects whose *identity as subjects* made them malleable to the dictates of the crown.

Although this chapter deals extensively with the question of how literacy mediates identity changes in the postcolonial world, with how the "uses of literacy" in non-Western settings both draw upon and transform Western textual legacies, such changes cannot be well understood without some sense of their historical, that is, precolonial *and* colonial, contexts. Thus, we begin with a discussion of the making of selves with the colonization of the New World at the start of the sixteenth century using the island of Hispaniola and the ancient societies of Mesoamerica and the Andean region as examples. Then we take up examples from postcolonial settings in South America, the Caribbean, and North America, pursuing the themes of hybrid identities and resistance to power in reading and writing practices.

Literacy as requirement: legitimating the conquest

Familiar literary and cinematic images of heavily armored conquistadores routing natives in military engagements mask the importance of reading and writing in the conquest of the New World. While military might took control of the land and the natives, "the *right* to rule was established by language and ceremony" (Seed, 1993, p. 111). As Columbus made landfall on what he believed to be the East Indies, he ceremonially took possession of the land for the rulers of Castile and Aragon, inscribing the act in legal documents which would constitute the proof of possession:

The Admiral went ashore in the armed launch, and... brought out the royal banner and the captains [Pinzon and Yañes brought] two flags of the green cross... with an F [Ferdinand] and a Y [Isabella], and over each letter a crown, one [letter] on one side of the [cross], and the other on the other... The Admiral called to the two captains and to the others who had jumped onto land, and to Rodrigo Descobedo, the escrivano [notary and registrar] of the whole fleet, and to Rodrigo Sanchez de Segovia; and he said that they should be witnesses that, in the presence of all, he would take, and in fact he did take, possession of said island for the king and for the queen his lords, making the declarations that were, at which at more length are contained in *the testimonials made there in writing.*   (Dunn and Kelley, 1989, pp. 62, 64, emphasis added)[2]

It was the very act of reading and writing of specific texts that established the authority of conqueror over both land and people, with authority over people taking precedence in the Spanish colonies (Seed, 1993). The authority of the Spanish crown over the lands entered in the New World was secured by a papal donation and sealed by a papal bull, *Inter caetera*, issued in 1493 by Pope Alexander VI (Williams, 1990). The right to rule was conjoined with an exclusive right to preach the Gospel; in fact, the right to rule was granted "in order to secure the right to preach" (Seed, 1993, p. 123). The ritual speech employed in such ceremonial practices was less important that the placing of physical signs – the placing of a cross, setting of landmarks inscribed with royal coat of arms – and the renaming of lands and their distinctive geographical features. These acts, even when observed by the inhabitants of the newly "discovered" lands, were directed not at them, but at other Europeans who might enter the territory newly gained at a later date.[3] Yet the ceremonies of taking possession were soon to be directed at the native populations and the reading and writing practices of the alien invaders, perplexing to the natives, were to be employed in the transforming of natives into imperial subjects and catechists.

The Order of Preachers (Dominicans) who began their evangelizing efforts as early as the second voyage of Columbus in 1495, first encountered the tribal societies, the chiefdoms, of Hispaniola. The process of baptizing, of Christianizing the pagan, was, to oversimplify, one of replacing an "oral" religion with a religion of the book. But the conversion of the aboriginal inhabitants of the first colonies during the first years of colonization was not only the preoccupation of the preachers. Spanish officials were also to assist in the efforts at spiritual conversion. These colonizers, however, had other interests, the rapid acquisition of fortunes being foremost. In 1504 Queen Isabella had ordered the *encomienda* system to be instituted in Hispaniola. This system of land and slave holding had devastating effects on the Indian population of the island. Of an estimated forty thousand Indians on the island in 1509, the year Columbus' son Diego Colón became governor, only a few thousand remained by 1514.

The abominable conditions under which the Indians were forced to live and work outraged many of the Dominican friars, especially two who arrived on the island in 1510: Fray Pedro de Córdoba and Fray Antonio de Montesinos. Montesinos, in a sermon on the text: "Ego vox clamantis in deserto" (John 1:23) condemned the atrocities committed by the Spaniards.[4] Upon hearing this sermon the Spaniards called upon the governor to punish the young friar. In response Colón sent a letter to King Ferdinand charging the Dominicans with creating instability in the colony. Córdoba decided to send Montesinos to Spain to plead the Dominican's case, but his numerous attempts to gain an audience with Ferdinand were unsuccessful. Córdoba followed Montesinos to Spain arriving just shortly after the promulgation of the *Laws of Burgos*, December 1512. These laws, meant to govern the behavior of masters towards their Indian slave holdings especially as regards their conversion to Christianity, had resulted from the criticism mounted by Dominican friars against colonial officials for their failure to treat the Indians in a Christian manner. After Córdoba challenged the Laws as too weak to ensure relief of the Indians, Ferdinand asked him to review the laws and recommend adjustments. As a result of his recommendations some modifications were made, though Córdoba continued to argue that the Laws were insufficient to protect the Indians.[5] In addition, from commentary on these laws a text was extracted, the *Requerimiento*, which, when read to the natives, required them to accept the Spanish crown as legitimate legal authority over their lands and themselves. Seed explains:

In the instructions issued by the Crown for discoveries and conquests after 1512, the Requirement was ordered to be read to the New World natives. In other words, from then on, the Crown specified a ritual speech to be used in enacting the authority of its empire over a people. No longer would any "appropriate ceremony and words," duly recorded by notaries, as we saw with Columbus, be sufficient; the words had to be those of the Requirement. (Seed, 1993, p. 125)

As part of this reading, the natives were asked to submit to the authority of church and crown. Should they refuse to admit preachers to spread the Gospel, "the Spaniards considered themselves justified in commencing hostilities" (p. 126).

The image of a conquistador reading in an officious manner an unintelligible language to uncomprehending Indians would be comical if the results of such incomprehension were not to be so tragic. It appears that few efforts were made to ease communication. Seed cites Gonzalo Fernández de Oviedo: "I would have preferred to make sure that they [the Indians] understood what was being said; but for one reason or another, that was impossible...I afterwards asked Doctor Palacios Rubios, the author of the Requirement, whether the reading sufficed to clear the consciences of the Spaniards; he replied that it did" (p. 126).[6] Seed continues: "No demonstration of understanding was required: rather, the issue of reception was studiously ignored. It was the *act of reading the text* that constituted the authority. The only other action needed to legitimate Spanish rule was to record that the act of reading had taken place" (p. 126, original emphasis).

By these first and following forays into the New World, the Spanish colonials succeeded in establishing dominion over native peoples, soon to be exploited for purposes of trade and commerce. Proselytizing goals and economic interests were inseparable in the actions of the colonizers, such actions throughout the sixteenth century having been legitimated by the reading of the *Requerimiento*. Thus, Seed concludes: "Spanish authority was textual imperialism par excellence: the reading of a Western text to uncomprehending natives" (p. 131).

The scriptural economy in Hispaniola, the Andes, and New Spain

At the conclusion of our second chapter we cited three descriptive elements de Certeau uses to characterize the scriptural economy of the capitalist West, namely, (1) a presumed blank space or tabula rasa, on which inscription operates; (2) a text constructed in or upon this place of blankness; and (3) a strategic intention to dominate or transform. These elements comprise, in the laboratory of New World exploration, the conquest of one episteme by another, of the tyranny of the written over the oral. Writing and reading in the languages of the imperium create the Other while justifying the ethnocentrism of the conquerors; alterity reaches its zenith in the confrontation of the civilized European with the primitive – the most purely "Other" is the savage. In this confrontation the humanity of the civilizational alter is progressively attenuated until the savage is reduced to object, a blank slate, upon which the knowledge (episteme) of civilized man can be inscribed. In the writings of Columbus, for example, we find the natives described as part of the landscape (Todorov, 1984). The *encomienda* gave the land and the native inhabitants to the European colonizers. The indigenous peoples' histories were erased; indeed, the very question as to their status as humans capable of being saved through baptism became a cause for theological debate (Williams, 1990). But granting that indigenes might be saved, as Spanish and papal law subsequently allowed, did not restore them fully as humans on a par with their European contemporaries. They were seen as pagans, nonbelievers; the word of God must be brought to them; and they must be remade as worshipers of the Lord God and as subjects of the lords of imperial Spain. Through the power of sword and book they would become incorporated into the political realm of the crown and subject to the papal dictates of the Roman church. They would become part of the history of the West as the exploits and deeds of the conquerors were recorded in the annals of conquest and colonization.

The authority of colonial writing

The framing of natives in writing as colonial subjects begins with justifying the writing process itself as imbued with the power to record history accurately and with complete disinterest, and, simultaneously, with the claim, and demonstration *in writing*, that since the natives had no writing they had no way to accurately record the past. Without writing, native history is delegitimated, native history is elided. Without history, the natives can more easily be remade (inscribed in the texts) using molds provided by the right of conquest and Christendom. As Rabasa reminds us, "Missionaries in the New World were practicing the writing of history as an instrument of change long before Vico advanced the principle that man makes history" (Rabasa, 1993, p. 66). We might trace this practice *ab initio* with a brief consideration of the work of the Hieronymite friar Ramón Pané, a missionary companion of Columbus during his second voyage.

Landing on the island of Hispaniola in January 1494, Pané went to live among the Indians of the province of Macoris to carry out the commission of

Columbus to investigate native "beliefs and idolatries," "and how they venerate their gods" (Arrom, 1992, p. 266; López Maguiña, 1992, p. 291). In 1498, after four years with the Taino people, having learned the native language sufficiently well, Pané translated and delivered to Columbus a compilation of mythical tales, beliefs, fables, etc., the *Relación acerca las antigüedades de los indios*. This result of what might seem a laudable ethnographic project was in fact ancillary to the real reason behind Columbus' request, viz. "the need to prove the presence of the devil among the Indians in order to justify their eventual punishment" (López Maguiña, 1992, p. 296). The brutality of the conquistadores in their mistreatment of the Indians is well documented, and Columbus was no exception (Zinn, 1980). But his need to "justify [the natives'] eventual punishment" springs not from any inherent sociopathology; rather, it stems from the ideology of Christianity itself. Punishment of those who refused to accept Christ was then an accepted practice in the process of evangelization. López Maguiña explains:

Let us recall that Pané writes during the early period of Spanish colonization ... [when] no one had yet questioned the Indians' humanity. It is evident that for Pané they possessed a soul; that is why he is preoccupied with pointing out that many of them were ready to accept the tenets of Christianity. The Indians were infidels or gentiles who could be Christianized either peacefully or *by force if needed*. Since Pané saw Christianization as a necessity, he needed to prove that the indigenous people who he was to evangelize had been deceived and controlled by the devil. Thus Pané's attention to the antiquities of native culture was prompted less by an interest to understand it than by an attempt to prove evil influences. (López Maguiña, 1992, p. 296, emphasis added)[7]

A series of cosmogonic tales comprises much of Pané's *Relación*. What is of the moment, however, is the rhetorical structure of the work itself.[8] The full title of Pané's work is instructive: *Relación de Fray Ramón acerca de las antigüedades de los indios, las cuales, con diligencia, como hombre que sabe la lengua de ellos, las ha recogido por mandato del Almirante* (Historical Account by Fray Ramón about the Antiquities of the Indians, Which, with Diligence, as a Man who Knows Their Language, Have Been Gathered by the Order of the Admiral). Pané chooses *relación* (historical account) to label his report. Arrom, citing the dictionary of the *Academia Real*, informs us that "[t]he term *relación* has, among other meanings, that of 'the act and effect of relating' and of a 'report that an ancillary official makes of the substance of a trial or any repercussion that it might have before a tribunal or a judge' " (1992, p. 272). Pané thus makes his report to Columbus as subordinate to superior. This is significant, as Arrom points out, because "[t]his legalistic formula allows him the use of the narrative first person ...: 'I, fray Ramón, a poor hermit of the Order of St. Jerome, by the mandate of the illustrious Admiral ...' " (p. 272). The narrative first person, later to become familiar from the Spanish picaresque novels of the second half of the sixteenth century, is important in the New World context. The authorial voice emanates from an eyewitness, a participant in the events recounted and in the event of recounting, and it thus underscores the truth of what follows in the narrative.

This same opening gambit will recur in the chronicles of conquest. For example, Bernal Díaz del Castillo's *The True History of the Conquest of New Spain* was written to counter the inaccuracies of the account of the conquest written by Francisco López de Gómara, who had never been in the New World. Díaz' chronicle begins: "I, Bernal Díaz del Castillo, citizen and Regidor of the most loyal city of Santiago de Guatemala, one of the first discovers and conquerors of New Spain and its provinces . . . speak about that which concerns myself and all the true conquerors my companions" (Díaz del Castillo, 1956, p. 3).

The narrative "I" of the eyewitness reporter may of course lull the reader into credulity regarding the veracity of what is written. The reader believes what is written because the author was eyewitness and because it is a written account. Pané thus tells us that he carried out his task of gathering the "antiquities" of the Taino Indians with diligence and in accord with his abilities in the native language: "Everything I write is as they narrate it, just the way I write it; and so I put it as I understand it from the people of the country" (Pané, cited in López Maguiña, 1992, p. 297).We should not forget, however, that Pané's overall purpose is Christianization. Pané does not believe in the truth of the myths the Tainos tell him, nor in the validity of their beliefs, because in his mind there is only one true religion and one true God.

Arrom (1992) points out that Pané's *Relación* is significant in that it opened a route, a map of scriptural conventions, of which the eyewitness testimony is one, which was followed by many later chroniclers and investigators (El Inca Garcilaso, Bernardino de Sahagún, Durán, and others) whose works provided the inquiring and educated European access to the ethnographic marvels of alien lifeways and worldviews. Yet native worldviews, contained in their myths, poetry, songs, and religious rituals, were expressed overwhelmingly in performance by oral means. Once entextualized, mediated by a European, much of their meaning was effaced (for a case from colonial New Zealand, see McKenzie [1987]). This reportorial sleight of hand – the erasing of native history and culture in the very cataloguing and recording of native customs and beliefs – opens a space for the creation of colonial subjects. The natives are known to European readers through the writings of conquistadors, missionaries, and various and sundry other travelers. The "natives of America" are in this sense the creations of writing; they are "simulations" of a possible or vanishing real (Vizenor, 1998), representations of natives by Europeans for Europeans, using those rhetorical conventions and narrative practices formed within the ideological framework of Western political and religious institutions.

The erasure of native writing

The whole process of making subjects is part and parcel of writing conquered peoples into the history of the conquest/colonization, i.e. subjects are remade through literate means. The colonizers write their histories, *relaciones, cartas,* using the rhetorical frameworks and within the worldview of the dominant society, within the episteme of the dominant world. Yet when the colonized peoples, "educated" by the colonizers as scribes to serve the colonial administration and the church, come to write their own histories, they will of necessity employ the communicative means (alphabetic literacy) imposed by the conqueror. It is insufficient to view this result simply as the successful imposition of one language on another, it is, rather, one in which the mind itself is colonized (Ngũgĩ, 1986). That is, in writing history, in adopting the canons of historical narrative of the conquerors, the native writers not only use the language of the conqueror, but use the communicative means of one episteme to write another. The contrast between the writing by colonizer and that by colonized is captured succinctly in Rolena Adorno's comparison of the work of Todorov and of de Certeau: "Whereas Todorov invites us to contemplate the power of the written word to crush the other (creating a dominant discourse in which the other as subject would not recognize oneself), de Certeau's work invites us to consider the other as a colonial subject who is not only the observed but also the observer" (Adorno, 1989a, pp. 202–203).

We have argued that the colonizers used their alphabetic literacy to write the history of conquest and of the native peoples, justifying their subjugation of the natives in terms of Christianization. In this process, the voices of the indigenous peoples were rendered in the language of the conquerors, and their actions were interpreted in the framework of Western knowledge and belief. Where the indigenes' world was oral, there would be no conflict over choice of written forms. When narratives were written in the language of the conquerors by the conquerors, the voices of the indigenes were effectively silenced, altered by their transformation to print in an alien medium. What the conquerors heard, and their European readers read, was not what the indigenes had spoken.

The colonial "scriptural economy" was, however, not simply a process of ignoring or erasing the native voice. In those societies in the valley of Mexico and again in the Andean world, where nonalphabetic systems of writing were in place, the conquistadores were to justify conquest with the *requerimiento* and the Bible, and the power of the sword. They ignored indigenous means of preserving the past, the centuries of history and sacred knowledge contained, for example, in the codices of the Maya and the Mexica (Aztec), and, in the civilization of the Incas, associated with the *quipus.* In the valley of Mexico and in the Andes, the conquerors were faced not with nonliterate peoples where they might easily uphold the primacy of literacy over orality. Here were complex civilizations, with literate traditions. How would the alphabetic literacy of the conquerors, in the context of the Andean highlands, influence "the nature of historical memory, which had formerly depended upon the interplay of oral narrative and mnemonic device" (Rappaport, 1994, p. 271; Rappaport and Cummins, 1997)? How, in the context of the civilizations of ancient Mexico, would the books of the native priests fare against the proselytizing zeal of the Spanish missionaries? Here the conquerors were faced with complex nonalphabetic systems of preserving the past not acknowledged within their own European historiographical tradition. Mignolo explains: "the encounters between people with different approaches to language, writing and recording the past led to the suppression of Amerindian writing systems and the transformation of their speaking and writing habits as well as to the dissemination of ideas among the European reading public that Amerindians were less civilized because they lacked letters, did not have history, and had painted books dictated by the devil" (1992, p. 303).

The conquerors destroyed the writings in the sacred painted books because such writings – the writings of pagans "dictated by the devil" – were against Christianity. Hence, the natives' "struggle for voice" would be a struggle to preserve, and later to rewrite, history; a conflict in which literate traditions employing differing rhetorical strategies competed. The power and influence of Western literacy, what Mignolo (1989, p. 53) refers to as "the tyranny of the alphabet," lies in its ability to write the history of conquered peoples, to incorporate them into the history of the West, and to *re*present natives to themselves through European eyes. The devastating result of this scriptural effacing of indigenous histories is captured by the anonymous Quechua-speaking author of the Huarochirí manuscript from Peru:

Runa yndio ñiscap machoncuna ñaupa pacha quillcacta yachanman carca chayca hinantin causascancunapas manam canancamapas chincaycuc hinacho canman himanam vira cochappas sinchi cascanpas canancama ricurin hinatacmi canman. If the ancestors of the people called Indians had known writing in earlier times, then the lives they lived would not have faded from view until now. As the mighty past of the Spanish Vira Cochas is visible now, so, too, would theirs be.   (cited in Rappaport, 1994)

The missionary friars ordered by the King of Spain to bring Christian doctrine to the indigenous peoples of the New World reached the valley of Mexico or New Spain in 1524.[9] They confronted a politically complex state society altogether different from Hispaniola. Here were societies where writing had been practiced for hundreds of years; and here a priestly elite wielded substantial power supported by their ability to perform sacred rituals in accordance with prescriptions recorded in sacred books. For the missionaries to remake the conquered population, to render them salvable, entailed not only the proselytizing efforts practiced on the islands, but the stamping out of an indigenous literacy: one religion of the book (the painted codices) was to be replaced by another (the Bible). For the colonizing power, one religion was a false religion, its worshipers suffering obeisance to false gods; the other, Christianity, was the true religion, and the Bible the word of God. Both were religions of the book, but each sacred book exemplified a different literacy and spoke of different deities. The codices were pictographic representations of Aztec lord-deities and rituals of sacrifice, while the Bible recorded in an alphabetic script the tales and prophets of Christendom.

For evangelization to be carried out successfully, for pagans to be remade Christian worshipers, one form of literacy *and* its meanings and functions in the lives of the native populations had to be superseded by another. That is, not only did the Bible portray true religion and must therefore replace paganism, the Bible texts were encoded in a form of writing considered on a higher evolutionary plateau than the pictographic representations which comprised the codices.[10] But while the missionaries strove to Christianize the natives, which entailed the destruction of their sacred books, they did not attempt to impose the Spanish language. Instead, acting as linguist/missionaries, they translated the Christian religious texts into the native languages and used them in instruction. Equating native literacy with demonic knowledge, they appropriated the language of the natives and inscribed knowledge of the one true God in new books.

In order to better understand the complex process of literacy destruction coupled with language preservation we offer an extended case study of Mexico. This investigation into the contexts for and functions of literacy in pre- and postconquest Mexico is no mere academic exercise. The colonial legacy of the clash of literate civilizations is still today very much a part of the thorny issue of identity for the descendants of the native peoples, comprised at present of some fifty-eight ethnic groups (King, 1994, p. 3). The indigenous peoples of Mesoamerica had elaborate writing systems predating the conquest by hundreds of years which they used for religious and secular purposes. Although the Spaniards destroyed the material manifestations of these writing systems, the great number of books (codices) produced by native scribes on paper made from the bark of a fig tree or deerskin (only a handful of preconquest codices of which are extant), the history of their attempts to colonize the writing process itself is complex. Thus, while the production of the painted books retreated to caves, and scribes recorded the sacred knowledge hidden from Spanish eyes, they also wrote "secret" books in alphabetic script. It is the legacy of this conflict between the alphabetic literacy of the Spaniards and the various literacies of the ancient civilizations of Mesoamerica that provides the cultural backdrop to the present struggle to sustain ethnic identity in the face of the powerful forces of nationhood carried out overwhelmingly through educational institutions by means of language and literacy. In other words, language and literacy are not only the means by which the battle is fought, they are the site of the battle itself. This means that even though literacy in the colonial period was restricted in Goody's sense, that is, it was the province of an elite, indigenous groups fighting for linguistic rights in the late twentieth or early twenty-first centuries may nonetheless look to these sources of elite but indigenous resistance to language colonization in the colonial period as earlier manifestations of their continuing struggle. This is so because beliefs about the nature and uses of literacy may well have been interiorized by these subordinate groups responding to the power of the elite. Therefore, careful attention to this legacy of struggle may afford a key to "why the many Indian groups are today largely agraphic despite an indigenous literary tradition in both pre-Columbian and colonial periods that is traceable through to the early years of this [twentieth] century" (King, 1994, p. 1).

Lounsbury informs us that "[a]s many as thirteen different systems or traditions of writing have been distinguished for the Middle American area" (1989, p. 203). The extensive use of writing in Mesoamerican civilizations by the beginning of the Christian era is evident in the archeological record, and by the time of the Conquest, "the Olmec, Teotihuacan, Toltec, Zapotec, Mixtec, Otomi, Tarascan, Tezcocan, Mexica, and Mayan peoples had developed writing systems and literary cultures that met the needs of their particular societies" (King, 1994, pp. 25, 27). In general, writing was in the control of a priestly elite and used predominantly for ritual, economic (e.g. tribute roles), and historical purposes, but this restriction should not be taken to mean that materials were not plentiful. King numbers sites for paper production at more than twenty-seven and notes that "[f]or the Aztecs, paper, which they also used in certain ritual contexts, was so important that they demanded it in tribute from the peoples they conquered" (p. 27).

The importance of writing and of books to the peoples of Mesoamerica was frequently documented in the writings of the missionaries and conquistadores: "Sahagún recalls how he brought together the *sabios*, or wise men, who answered his questions about their customs and beliefs by consulting their painted books" (p. 28). Sadly, as noted, most of these books were lost early in the conquest in the destructive acts ("rituals of purification") carried out under orders of priests and bishops who sought to exorcize the work of demons contained within their painted pages; later, many of the friars came to regret the actions of their compatriots.

What the missionary priests confronted in Mesoamerica was not a monolithic literacy analogous to the Latin *lingua franca* employed by the Roman church throughout Christian Europe. Although the Aztecs understood the importance of facilitating the administration of empire by imposing one language (Nahuatl), what existed in Mesoamerica at the time of first contact was a plurality of literacies different in kind and use. King discusses three, the Mixtec, the Mayan, and the Aztec, and we follow her here to briefly underscore the similarities and differences.

As is well known, writing developed with the rise of state societies, and schools were not far behind. The Mixtecs, the Maya and the Aztecs all had special schools in which writing was taught. This is important because the missionary friars could later build upon an indigenous schooling tradition in training scribes in alphabetic literacy. The Mixtec scribes employed a mixed iconographic, ideographic, and phonetic writing to record dynastic history:

The particular significance of the surviving Mixtec codices is their central concern with the recording of dynastic and historical information. Writing, we may deduce, was essentially bound up with the transmission and fixing of knowledge from generation to generation. The codices were both legitimizing and educational, securing the rights of the Mixtec nobility and their descendants by recording for posterity and providing the means by which the young might learn of the exploits of their warriors in battle and of their rightful identity as Mixtecs.   (King, 1994, p. 30)

As one of the means to secure their rights, the Mixtec nobles, as elites else-where, whether religious, military, or secular, recognized the power of literacy to inscribe and thus fix their history in writing. Thus the control of literacy through the establishment of scribe schools is linked to writing the history which legitimated the nobles' position in the top stratum of society.

Of central concern to the Maya, in contradistinction to the Mixtecs, was the recording of calendrical and astronomical information used for the religious purpose of divining when to carry out certain activities, a kind of religious Farmers' Almanac. Although thousands of codices were produced, only three survived the ravages of climate and the rages of priests. Today we know Mayan writing from these three codices and the glyphs preserved on the temple stelae to be "a mixed system using phonetic and logographic glyphs and presenting various forms of alternatives for aesthetic choice" (p. 34). Due to this "mixed" writing system, a definitive meaning for many of the glyphs has not been estab-lished despite the best efforts of archeologists and linguists to decipher them (Justeson, 1989). This may very well be because "[p]ictographic and ideo-graphic writing were not intended to be reduced to speech in the same sense as phonetic writing" (p. 35). That is, a shaman reading one of the texts may derive any one of several possible interpretations because the signs are pluridimen-sional; a sign may provide an opening to elaborations of meaning. However the Mayan codices were read, "[they] were not intended to be read in a quotidian sense; they were essentially esoteric in nature and required lengthy study and preparation because only shamans could decipher the secret knowledge locked in the texts" (p. 35).

At a level nearly commensurate with the uses of literacy in the Old World empires, with the Aztecs we find writing used for a multiplicity of purposes directed at administering an empire. Although few of the Aztec codices sur-vive, those that do provide evidence for the use of written records in legal disputes, for accounting purposes (recording tribute), for recounting history, and, like the Maya, for recording calendrical and astronomical information for religious purposes. Aztec writing was basically pictographic, as Sahagún men-tions "they communicated with each other by means of images and paintings" (cited in King, p. 37). In a maneuver that foreshadowed the acts of the Span-ish priests, once the Aztecs embarked upon imperial expansion, they burned codices, rewriting their histories to give greater prominence to themselves and their conquering exploits.

In order to carry out the administrative and religious functions of empire specialists are needed and schools were established to prepare male youth[11] for their future roles:

> The Aztecs had two types of schools: the *telpochcalli*, where the sons of commoners studied to be soldiers, policeman, or petty officials, and the *calmecac*, schools attached to the temples where the sons of noblemen studied the arts of writing and oratory and the history and accumulated knowledge of Aztec culture. In the calmecac, the young men learned the correct oral accompaniment to the painted books and techniques in oratory and the different styles of language. They learned the songs of the gods, the count of the days, the book of dreams, and the book of years. . . . In the calmecac . . . the students learned the verses to accompany sections of the different books, each page functioning as an aide-mémoire opening the way for oral explanation and elaboration. Reading in this context was not a solitary act but a communal or social activity with didactic and ritual components.   (p. 39)

Reading was not a solitary act, but a performance, one which allowed the reader to use the pictographs as signs which trigger the memory. While the dates of terrestrial and celestial events contained in the books was essential knowledge, such knowledge was incomplete without its actualization in performance. Because knowledge was not contained solely in the text, the conflagration which destroyed many of the written and painted artifacts did not completely erase the history and culture captured in the writing systems of pre-Columbian Mesoamerica. Aspects of the indigenous literacies would remain as a legacy from which to define and defend the identities of the native peoples through the colonial period and beyond.

What the Spaniards brought to Mesoamerica, then, was not literacy as such, which pre-existed widely, but *alphabetic* literacy. Traditional practices of reading remained and missionaries, recognizing the extent of literacy among the "barbarians," used it to their advantage in their efforts at Christianization by preparing texts in the native languages (very much like the Wycliffe Bible translators were to do in the twentieth century). Interestingly, the Spaniards at times adopted pictographic writing, and it was employed by the natives in official record keeping. Alphabetic writing was used to provide explanations for the pictographs (King, 1994). Gradually pictographic writing died out, replaced by alphabetic script, but the scribes did not use it to record in Spanish, rather to record the native languages. Spanish may have been the language of domination, but it was not the dominant language. The official language policy was to impose Spanish in administering the colonies and in converting the Indians, but due to the linguistic complexity and the geography of the region it was difficult to establish Spanish as a *lingua franca*. Indian communities distant from the centers of commerce and administration might not be exposed to Spanish directly, except in the person of the priest. But as in most things regarding colonial Mexico, capturing the gist of the official language policy in one concise statement is difficult. No one fixed policy was instituted and promulgated unchanged throughout the colonial period. The relative importance of the Spanish language to the goals of church and crown shifted, with Spanish being emphasized more strongly later rather than earlier. But which language to use for administrative purposes, proselytizing, in education, and so forth, was all hotly contested between church and state and even among the secular clergy and religious orders (Heath, 1972). Nonetheless, due to the empire building of the Aztecs, for example, Nahuatl was widespread and as a *lingua franca* could be adopted by the church to facilitate its evangelizing.

Recall that the *Laws of Burgos* had required the *encomenderos* to educate the Indians in the Spanish language (Castilian) and in the Christian faith. The realities of the Mesoamerican context doomed this "civilizing" process from the start as the *encomenderos* simply ignored the dictates of the crown. By 1542, Charles V had turned over the education of the Indians to the mendicant friars. The priests, in accepting this responsibility, interpreted it not strictly in political terms, but also in spiritual. Because some religious orders viewed the Spanish culture as morally tainted and fatally polluting to the indigenous peoples, they sought, as adjunct to their evangelizing mission, to maintain a separation between indigenous and Spanish social spheres. That is, "the early representatives of the orders came to evangelize, not to Hispanicize" (Heath, 1972, p. 15). With conversion as the goal, teaching and preaching in the indigenous languages (while retaining Latin for liturgical uses) was the most expedient means to spread the Gospel. Not only did the friars resist the use of Castilian, they proposed Nahuatl as an alternative, clearly avoiding strict adherence to the wishes of the crown.

The success of Aztec empire building had made knowledge of Nahuatl widespread. The Franciscan friars proposed extending the range of Nahuatl beyond the valley of Mexico and argued that Indians learned Nahuatl easier and more quickly than they did Castilian. This proposal was unacceptable to Charles V, who was concerned less with the outright disobedience of the Franciscans than with the success of the Christianization process itself. It was one thing to teach the Indians common prayers, the seven deadly sins, and the most basic tenets of the Christian faith; it was quite another to instruct them in "the deeper mysteries of the Catholic faith in Nahuatl or any other Indian tongue" (Heath, 1972, p. 19). Thus in 1550, in a move meant to preserve and strengthen the teaching of Christianity, Charles V mandated that formal education no longer be restricted to the elite, but to accommodate any Indian wishing to learn Castilian. The idea behind this was a simple one: create a ripple effect. Once the friars educated Indians in Castilian and in "the deeper mysteries of the Catholic faith," they would now serve the friars, carrying their training to others who in turn would carry it still further (p. 20).

If the church had an ambiguous relationship to the sources of political power, at times supporting the forces of empire, at times defending the natives against them, one thing is certain: the education offered through the schools and through religious instruction has been a significant factor in indigenous peoples' struggle to maintain their identity. Once Indians educated by the friars had acquired literacy in Spanish, they could now employ it in defense of their claims against the crown, and later against the state. Many leaders of popular uprisings in the eighteenth century were educated under the auspices of the church (Rockwell, forthcoming). Contemporary movements for linguistic and ethnic rights throughout Latin America are often led by those who have adopted the teaching of liberation theology from the activist clergy in their communities.

Thus far we have focused on ritual uses of native writing systems and their suppression as part of the spiritual conquest of souls, mentioning proselytizing friars and a counter-discourse of "secret" ritual documents in caves. But such "acts of resistance" by underground shamans by no means comprise the entire story of how the indigenous peoples survived the conquest. Mention must also be made of the immensely important process by which indigenous peoples appropriated and used alphabetic writing for public record keeping and daily life. To do justice to this highly complex appropriation process is beyond our means here, but let us briefly address the matter.[12]

Relevant to our purpose here is how the incorporation of native communities into the colonial order was both facilitated and subverted by native-language literacy and the adoption of textual genres into native languages, as well as the inscribing of native history into world history by native and mestizo historiographers. As de Certeau so pointedly observes of the native peoples of the Americas:

even when they were subjected, indeed even when they accepted their subjection, the Indians often used the laws, practices, and representations that were imposed on them by force or by fascination to ends other than those of their conquerors; they made something else out of them; they subverted them from within – not by rejecting them or by transforming them (though that occurred as well), but by many different ways of using them in the service of rules, customs or convictions foreign to the colonialization which they could not escape. They metaphorized the dominant order; they made it function in another register.   (1984, pp. 31–32)

The adopting and use of alphabetic systems in the creation of oppositional practices is a complex and fascinating subject. For our purposes, let one case from Mexico suffice,[13] that of the native historian Don Fernando de Alva Ixtlilxochitl, a descendant of one of the ruling houses of the Aztec Triple Alliance. Educated by the Franciscans, he was employed in government work and adopted Spanish ways as conditions required. His "taking pen to paper and asserting adherence to the Christian faith and loyalty to the Spanish crown served simultaneously to reorganize cultural space and affirm a place of utterance" (Adorno, 1989a, p. 210). In his histories, written during the first years of the seventeenth century, Alva Ixtlilxochitl "renegotiated" the narrative terrain of accounts of the Spanish conquest by writing the heroic actions of native peoples who would be otherwise lost to world (written) history because missing from the histories and chronicles written by Europeans. The sources used in his research included paintings and the oral traditions of his people. He celebrates the contributions made by his own ancestors in the wars of conquest and emphasizes military values from his own culture – prudence and valor. In the Spanish accounts, such qualities had been attached only to European warriors.

Because Alva Ixtlilxochitl has accommodated himself to the culture of the conquerors (as an educated, Christian, government functionary), his is not an independent, uncorrupted native voice. Rather, his life and his histories are an expressed hybridity, drawing on both the paintings and oral traditions of his people as well as alphabetic literacy. As Adorno concludes: "Alva Ixtlilxoxchitl's subject position is not that of the pure indigenous prehispanic past, but that of a colonial subject . . . whose conscious attempts to accommodate himself to new doctrinal and discursive norms bespeak an ethnic ambition and a search for identity" (1989a, p. 216). Any current struggle of indigenous peoples for ethnic identity will have to acknowledge such an hybridity at the core of their struggle and in themselves (for Andean cases see Rappaport [1998], Howard-Malverde [1997] and Adorno [1985]).

Given the complexity of the sociolinguistic history of Mexico, the duration of the struggle to retain native languages, to recognize indigenous literacies, to acknowledge the achievements that are the native language literature of the pre-Columbian and colonial eras, one is struck by the need, in the present, to address the question formulated by Rockwell (1999). Pertaining to the current perception of the Maya, she asks: "How did the Maya people of Chiapas, who in the past possessed what is increasingly recognized as a sophisticated writing system, come to be considered over a period of 400 years members of 'oral cultures'?" (p. 1). The question, essential for any adequate understanding of educational interventions, is intriguing because it seemingly reverses the evolutionary trajectory of development through literate means. We have a case, to borrow the words of Andre Gunder Frank, of the "development of underdevelopment." "Mayan literacy," to the educationists and policy makers, disappeared long ago; the term returns us to a distant past of scribes using a nonalphabetic script for special purposes, of interest now only to archaeologists and antiquarians. But as we have shown, the literacies of the ancient peoples of Mexico were central to their history and to their struggle against the forces of domination. Those concerned with contemporary issues of educational policy which deny this history continue a process of disempowerment relegating native peoples to a negative category of "oral" peoples who must be saved, in a secular sense, in order to be assimilated fully into national consciousness.

Rockwell adopts the concept of "appropriation" from Chartier's (1995) discussion of popular culture to provide examples of how native peoples over a period of four centuries "used [writing] for their own ends, while at the same time *defending* themselves against some of the abuses exercised through writing by those in power" (1999, p. 2, original emphasis). What we are concerned with is the ways in which an alphabetic writing system, that in which Castilian Spanish is represented, is understood *and* transformed by literate indigenous peoples, or rejected. As Rockwell stresses, "[i]n encounters with dominant groups, appropriation may involve strategic *avoidance of writing* as well as *strategic uses of literacy*" (p. 2, original emphasis).

The disappearance of preconquest (and later postconquest) books among the Maya had various causes. In addition to the book burning already noted, some genres of writing disappeared because the contexts in which they functioned, for example temple rituals, disappeared. Some were hidden away and some fell victim to the ravages of tropical climate. But the disappearance of books did not entirely extinguish the entire array of pre-Columbian literate practices. While in regions under control of the Aztecs friars had immediately begun to produce books in Nahuatl for the use of their fellow missionaries, missionaries in Chiapas used oral and visual means in their proselytizing efforts. Yet Rockwell informs us that literacy did not die out completely as Mayans over the next two centuries "developed clandestine religious practices (in caves, fields and homes) involving written scripts, and registered current versions of their beliefs and practices using the alphabetic system taken – or stolen – from the Spaniards. These books were kept in hiding and [as none survive] presumably used to reconstruct ritual calendars and interpret ongoing phenomena in the light of Maya history" (p. 4).[14] If we now recall that ancient Mayan writing was not purely pictographic, and that readers of the sacred books, shamans, would interpret the symbols in performance, what these postconquest books might have contained were records of performances.[15] If this is so, we have a case where "[t]he appropriation of alphabetic writing seemed concerned with preserving an *oral tradition*, as well as inventing written text" (pp. 4–5, original emphasis). In other words, "In Chiapas, it is possible that destruction was so thorough that it forced communities to inscribe texts in collective memory using different means, including elaborate oral ritual genres, and writing without words (such as textile designs)" (p. 5).

Rockwell discusses what she calls the denial of literacy using cases of rebellion which occurred in Chiapas during the eighteenth century. Even in the face of evidence that writing has been appropriated by rebel leaders, fluent in Spanish, for use in formulating demands and writing proclamations, "official accounts tended to deny the presence of writing and the understanding of written documents" (p. 7), casting the rebellions as the work of ignorant peasants. In short, "the discourses of power tend to negate subaltern uses of literacy" (p. 8) resulting in legitimating in the eyes of the powerful the imposition of a particular form of literacy on the indigenous population through schooling.

In recent years native voices have been heard through a spate of writings in the literary genre *testimonio*, one of the most famous, and controversial, being that of Rigoberta Menchu (1984). Rockwell mines some of the testimonies of Chiapas natives searching for evidence of the appropriation of literacy and of the history of writing in the twentieth century. Her examples from stories of schooling collected by Andrés Aubry are instructive because they highlight the abuse of power through schooling. The stories (testimonies) recount the introduction of schools to the indigenous communities at the start of the twentieth century. One is a story of resistance in which a father disguises his son as a daughter and later takes him to work on a *finca* to protect him from the influence of schooling. The other story is the converse. A young boy, Antonio, is sent to school by his parents after they had been "harassed by soldiers bearing papers . . . After ridiculing the soldiers' bad manners and rude talk, they conceded that it is best 'to learn the weapons of the enemy,' [and Antonio adds that] 'I want to learn Spanish so that they will respect us . . . I want to learn to read, and also to write, to understand what those papers say' " (pp. 9–10).

Taken together the two stories point up opposing strategies in dealing with schooling: resist or acquiesce. The first preserves native identity leaving the native in an existence marginal to the economic and political mainstream. The second offers at least the possibility of acquiring "the weapons of the enemy" which may be used to defend ethnic identity and native lifeways. But for this later strategy to be effective, children must actually learn what they will later need as adults to counter the oppressive intrusions of the national government into native culture. What children are learning is how to behave in non-Indian ways. Rockwell reports that "Grievances expressed by parents include not only the fact that their children's manners changed, but also that they finish elementary school *without* having learned basic Spanish literacy." And that, "In the past two decades, many communities have submitted to educational authorities the minutes of the town meetings in which they decided to dismiss a local teacher, on grounds that often involve failure to teach effectively, violation of local custom, and undesirable behavior" (pp. 10–11). Rockwell's concluding comment on these stories of schooling underscores the necessity of attending to both power in literacy and the historical dimension of literacy practices: "In these cases, it would seem that the *demand for literacy*, and the exercise of collective rights through literacy, counters the abuse of power that offers nominal schooling, while continuing to undermine effective access to literacy" (p. 10, original emphasis). At a time when literacy instruction is offered as a panacea for the amelioration of economic, social, and political marginalization, whether ethnic or racial, we would do well to attend also to the appropriated uses, the history and power of reading and writing in the communities denigrated as "oral."

Reading beyond the text: postcolonial responses

How power is implicated in the multiple performance genres comprising Street's (1984) oral/literate "mix" of modes of communication is exhibited in a case from the Andean region documented by Digges and Rappaport (1993). The case calls into question any attempt to delineate clear functional meanings for one or the other, oral or literate, as distinct, separable categories, or to weigh the relative importance of each in the uses of literacy comprising the oral/literate mix. Rather, the representational means exploits orality and literacy for different ends in the struggle for social and political recognition and legitimation. What an official document may represent and what is "actually" represented in such documents is read differently by different social segments of a particular society or state. Said differently, one and the same document may hold different places, have different meanings, in the separate discourses of competing social groups. Such discourses incorporate representational or symbolic forms beyond the textual (read "alphabetic") such that what is inscribed may be taken to include nontextual practices, such practices being read by some readers, and read out by others. What this means is that the readers' knowledge of what is inscribed in any given text is only partial knowledge. Due to the elevation of the written word over the oral, however, written text is often assumed to be full, nearly complete, its incompleteness due to "weaknesses" in the readers' schema or epistemic knowledge, not to any lacunae in the text as authored. That readers might be "reading" texts in relation to events and practices not actually inscribed therein is thus given very little credence.

If orality is the underspecified term in the oral/literate dichotomy, causing much of what occurs in oral performances to be lost in inscription, so much more so for practices not easily transferred to print, such as rituals performed by both colonizer and colonized. If their inscription is incomplete, faulty, or, in some readings simply absent, such practices may nonetheless be "read" in the documents. The meaning of historical events lies in the amalgam of interpretations constructed or extracted by different readers – from the writings of chroniclers who recorded eyewitness accounts to the narrative interpretations of later historians in support for legal claims in the present. Historical meaning has always been contested terrain.

The case reported by Digges and Rappaport is instructive in this regard. By contrasting readings of an official document by Indians and state officials, Digges and Rappaport examine reading as ritual practice in Cumbal, a community located on the border between Colombia and Ecuador. In this case, the text of colonial documents (titles) serves both as a means to establish land claims and ethnic (native) identity and as a symbol of political power. In Cumbal we find an oral/literate mix in the selection and use of evidence in constructing and supporting a history of the community. For Cumbales, the "selection of specific pieces of evidence from the written record is governed by nontextual criteria, in particular, by ritual and practical activities in the present" (p. 139). Further, "the texts they choose to examine are often no more than a prompt for oral elaboration, and the meaning of these texts only emerges in the course of such performative acts as ritual" (p. 139). While state officials charged with the administrative tasks of determining mineral rights read titles to land within the framework of a well-established legal discourse, in which what is written holds sway over attempts at oral suasion, community leaders have recourse to oral tradition and ritual practice as justification for their claims.

Cumbal is comprised of four "resguardos, communally owned territories administered by semiautonomous political authorities (*cabildos*)...[and] legitimized by eighteenth-century titles granted by the King of Spain" (p. 140). Through the years, many of the lands have come under the control of non-Indian landlords, shrinking the land under the control of the cabildo. As the native population grew, communities had recourse to the courts, attempting to legitimate their claims and to have lands returned to Indian control. When their attempts failed in the courts, the cabildos "of the early 1970s [embarked] upon a militant program of land claims that has included the peaceful occupation of those ranches that lie within resguardo boundaries, as well as the revitalization of native culture and historical consciousness" (p. 140). One result of this militancy was the *rereading* of colonial resguardo titles.

The case reported by Digges and Rappaport specifically concerns the defense of mineral rights, the sulphur deposits of Mount Cumbal. The authors provide alternate readings of a letter written to the Minister of Mines and Petroleum by the cabildo of Cumbal in support of their argument that "[t]he ethnography of reading cannot be examined independently of the ethnography of writing and ritual practice" (p. 139). In their petition, the members of the cabildo of Cumbal ask that their rights to Mount Cumbal be respected. They refer to the securing of rights by royal decree in 1758, rights later recognized in the first constitution of newly independent Colombia, and they include a description of a "possession ceremony" carried out by one "Spanish Infantry Captain...by commission of the ROYAL COURT OF SAN FRANCISCO DE QUITO." This description comprises the main body of the letter:

And one and another time, the Spanish Infantry Captain and Magistrate of HIGH JUSTICE OF THE PASTOS...by commission of the ROYAL COURT OF SAN FRANCISCO DE QUITO – legalized the possession, he made it good, and he also made good the dominion of the four hereditary chiefs.... For a week the Infantry Captain had to identify, one by one, the natural boundaries within which the expanse of land granted to the Indian masses, with their chiefs at their head, was encompassed by boundary-markers. ACCOMPLISHED the patient tracing of boundaries, to which chiefs from other towns were invited, the Spanish Infantry Captain knelt on the plain, and then, assuming the gold crown of his king, his natural lord, handed over in a loud voice, the land in its tenancy, its possessions, and its very dominion, to the chiefs, the genuine representatives of the peoples of CUMBAL.   (p. 142)

The government attorney's response to the letter is dismissive, even patronizing: "In view of the fact that this is a matter concerning a community of indigenous people who, perhaps, are not familiar with the laws and decrees concerning mining concessions..." (p. 143). More significantly, it ignores the description of the possession ceremony entirely. Instead, the attorney informs the petitioners of the proper procedures to be followed in pressing their claim, and thereby provides himself with an excuse for not acting on their petition. The attorney, by ignoring the main body of the letter, the description of the possession ceremony, has read out of the letter that which is ostensibly of most importance to the Indian petitioners. It is enough for him to assert that procedures were not followed. They have not followed the legally prescribed means of formally petitioning; he reads the document from his position in a bureaucratic state structure within the framework of legal discourse.

The Spanish provenance of the possession ceremony made it no less legal than the written law for the Indians, but a question remains: why place emphasis on a description of a ceremony to press their claim when documents which could be read within the realm of legal discourse were available? Digges and Rappaport explain that the modern "possession ceremony by which the cabildo grants usufruct rights to communal lands to resguardo members," and which "faithfully reproduces similar Spanish rituals that are described in detail in colonial land titles ... operates as a conceptual filter through which colonial titles are remembered and reinterpreted. Although the colonial chiefs won their right to the lands only after protracted struggle documented in the title, their claims were only validated through the possession ceremony that is still relived, week after week, by resguardo members" (p. 144).

In this case we are not faced with an illiterate or nonliterate population unable to read the written documents validating their legal rights to the sulphur deposits on Mount Cumbal. Rather, the Cumbales, fully recognizing the importance of the documents, nonetheless reject the written testimony as alone validating their claims. It is the weekly rehearsing of the possession ceremony as it is recorded in the documents that holds symbolic power, for the ritual practice of taking possession enforces their claim. Thus, for the Indians, the ritual is a *re*reading of the document in which neither the oral nor the literate supersedes the other:

[The Cumbales] read their titles in culturally specific ways dictated by contemporary political practice, extracting from the documents only those features of colonial ritual that *they* recognize as bestowing legitimacy upon modern reservation members: walking the boundaries, kneeling on the land, calling together eyewitnesses, declaring possession. Those who do not have access to the titles, or who have not consulted them in a long time, remember and recount their contents in oral form, focusing in particular upon the possession ceremony.   (p. 144, original emphasis)

In any event, a contemporary reading of the titles themselves, whether by Indian or government official, is not a straightforward task. Such a reading is complicated by the multiple layers of documents and varied types of record comprising the titles[16] created over a lengthy time span. First, what was recorded in the documents by scribes during the colonial period was what was said and done during rituals of possession through which the laws were enacted: the "laws and statutes [of the colonial administration] were validated, enacted, and experienced by most people through ritual practice" (p. 145). Second,

Cumbal's titles contain a variety of records spanning some forty-six years, from 1712 to 1758, including multiple testimonies of local chiefs and with non-Indians residing in the area; written records of ceremonies granting land rights to any of a number of parties to the dispute; documentation of the numerous requests for testimony, judicial considera-tion or investigation that kept the lawsuit going for more than four decades; copies – and occasional originals – of earlier documents, especially royal decrees, granting Indians territorial autonomy in the seventeenth century. (p. 145)

Digges and Rappaport also point out that due to the complex intertextual-ity exhibited in the titles, a competent literate lacking the specific training to "read" the arrangement of different forms might easily read them in a different manner. As an example of the latter, the authors return us to the letter/petition and tell us that the phrase "one and another time" indicates that the petitioners, "instead of perceiving the title as an amalgam of documents produced at dif-ferent times by different individuals, many of which included descriptions of the same possession ceremony . . . read it as a collection of repeated identical images that, moreover, are significant only so far as they legitimize current practices" (p. 147).

Further, the ceremonies detailed in the documents, although quite similar, are not identical to those performed today. Indians, quite familiar with current ritual practices (since the possession ceremony is performed almost weekly), reinterpret the ceremonies described in the documents in light of current cere-monial practices "and transmit this knowledge in oral form to other community members. The memory of the existence of the colonial document has thus prin-cipally been maintained through oral means, as well as through reference to symbols" (p. 147).

In the confrontation between the farmers of Cumbal and the legal system of the Colombian state we have a complex textual archive, a complex legacy of colonial and contemporary ritual practice, and distinct ideologies of reading. In this case the Indians' reenactment of the possession ceremony is not purely oral, nor is its entextualization purely literate. The Cumbales practice of reading is a defiance of what de Certeau characterizes as "the assimilation of reading to passivity," appropriate to a "scriptural imperialism" (1984, p. 169). Instead, theirs is a reading that conjoins text artifact and ritual practice in "a circular and constant movement." It is also a reading and a writing that violates the authorities' expectations and most likely leads to their rejection of the cabildo's petition:

While it is true that the Cumbal readers of colonial documents are employing the same technology of writing common to other regions, the nature of their reading of the Spanish language is conditioned by other factors. There is no linear "fixity of text" that literacy supposedly promises, but instead a circular and constant movement between literacy and orality, between orality and ritual practice, between ritual practice and literacy. This movement cannot be simplified into an oral/literate dichotomy. Moreover, it cannot be generalized across political, historical, and cultural situations. Ultimately, the lack of "fixity of text" proved to be all too confusing to the Colombian authorities who read the council's petition.   (Digges and Rappaport, 1993, p. 149)

Ambivalent acceptance of and resistance to the standardization and institutionalization of the language of the colonial power, both oral and written, is characteristic of the postcolonial world (Foley, 1997c). As Ngũgĩ wa Thiong'o (1986) argues, the subaltern, struggling to create and elaborate a self in and through writing, must choose to either reject the language of the colonizer or appropriate it to his own uses. The first alternative, outright rejection of the authority of the colonizer's language, rarely occurs. It seems a bold first step on the path to the creation of a pure decolonized self but is, in actuality, a surrender. The reality of the postcolonial world, in which political independence has been won or granted, remains one of struggle: simultaneously to define a political entity *vis-à-vis* the former colonial power and to create a new cultural identity which reflects not only a distant historical or even mythic preconquest past, but also incorporates the lessons learned as colonized people. To deny the reality of conflicting modes of communication which comprised the communicative economy of the colonial world in an attempt to return to pure forms of a preconquest past is to deny the struggles which led to independence. These were struggles carried out as much with words as with arms.

A second alternative available to newly independent peoples is to appropriate the language of the former colonizer shaping it to their own purposes, using it in ways which contain the history of their struggles for freedom, elaborating selves through literacy practices, in writing and by reading, in ways which challenge the dominance of the standard language of the schools and the sacred books of the missionaries. In the Cumbal case just discussed, we have seen how indigenous practices of reading emphasize local ritual practices in ways that disrupt formal legal expectations about petitions, arguments, and textual warrants. This points up the irony of postcolonial situations: that the standardized legal and religious institutions of the colonial powers typically become those of the decolonized nation state. This is evident in a country like Jamaica, which has had a long debate about the relation between an elite Standard (British) English and a popular Creole as media for education, government, and religion (Trudgill, 1974). In the Jamaican context, Standard English is associated both with the colonial past and a desired modernity, for the standard is an international language of business, culture, government, and learning. Creole, conversely, is emblematic of the colonial past and mass opposition to that past. Creole is also a preferred medium of communication and affiliation in the Caribbean diaspora in the UK and (continental) North America (Gilroy, 1987; Rampton, 1995). It is a "voice" of cultural practices such as reggae and Rastafarianism which challenge settled hierarchies in fields as diverse as popular music and religion. In what follows we will examine a case which demonstrates the appropriation and transformation of literacy practices for salvation, involving reading practices in contemporary Jamaica.

In a number of recent works on language and literacy among the Rastafari of Jamaica, John Pulis (1993; 1999; forthcoming) describes their reading of scripture, an interactive discursive practice known as "citing [sighting]-up," as a "subversive activity in which [practitioners] subordinate the text, the printed word, and associated understandings of literacy to the spoken" (1999, p. 357). This is a noteworthy reversal: not only is the spoken the privileged medium of meaning making, contrary to typical expectations in a literate society, but reading is perceived as an aural, in contradistinction to an oral, activity. The ear, in short, has replaced the eye, as the organ of reading. In order to understand such complex practices as "citing[sighting]-up" it is necessary to jettison the oral/literate dichotomy, replacing it with the nondichotomous, overlapping categories "power," "authority," and "identity." To do so enables us to understand "how a local practitioner has brought a tradition of resistance and struggle to bear in transforming the printed text into an orally recounted Bible or 'living testament' of African history and culture" (1999, p. 358).

The Rastafarian Brethren proclaim the now-deceased Ethiopian Emperor Haile Selassie the black Messiah, Jamaica a New World Babylon, and themselves the "chosen" people of biblical renown. Once subjected to attempts at suppression by first colonial and later postcolonial officials, as much for their unique style of speech (Dread Talk) and comportment as for their religious beliefs, these former " 'outcasts' of colonial society" had, for a brief span of time in the 1970s and 1980s, a profound influence on "the vanguard of postcolonial art, fashion, and cultural identity" (pp. 358, 359). Reading scripture is an activity central to their religious practice.[17]

Bible reading is a practice variable across time and place, yet quite familiar to us as an interpretive process of exegetical reasoning from text. Put most forcefully in Protestant theology and literacy ideology, the meaning of God's message is "in the text." The situation appears to be quite different in the world of the Rastafari. In contrast to many scenes of scriptural engagement in the Christian tradition (e.g. D. Boyarin, 1993; Long, 1993) "citing-up . . . is not a passive, contemplative, or solitary ritual performed in silence, but an aural and a multi-vocal event" which "mediates between and subordinates the text, the printed word, and associated understandings of literacy to the spoken" (Pulis, 1993, p. 359). More dramatically, "the meaning produced by citing-up is not carried by the text nor are literary conventions such as voice, narration, and textuality bounded by the ink and pages of a book. Attention to the performative will shift the focus of description and analysis from the text (and a text-centered exegesis) to the relation between biblical texts, historical events, and everyday life" (p. 359), and thus, to the relations between language, power, and social identity.

Pulis (1999) provides the reader with a history and analysis of his encounter and numerous "reasonings" with a "rootsman" he calls Bongo, who lives in a rural parish about eighty miles from Kingston. It was said of Bongo that his "countenance shined"; that is, his comportment and "his 'words' or rhetoric did not contradict his 'livity' or way of life"; and that his "gates" (household) "were open to dread and nondread, African and European alike, and was [sic] noted for . . . lively debates or 'reasonings' " (p. 361). Bongo's day was bisected by two essential activities: morning horticulture ensured the production of his material subsistence, while afternoon Bible reading and "reasonings" provided spiritual sustenance. Pulis tells us that "one of [Bongo's] favorite expressions was 'a chapter a day keeps the devil away' " (p. 362) and that for Rastafari "[t]he books and chapters that constitute the Bible are of central importance . . . [because] they are considered by most practitioners to be an encyclopedic resource of African culture and history 'buried' or 'locked off' within the ink and pages of a book" (pp. 362–363).

The Bible, however, was viewed as incomplete, as not whole. Key books and chapters, those containing " 'crucial I-tations (meditations),' books and chapters about African culture and history" (p. 362) were missing. While it was necessary to act upon the Bible, it was also necessary "to transform . . . the 'dead letters of print' into 'livical' sounds . . ." (p. 363) through "reasoning," a process not simply of the discovery and extraction of hidden meaning, an intellectual mining process, but rather of the *freeing* of meaning long suppressed by translators and compilers of the "authorized King James Bible" version. "Reasoning," then, is not a passive decoding, nor is it an hermeneutic move opening up meaning, but rather a process of reconstruction. The results of such "reasonings" are profound: from the meanings liberated from the text an historical and cultural identity is forged, the place of the Rastafari as the "elect," the chosen people of the Old and New Testaments is validated, and the knowledge necessary to a sound spiritual daily way of life in the contemporary world is made available.[18]

Reading scripture was not a contemplative activity, done in silence and solitude, but an oral/aural transformation of the textual into the "livical." The subordination of the written to the spoken begins, for Bongo, with a scriptural prescription. In First Samuel, chapter 1, verses 12–15, Anna, her heart full of grief, prays to the Lord to open her womb and give her a son. But she prays in her heart and only her lips move, so her voice was not heard. And the priest Eli, observing her, thinks her to be drunk. For Bongo, this means that reading the Bible silently, without speaking, is equivalent to praying without speaking. In addition to acknowledging the scriptural prescription underlying Bongo's reading aloud, there is also a critical knowledge of sound-based semantics necessary for transforming and subordinating the written text to the spoken word. This entails the "busting" of words and subsequent constructing of "up-full" or "livical sounds." As this "busting" process in the speaking/reading of scripture lies at the core of Rastafarian practice of textual transformation whereby reading becomes a subversive activity, it is necessary to quote Pulis' description at length:

> Language, for Rastafarians, is an arena, a site of struggle and transformation. Since English is considered the language of enslavement and captivity it was not deemed "heartical," capable of expressing black culture and consciousness. Upfull sounds were created by bringing the "word-sound-power," the tonal or sound-based semantics of Creole to bear on transforming English (spoken and printed) into a way of speaking known as I-yaric, I-ance, or Dread Talk. The acoustic or phonetic structure of English was interrogated, that is, sounded out loud, broken apart to expose contradictions between sound and sense, and reassembled into a vocabulary of spoken or livical sounds. For example, the /un/ sound in the word understand was replaced by the /o/ as in over to create the word-sound /overstand/ because the negative sound associated with /un/ implied one speaker was under and below and hence less competent, fluent, and literate than the another....
>
> Unlike the [example] above, in which sounds were added and deleted, the similarity in sound in the homophones /cite/ and /sight/ led to the compounding and convergence of their meaning in the word-sound /cite[sight]-up/. In this case, the tension or antagonism between a spoken and printed literacy (understood here as that between cite as aurality or the sounding of words and sight as a reference to visualizing the scribal or printed word) signified a way of reading and a form of interpretation that compared, contrasted, and realigned textual citation with historical events and cultural constructs. This was not an either/or negotiation. Rather than simply delete sounds (replace one literacy for another), the tension between the two enabled local folk to contest normative or accepted interpretive frames as they subordinated the printed to the spoken.   (pp. 363–364)

[Thus, when "citing-up," from the Bible,] the books and chapters that constituted the Bible were sounded out loud, interrogated for contradictions, and reassembled into an orally recounted Bible or "living testament."   (p. 364)

A challenge to the oppressive nature of English, "the language of captivity," is clear in an extract from a "reasoning" engaged in by Pulis, Bongo, and a visiting neighbor, Gerte. Bongo and Pulis have been reasoning about evidence for the divinity of Selassie now that Selassie has departed from the earth. Gerte approaches and asks Pulis: "Wha da man seh?"... "Da man know Selassie king?" Pulis' response, "Hum, well, I believe..." is interrupted by Gerte: "Believe? Black people na believe, dey KNOW!" Here, Pulis explains, Gerte's retort serves less to chastise him for his lack of deep faith than to call attention to a word, "believe," that needs "busting" and, ultimately, rejection:

> words like belief function as ideophones, cues or markers to a language that masks the signs and sounds of enslavement. According to this logic such words have "buried" or submerged within them sounds (be/lie/f) that negate their meaning, and the formation of such words was considered a form of politics intended to perpetuate "mental slavery," i.e., to deceive speakers into accepting the meaning associated with a word as natural.   (pp. 367–368)

The reasoning continues when Pulis, now instructed by Bongo on the importance for Rastafarians of interrogating the Bible ("I-n-I mus cite-up more times, cause dem dat have eyes SEE, an dem dat have ears HEAR!"), is surprised to learn that the Revelation of John the Apostle, the last book of the authorized King James version, is considered by Bongo to be the first: "dis here de FIRST book, Yes I...dem mek it LAST, try ti kon-fuse-I, hide-up HIM words" (p. 368). Bongo, having placed Revelation in its rightful place for Pulis, proceeds to "unlock" the hidden meanings: "What I tell da man [about the image of Selassie], him na a little dream like duppi-spirit ting, him come as de Word, siin! [understand]," Bongo explains as he reads aloud from chapter 1, verse 5: " 'Blessed dem dat readeth ana dey dat hear da word [of this prophecy],' ana check der so [verse 8], 'I AM ALPHA AND OMEGA, THE BEGINNING AND THE END,' Selassie dat!" (pp. 368–369).

Pulis attempts to interject that the verse quoted refers to Jesus Christ, but Bongo continues to explain, using verse after verse from Revelation, how Jah (Selassie) is not a spirit, but has come into the world as the Word, and has a material existence as the Word. What follows is a concise, yet profound example of the transformation of the written into the spoken, a scriptural justification of the subordination of the textual to the oral/aural, and of the materiality, the "word-sound-power" of the spoken word:

[Pulis]   Bongo, the book reads, ah...says, "I was in the spirit." What does "in the spirit" mean, then, if not a dream or vision?
[Bongo]   Bradda John, tell I, da man in school?
[Pulis]   Yes.
[Bongo]   Siin! Tell I, how da bredren see sound?
[Pulis]   What?
[Bongo]   Da book na talk! I tell da man da system, da system jumble-up de book, da man mus penetrate da words to overstan dem! Yes I...Vision now, said bredren have him vision, vision na a spirit-ting. Faawod, I-aya, see wha him a deal wit, [he added as he pushed on to verse 12]: "Ana I turned to see the voice dat spat wi me." Wha I tell de man, how said I-dren see a voice? It WORDS I-aya! Jah na a spirit, Him a mon! Look der so, tree [three] times him say, "him dat have ear, I tell da man, dem try to kon-fuse-I, da man no see?"   (p. 369)

As Bible reading, this is a literacy event of an extraordinary kind. For Bongo the prophecy of John refers not to Jesus Christ, but to Jah, the Emperor Selassie. Bongo has here read and interpreted the Bible passages in a way which expunges Jesus from the geneaology of prophets leading to Selassie. Pulis informs us that some Rastafari consider Jesus "a fabrication, a textual icon created by false prophets" (p. 389, note 44) and reminds us that Bongo's activity in this instance recalls the literate practices of reading that de Certeau (1984) calls "poaching." Bongo acts; he is not a credulous consumer of an "authorized" text. The Bible cannot be accepted as literal truth, nor can it be approached as a cipher whose hidden meanings must be decoded with the special knowledge that is belief. The text must rather be interrogated from the experience of a subject people and "busted" using the word-sound of the oral language. To hear the voices of

Africans imprisoned within the text one must listen, but this listening, an aural activity, occurs conjoined with the oral. As Bongo reads (and hears), he frees from captivity the voices locked in the text.

With these voices, now free, a history and tradition for a present generation are constructed. For de Certeau, the readings gained through poaching leave mere traces, they are ephemeral, because the poachers are marginalized readers, readers not partaking of bourgeois sensibilities and accepting of bourgeois authority, textual and otherwise.[19] But here, Bongo, Gerte, and others who reason together, form a community of interpretation, a community of speakers, whose renderings of textual meanings, while contentious, form a bedrock of Rastafari belief and the source of power and identity. That is, the voices of the participants in the reasonings authored a new text, not through any fixing or entextualization in writing, but through linguistic practices, "citing-up" and "reasoning," which are authoritative within a religious community of practice (Bauman and Briggs, 1990; Silverstein and Urban, 1996). The voices unlocked and freed from the text are recontextualized within the worldview of Rastafari. The Old and New testaments thus transformed become a new, living testament, in which the unlocked voices now live and speak, and in which an oral tradition becomes a "living testament" guiding the everyday practices of the Rastafari. As Bongo insists, to read it is not enough to see, one must hear as well. Through the literate practice of citing [sighting] up and reasonings, the message of the "authorized" King James Bible is subverted in order to remake colonial subjects as free, "chosen" people, a spiritual elite.

Agency within and against a scriptural economy: invented writings and the crafting of hybrid selves

We have argued at length in previous sections that in colonial and postcolonial contexts non-Western peoples have been dominated by Western languages and the alphabetic literacy the colonial powers imposed. As Seed asserts, "conquest of the New World also entailed a conquest *of* language and a conquest *by* language (Seed, 1993, p. 12). In response to colonial legacies, native peoples have adapted traditional practices to the dominant literacies in which they have often been schooled. In so doing, they transform the received literacy, they find a space to voice their selves within literate practices which are never neatly oral or written, traditional or modern. Such hybridizing practices have long histories, as shown, for example, by Burkhart's subtle studies of missionary-educated Nahuatl scholars who worked with Franciscan friars translating Catholic religious drama into Nahuatl in the sixteenth and seventeenth centuries (Burkhart, 1996; 2000).[20] As our two cases of disruptive readings illustrate, such hybridizing practices are common also in postcolonial settings, perhaps indeed typical of postcolonial cultural identities and literacy practices (Besnier, 1995; Bloch, 1993; Kulick and Stroud, 1993).

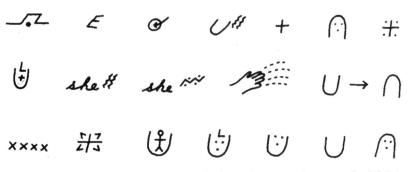

Figure 6.1   *Western Apache writing of Silas John. Text of "prayer for life" in correct reading form, from left to right in descending order*

For those subaltern individuals and groups who must engage with an imposed scriptural economy, power comes in many forms. Sometimes it comes through the forging of identities that use literate means in ways that partake of the dominant but in service of indigenous needs and lifeways. This complex dynamic of literacy, power, and identity can be seen in striking form in our last case, which concerns an example of "invented writing," in a situation that straddles the colonial and postcolonial, the traditional and modern.

We refer to the case of the Silas John Edwards, a Western Apache who designed and promoted an indigenous writing system in the early twentieth century. As described in Basso (1990a), this is an intriguing case of "revealed" rather than acquired literacy. In 1904, when Silas John was twenty-one years old and living on the Fort Apache Indian Reservation, he experienced a vision, and in this vision "he was presented with a set of sixty-two prayers and an accompanying set of graphic symbols with which to write them" (p. 29). He later became an influential Western Apache shaman and the leader of a nativistic religious movement which combined Apache ritual traditions with elements of Christian theology. His writing system played an essential role in the recruitment of adepts and the performance of ritual.

In the system of writing that Silas John fashioned subsequent to his vision, written symbols represented both language and action, providing highly detailed cues for the reader as to what was to be said and done during the performance of a ritual. Figure 6.1 provides the text of a "prayer for life." As we can see, the writing used stylized designs, such as [✝] which may be from Apache sand painting, and it also used elements from a roman orthography, such as [ℓ⁄ᵗ] or the cursive form [she#]. The symbol [ℓ⁄ᵗ] simultaneously required speech and action: the linguistic utterance *yo'o'sn bi ha'dndi'n* "God, his sacred pollen," and the speaker sprinkling a pinch of cattail pollen upon ritual paraphernalia, thereby blessing it (p. 45).

Silas John apparently waited for twelve years after his visions before he proclaimed himself a prophet and began to preach. When he began to preach, he also wrote down his prayers with paints on tanned deerskins, using symbols such as shown in figure 6.1. Four years later (1920), he selected twelve "assistants" to spread the word, traveling among Apache people, conducting ceremonies and holding religious gatherings. The assistants were first taught to read and write, then they went through an initiation ritual during which they were given prayer skins. Afterwards, they were assigned a holy place, at which they were to regularly perform ceremonials, using their prayer skins as memory aids (p. 30).

Access to knowledge of the system of writing was restricted to a small group of specialists, and correct reading was imbued with great significance. As one Apache consultant told Basso:

Silas John just let a few people know what the writing meant. He once told my father that it had to be kept just like it was when he heard about it from God. *If some person ever tried to change it, he said, God would stop listening to the people when they prayed.*
(p. 31, emphasis added)

Not only was access to the writing tightly controlled, knowledge of the writing was also essential to successful performance of a ritual:

So fundamental is the knowledge necessary to read these instructions, Apaches claim, that any attempt to execute the role of "ceremonial leader" (*diiyin*) without it is certain to be flawed and unacceptable.   (p. 39)

In order to more fully appreciate what is involved in this practice of writing and ritual, let us first consider what Silas John said about the original vision in which he received knowledge of the prayers and of the script:

There were sixty-two prayers. They came to me in rays from above ... They were presented to me – one by one. All of these and the writing were given to me at one time in one dream ...
God made it [the writing], but it came down to our earth. I liken this to what has happened in the religions we have now. In the center of the earth, when it first began, when the earth was first made, there was absolutely nothing on this world. There was no written language. So it was in 1904 that I became aware of the writing; it was then that I heard about it from God.   (p. 29)

Based on this account, plus what we know about his religious movement, it appears that Silas John has appropriated the Christian belief in the divine power of God's word. Silas John refers to a single "God"; to the time "when the earth was first made"; when "there was absolutely nothing on this world. There was no written language." Christianity, as Goody (1986) among others has instructed us, is a "religion of the Book." Apache shamanism before Silas John's innovations was part of an "oral religion," and therefore in the Goodyesque account fated to succumb to the superior organization, theology, and textual practices of Christianity. In such an account, Silas John would be the mediator of the unequal encounter between a religion of the Book and a local spiritual system.

In this case, however, rather than the institutional power of entextualized religion (Christianity) simply transforming or eradicating the local religion (Apache shamanism), something more subtle was going on. Silas John has not accepted the Christian Book. That acceptance would have required submission to another language, English, and probably submission as well to the personnel of a Christian church, in the form of a local mission. Instead, Silas John drew upon the idea of the power of divine writing, creating a written code, quite unlike English, knowledge of which is necessary to successful performance of ceremonies. A "traditional" practice of rites is continued, but only through the agency of new literates, readers who control access to the divine through their manipulation of an esoteric script. As one Apache consultant put it "Only the ones who can read can pray" (p. 40).

It is common enough that hybrid forms of spiritual practice, resulting from colonial encounters, involve non-Western peoples appropriating the idea of the supernatural power of sacred text. This is the case among the Mende of Sierra Leone, who make spells and talismans with fragments of Classical Arabic script (Bledsoe and Robey, 1993); it is the case with the Gapun villagers of Papua New Guinea, who manipulate the biblical text in search of the material benefits promised by Cargo religion (Kulick and Stroud, 1993). In a case strikingly similar to the Apache, the Aladura movement in colonial Nigeria of the 1920s involved a prophet, Oshitelu, who received prayers in a vision, along with a writing system for recording them, a writing system distinct from English orthography and accessible only to the specially trained (Probst, 1993). In such cases the superiority of the "religion of the Book" is not simply accepted; nor, however, is a pre-encounter "oral" religious tradition simply reasserted. Instead, text and voice are refigured in a quest for a divine authority that appropriates and subverts the traditional power of Christian/colonial letters.

In cases such as the Gapun, Oshitelu's Aladura movement, and Silas John's writing, we seem to deal with twentieth-century holdouts to the "civilizing mission" of Christianity and modernity. In order to sharpen our sense of what is being resisted and reworked in Silas John's case, let us recall the US-based ideology of literacy–identity–progress which was discussed at some length in chapter 4. This ideology can be said to begin with the figure of Benjamin Franklin, for whom the anonymity and rationality of print discourse was to provide the discursive wherewithal for a new "republican" political subject, the participating citizen, endowed with inalienable rights, including the rights to speak and publish freely. Frederick Douglass, for whom reading and writing were first encountered as prohibitions, represents the emergence into full equality of a previously repressed category of person: the slave. Literacy as emblem of liberation – with a pass forged by his own hand, Douglass "took the *ell*" and fled to freedom – signifies also the attainment of fully modern political subjectivity: to be adult, free, and financially independent. Women were the other great class of partial or repressed political subjects in US history. As we have seen, in the latter decades of the nineteenth century and early decades of the twentieth, the time of Silas John, women from settled as well as struggling backgrounds used reading for resources to imagine fuller, more independent selves, social identities more able and inclined to insist on fully modern political status. With the case of Silas John, however, we reach a limit or boundary; the narrative of literacy and modernity no longer coheres. Neither Christian nor traditional, but drawing upon and reworking the resources of both, Silas John's writing-and-religion represents a spirited attempt (pun intended) to establish the conditions for a special – we would now say "hybrid" – religious community, practice, and identity.

Silas John's life and writing illustrate two contradictory aspects of identity, which we have not been able to discuss as fully in our other cases. The first aspect concerns whether identities are essential to a person or group, that is, rooted in some primordial attribute, such as common descent, language, or territory, or whether they are, conversely, nonessential, changeable, and constructed from diverse sources. The second aspect, related to the first, concerns whether having or holding an identity binds an individual to the authority or expectations of a group or whether the individual's "freedom to choose," the characteristic ideal of liberal political orders, extends to the question of belonging and identity (Bauman, 1992; Kuper, 1999). Put simply, is identity ascribed or chosen?

In the case of Silas John we see each possibility. We have a man who did not leave the reservation for the city, forsake his native tongue for English, or reject traditional religious practices for Christianity. On this basis it would appear he held a firmly rooted traditional Apache identity. But he grew up on a reservation, established after military conquest by the US, at a time when national policy and elite consensus both called for demolishing indigenous customs and societies in order to hasten the assimilation of Indians, as individuals, to American civilization (Spicer, 1969). In addition, as a youth he associated with Lutheran missionaries on the Fort Apache reservation, from whom he apparently learned of Christian cosmology, and he went on, as an adult, to recast Apache rituals as part of a text-legitimated, syncretic Apache/Christian religion. This suggests a remade, hybrid, constructed identity. Although Silas John's individual agency is clear enough in the crafting of a system of writing and ritual, suggesting an identity itself chosen and crafted, his work was in the service of communal-religious authority, suggesting collective constraint.

Conclusion: identity, power, and poaching

We have used de Certeau's notion of a scriptural economy as an orienting concept for characterizing colonial literacy practices. Prominent in this economy is a practice of writing which through inscription transforms a "blank page" into a "text." Thus were eye-witness accounts of the natives of Hispaniola rendered into authoritative Spanish texts; thus were royal titles to indigenous lands recorded and archived in the Cumbal case; and thus were the slaves of Jamaica brought the Christian civility of the King James Bible. As a strategic resistance to the scriptural economy, de Certeau advances the idea of reading-as-poaching, a recalcitrant, subversive, or simply "undisciplined" reading, which de Certeau terms "ephemeral" and "nomadic," but which we would argue can have its collective stabilities, whether those of land tenure or radical religious dissent. The concept of poaching reminds us, however, that the terrain of literacy practices – the zone of engagement as well as the means of engagement – is profoundly historical. It combines at once the long-term hierarchies, inscriptions, and regulations of colonial or nation-state power with the shorter-term adaptations and strategies of situated practical life, both "everyday" and "organized-resistant."

Power is pervasive in the official literacies of nation states and colonial regimes, but it is a multifaceted power. It is a power of imposition, of conquest "*of* language and *by* language," but also of self-fashioning "in language." What Marx remarked long ago – that people make their own history, but they do so in conditions not of their own choosing – applies to literacy practices and identity-fashioning in colonial and postcolonial settings. When the Cumbales read and petition, asserting their collective identity and rights, they do so by engaging the Colombian state and Spanish colonial documents. When Rastafari "bust words" the words they bust are those of the "authorized" King James Bible. Silas John's writing displaced the colonial-national language of the US reservation mission with what would appear to be both a "new writing" and an indigenous "picture writing" (as we discuss more fully in the next chapter), but Silas John nonetheless sought the power of writing, and, it must be noted, he sought to harness and maintain this power through a careful control of reading and ritual practice.[21]

Whether we deal with identities imposed through the arrogance of colonial inscription, shaped in response to the procedures and promises of schooled literacy, or claimed in defiance of such arrogance or procedure, questions of text, power, and identity pervade the history of literacy. As we argue in our concluding chapter, drawing on post-structuralist insights as well as ethnographic details, this history has many beginnings, and it concerns the future as well as the past of literacy practices.

7

CONCLUSION: LITERACY LESSONS – BEGINNINGS, ENDS, AND IMPLICATIONS

This development, coupled with that of anthropology and of the history of writing, teaches us that phonetic writing, the medium of the great metaphysical, scientific, technical, and economic adventure of the West, is limited in space and time and limits itself even as it is in the process of imposing its laws upon the cultural areas that had escaped it.   (Derrida, 1976a, p. 10)

It's our cultural fears – of internal decay, of loss of order, of diminishment – that weave into our assessments of literacy and scholastic achievement.   (Rose, 1989, p. 7)

Introduction

In the preceding chapters we have engaged with a number of complex conceptual issues concerning literacy, in particular those of text, power, and identity, and we have developed our arguments via a wide range of ethnographic and historical cases. What we wish to do at this point is revisit certain of those issues, developing arguments and questions further, making connections between chapters, cases, and conceptual positions. That is, and against convention, we will try to make this conclusion an opening as much as a closing. Because the theme of the "origins" of literacy continues to fascinate both scholarship and popular culture, we will return to this topic by means of the Tolowa case with which our book opened. As we examine the late-twentieth-century advent of writing among these Northern California native people, we are brought to issues and questions raised by Derrida about the theme of origins in writing as well as to recent criticisms made by Goody about Derrida's relativist arguments concerning writing, reading, and books. It may seem somewhat wrongheaded to be discussing the origins of writing at the beginning of a new millennium, when there are so many breathless pronouncements about the "death of the book" and "the end of print literacy." However, as we will see, in a reworking of Mark Twain's saying: rumors of the death of the book may be greatly exaggerated. More to the point, the ends we foresee for literacy often have much to do with the beginnings we imagine.

The question of text and textual origins

Prehistoric and fictive origins

There is a substantial research literature on the origins of writing and a notable interest, in literature and film, in what can be called the origins of reading. Scholarship on the prehistoric genesis of writing, whether in the Ancient Near East (Schmandt-Besserat, 1989), Classical Egypt (Baines, 1988), or the New World Mayan civilizations (Justeson and Mathews, 1990), has identified two primary functions or loci of concern which accompany inscription. The first, as we discussed in chapter 2, has to do with recording economic transactions. As Schmandt-Besserat's work suggests, the clay tokens and *bullae* found in the sites of archaic Mesopotamian city states were used to record and thus coordinate the storage and long-distance exchange of foodstuffs and manufactured items. The second function or concern has to do with what Derrida has called "genealogical anxiety." As Justeson (1989) has shown of the ancient Mayan inscriptions on stone columns, the primary recording was of dynastic succession, of the deeds of rulers to be sure, but more important, of their legitimate descent.[1]

In a curious way, the origins of writing in economic calculation and genealogical anxiety are reflected in more contemporary imaginings of the origins of literacy, typically cast as the entry of literacy into individual lives. Charles Dickens' classic novel of social mobility, *Great Expectations*, features a prominent scene in which the protagonist, Pip, struggles with early writing, using a stylized invented spelling to write a letter to the blacksmith, Joe, who is in fact sitting next to him by the fire. "mI deEr JO i opE U r krWitE wEll" reads the first line of the missive. But even this much writing is beyond the capacity of Joe, who pretends to read Pip's letter, but is restricted to commenting on individual letters: " 'Why, here's a J,' said Joe, 'and an O equal to anythink'." Pip's initial efforts at writing reach fruition in the classical education afforded a mid-nineteenth-century English gentlemen; his magical elevation from poor orphan to monied gentlemen, and all that entails, financially, morally, socially, and cognitively, are the "great expectations" at the heart of the novel. Joe, however, is another matter. He professes a love of reading, but is unable to read Pip's or any other text; he is unnoticing when Pip accidently holds "our prayer-book upside down." One of the kinder hearts in literature, Joe "goes nowhere" in this novel of mobility. Although Joe saves Pip from an orphan's poverty and is willing to apprentice Pip in his blacksmith's trade, when the news arrives that the rich and secluded Miss Havisham is interested in helping Pip, Pip leaves Joe, at first emotionally and then physically. It is part of the dramatic tension of the novel that the evening when Pip struggles at his new writing ability, discovers Joe's inability to read, and resolves to teach Joe to read, is the very evening when the call from Miss Havisham comes, and Pip's life begins to separate from that of the unlettered Joe and the laboring classes more generally (see also Howard, 1991; Webb, 1950).

For those inclined to boys' adventures rather than nineteenth-century realist fiction, Edgar Rice Burrough's (1963) *Tarzan of the Apes* offers another dramatic rendering of the passage from barbarous orality to civilized letters. Acquiring literacy is part of Tarzan's journey from scantily clad wild man to English gentleman, to becoming Lord Greystoke. In the sixth chapter of this novel, we are treated to descriptions of Tarzan learning to read and write. Indeed, he does this before he learns to speak the English language. It is in keeping with his ape-man persona that he initially thinks that the letters on the page are little bugs.

The theme of learning literacy as part of social betterment is also part of contemporary television and films. A recent and rather anachronistic British television drama, *Mr. Tom*, features a curmudgeonly but warm-hearted widower, Mr. Tom, who rescues a young boy from an abusive mother in England during the early years of World War II. Along with the boy's considerable emotional distress, it turns out that he is also unable to read. It is part of "Mr Tom's" nurturing that he teaches the boy to read as well as to trust others. Perhaps a better-known cinematic representation of the beginnings of literacy is given in the film *Stanley and Iris*, a love story in which Robert De Niro and Jane Fonda play fellow bakery workers. When the divorced Iris discovers that unmarried Stanley is unable to read, part of her concern for him, which develops into love, is expressed through her determination to teach him to read. As is true of any tale worth telling, there are setbacks and difficulties on the road to romance and literacy, but in the happy ending Stanley/De Niro and Iris/Fonda are together in love, and Stanley, now in possession of reading and writing skills, is launching a career as a successful inventor.

This intertwined theme of social and economic rebirth with an entry into literacy is common enough in memoirs, fiction, and film to merit a detailed treatment. Suffice it for our purposes to note that from troubled, marginal places, orphans, abused boys, angry loners are granted access to the social legitimacy of love, families, money, and careers *if* and *as* they acquire knowledge of reading and writing. However, the idea of social rebirth through literacy practices can be seen as well in other genres of accounts of the "origins of writing," in particular, in the projects to document, classify, and record the lives and languages of indigenous, native, or non-Western peoples.

The Tolowa case: transformative origins

As we have discussed in the preceding chapter, colonial missionary projects frequently involved translating the Bible into a heretofore unwritten native tongue. It was not, of course, simply a matter of writing previously unwritten languages. In the case of Mexico's Aztecs, and the other great civilizations of the Maya and Inca, what was at issue was replacing one system of writing, its political, economic, and cosmological intentions, with the script and holy book of Catholic Spain. During the twentieth century and, in particular, in the post-World War II period of American imperial dominance, this missionary practice continued, spearheaded by the Dallas-based Summer Institute of Linguistics, which was funded by a consortium of Evangelical Protestant organizations and supported scores of projects for translating the Bible into "unwritten" indigenous languages (Colby, 1995; Wallis, 1964). Here also we should note that often the indigenous languages had been the object of prior writing: usually there were writing systems, of indigenous, colonial, Catholic, or national origin, which predated the SIL effort, but these were deemed inadequate.

In the post-1960s decades, the articulation and assertion of cultural rights, including linguistic rights, has gone hand-in-hand with projects to document indigenous language "for preservation." This has occurred in the United States as well as internationally (Grenoble and Whaley, 1998; Nettle and Romaine, 2000). In order to consider specifics, let us now return to the Native American case used to open this book, which also involved an effort to document an endangered language. It was during this post-1960s period of general movements to assert native rights that the Tolowa of Northern California began to record their ancestral language in writing.

One of the early Tolowa language activists was Eunice Bommelyn. In the mid-to-late 1960s, as part of her work with the Indian Health Service, Eunice had contact with many elderly Tolowa people. While doing her social welfare work, she had grown increasingly interested in "genealogies," for as she talked with elderly Tolowa, many of them her relatives, she learned more and more about the ties of kinship that connected people of Tolowa descent. She also learned, or at least heard, many of the "old stories," that is, traditional Tolowa lore.

Eunice's "genealogical anxiety," if we may echo the Derridean argument, sprang from a sense that a rich repository of social knowledge about kinship relations connecting contemporary Tolowa to each other through prior generations would be lost when the elder generation passed away. Also lost would be the knowledge of traditional stories, and, more basically, the knowledge of how to speak the Tolowa language. For English had been the dominant language in the area since the beginning of the century, and not many people of Eunice's generation, let alone subsequent generations, spoke the Tolowa language well at that time, the late 1960s.

As part of her efforts, Eunice made contact with Tom Parsons of the Center for Community Development and, with his encouragement, a group of local people began meeting. They subsequently formed the Tolowa Language Committee, in which Eunice and her son, Loren, took leading roles. The committee and its language activists used the Unifon Alphabet for more than two decades for recording, analyzing, and publishing story collections, dictionaries, and other pedagogical materials (Bommelyn, 1994; Bommelyn and Humphrey, 1989;

Collins, 1998b). We have discussed in chapter 2 the controversies that arose between those Tolowa committed to the Unifon writing system and academics committed to an IPA or International Phonetic Alphabet system of orthography. We need not repeat the details of that dispute at this point, but should note that it was a dispute about transcribing. It raised what Derrida (1976b) has argued is an inherited Western preoccupation with linguistic and political representation. In brief, getting the linguistic details right was important for claims to being culturally authentic or legitimately representative.

We should also note that although the foregoing describes a first effort by Tolowa people to "write their own language," it does not refer to an originary event. Other efforts at writing Tolowa had preceded their undertaking by nearly a century. In 1877, in the period just after the American conquest of Northern California, the journalist Stephen Powers published *The Tribes of California* (Powers, 1976), which included numerous phrases and place names, in an approximation of the native language, as part of his description of several Tolowa towns. In 1889, J. Owen Dorsey, a researcher for the Bureau of American Ethnology, published "Indians of Siletz Reservation, Oregon" in one of the first issues of the journal *American Anthropologist* (Dorsey, 1889). This article included extensive kinship terminology from Tolowa sources, as well as from those of Southwestern Oregon Athabaskans, with whom the Tolowa had political and economic as well as kinship relations.[2] In the first decade of the twentieth century, the linguist Pliny Earle Goddard had collected extensive vocabulary lists (Goddard, 1909–1911a) and a body of traditional myths (Goddard, 1909–1911b), as part of an uncompleted project to analyze the structure of the language. In 1937, Phillip Drucker published "The Tolowa and Their Southwestern Oregon Kin," a modern ethnography covering such topics as "ethnogeography," "subsistence," "material culture," "money and property," "social life," and "the life of the individual." These sections featured lists of Tolowa terms for place names, fishing sites and songs, household items, *dentalia* and other ceremonial wealth, ritual names, and personal names. In the early 1960s, the linguist Jane Bright had recorded extensive lexical and grammatical information, as well as tellings of numerous myths. This formed the basis for a brief sketch of the sound system "The Phonology of Smith River Athapaskan (Tolowa)" (Bright, 1964), but her research archive was lost after her untimely death in a automobile accident.

Given this chronology, we may suspect that there *is* no single origin of Tolowa writing. Rather, as Derrida argued in his critique of Lévi-Strauss, as De Certeau reminds us, and as advocates of a situated approach to literacy would concur, writing occurs embedded in ongoing social practices. In the case at hand, writing occurs and recurs as part of journalistic and academic efforts to record and understand a people seen as vanishing primitives, and it occurs as part of an indigenist effort to represent themselves, their endangered language, their disrupted history.

In addition to this already complex chronology of phonetic writing, we should also note that there is evidence of other forms of Tolowa inscription, which precede any attempt at orthographic rendering, and which further complicate our sense of a writing/speaking dichotomy. Here the question concerns how far we should follow the argument, made by Derrida (1976a) and, subsequently, by a host of situated literacy scholars, that writing involves more than, or other than, the representation of language. Most radically, in Derrida's argument it appears that "writing" encompasses all inscription of social difference.[3]

If we follow Derrida's lead, as well as suggestive scholarship on American Indian "picture writing," we must entertain the hypothesis that traditional, pre-contact Tolowa society – as it can be reconstructed (Bommelyn, 1994; Collins, 1998b) – had "inscription practices." Among these practices were the making and displaying of dance regalia during major ceremonies and rituals as well as the performance and transmission of songs and stories that were part of such ceremonies and rituals (Bommelyn, 1994; Collins, 1998b; Drucker, 1937). Among such ceremonies and rituals were the "First Catch Rituals," with which annual fishing cycles were begun and a given village's rights to certain fishing sites established; or the "Girls' Puberty Ritual," a ten-day affair involving isolation, prayer, special foods, ministrations by a female shaman, and public dances, in which songs and regalia marked a girl's entry into womanhood. The dance regalia as well as ritual songs were themselves traditionally viewed as valuable forms of wealth and "property," to be owned, and, more pertinently, to be displayed by individuals and families on ritual occasions. As property, they were transmitted through kinship lines, although in recent decades they have been passed along lines of aptitude and inclination, as well as kinship.

This is where the Tolowa case leads us, to a conception of writing that would include ritual insignia, ritual artifacts, and the prayers and songs attached thereto. Such a conception extends well beyond alphabetic inscription and, indeed, blurs the line between speech and writing as these are commonly understood in debates about literacy. It is perhaps no surprise that such an extension has been directly attacked recently. In *The Power of the Written Tradition*, Goody (2000) presents his first book-length argument about literacy in over a decade. In this work he devotes a short chapter to "Derrida among the Archives of the Written and the Oral," which is pertinent to our immediate concerns. In this chapter Goody argues again for a clear distinction between speaking and writing, in which the crucial characteristic of the latter is that it represents language structure. He argues of Derrida that "Writing (and reading) comes to mean for the author [Derrida] not only the use of graphic signs in writing, in the systematic transcription of language in a visual form, but the use of other signs that may take a graphic form ... [for example] the mnemonic graphemes of American Indians" (p. 113). This expansive view of the activities of writing and reading, Derrida's *arche*-writing (see note 2 above), is too broad for Goody, for it fails to "distinguish between a graphic absence and a phonemic presence" and threatens to "equate a premonition with an inscription" (p. 114). These arguments are worth considering. The insistence on "phonemic presence" suggests that the alphabet provides the touchstone of all writing. Giving this priority to the alphabet is quite common in our Western academic traditions as well as in the general culture. We are heirs to a long line of thinking, epitomized by the European Enlightenment, which assumed that written communication was the hallmark of rationality, and further, that the alphabet was the precondition of "civil," that is, democratic, society (Asad, 1993; Derrida, 1976b; Gates, 1986). The boldest claims for phonetic writing are perhaps found in the arguments about "the alphabetic mind," common in the 1960s and 1970s, but continuing recently as well (Sanders, 1994). However, as we discussed at some length in chapter 2, the "alphabetic" aspect of the literacy thesis has been quite effectively criticized. It cannot hold up to historical-comparative scrutiny, as Gough (1968) pointed out early on. In addition, careful efforts to explore the psychological effects of scripts have found nothing like the sweeping *cognitive* effects originally claimed (Cole and Scribner, 1981). As we discuss more fully below, Goody himself withdraws from the alphabetic mind thesis in other chapters of *The Power of the Written Tradition* (e.g. pp. 139–140).

The warning not to "equate a premonition with an inscription" also seems to have merit. It is aimed at Derrida's assertion that "reading the stars" is indeed a form of reading, which strikes Goody as an unduly metaphoric extension of the concept. On initial consideration, it seems sensible to distinguish between decipherment in general and the more specific act of deciphering a script that encodes language-writing (that is, representations of spoken language).[4] But we have to ask what is lost as well as what it gained by restrictive versus expansive conceptions of an object of interest. How we conceptualize "reading" may be problematic if it is too narrow or too narrowly focused on present circumstances. For example, it is now well established that in the Western cultural tradition "reading" has meant many forms of activity, in which an inscribed text was part of, though not necessarily central to, a given literacy event (D. Boyarin, 1993; Clanchy, 1979; Howe, 1993). In addition, if we turn from historical considerations to a more present-day concern with the activity of reading, reader-response literary studies (Radway, 1984) as well as cognitive schema research in psychology (Anderson and Pearson, 1984) argue that the meaning of a text is a result of reader/text interactions. These interactions include, we may hazard, a reader's premonitions (or anticipations) of what kind of text is at hand, what intentions it might articulate, what purposes it might serve, and so forth. In short, we are reminded by diverse fields – "Whole Language" pedagogy, cognitive psychology, literary criticism, as well as by anthropology and post-structuralist philosophy – that mental states, speaking practices, and inscriptions correlate in highly diverse fashions. Hard and fast distinctions between inscription and sense can be hard to maintain.

At issue in this debate is not a distinction between inscription and sense, but rather how or where the distinction is drawn. Must inscription be marks signifying language in the strict sense (vocabulary and syntax), or may it include others forms of figuration? These other figurings could include "dots and zigzags on...calabashes" among the Nambikwara (Derrida, 1976c, p. 124) or, for that matter, the patterning of constellations, which have been "read" as navigational points (Frake, 1985) and occasions for stories for millennia.

Also not at issue is Goody's argument that alphabetic literacies have been instruments of significant social change. In Derrida's words chosen as an epigraph for this chapter, "phonetic writing" has been the "medium of the great metaphysical, scientific, technical, and economic adventure of the West." But an instrument is not a primary cause. As Diamond (1999) reminds us in *Guns, Germs, and Steel*, the success of "the West," and of centralized states more generally, is undeniable: states, Western or otherwise, have relentlessly conquered, exterminated, or assimilated peoples living in decentralized tribes and bands. But the causes are multiple, not singular. Often the causes for the historical dominance of some societies over others are prosaic: food domestication versus its absence; germ resistance versus the lack thereof; superior weapons of war. As Goody, Derrida, and numerous others have noted, writing allows the coordination of complex social action, but it does not, by itself, create such action. What a modern, centralized state does with writing is likely to be quite distinct from what a hunting and gathering group, such as the precontact Tolowa or most other indigenous North American peoples, would do.

Writing, archives, and power

"Picture writing" and archives

The thrust of Goody's criticism of Derrida is that the latter's view of writing does not give sufficient weight to the technical aspects of writing which distinguish it from speech. In particular, Goody refers to the ability, with writing, to have *archives*, that is, repositories of knowledge in the form of inscribed language. The archive literally represents the way in which writing-as-technique achieves permanence, such permanence contrasting with the presumed evanescence of speech. To recall again the arguments discussed in chapter 2, such permanence, as archive, allows for the organization and retrieval of information, enabling an unprecedented coordination of action on a large temporal and spatial scale. The centralized palace economies of Mesopotamia typically contained an archive, most notably those of the Syrian town of Ebla, in which "70 per cent of the... texts...were administrative" (Goody, 2000, p. 115). Against this technicist view of writing/archive, Derrida (1996) has argued for a conception of archive that encompasses the interaction of human minds and the world broadly available and inscribed, which would include, but not be limited to, repositories of alphabetic (or, now, digital–alphanumeric) texts.

The relevance of this argument to the Tolowa case is that the dance, songs, ritual, and regalia (shell dresses, Deer and Woodpecker headdresses, bows, and flint knives) were and are part of a practice of social memory. This practice marks divisions in society – of wealthy versus dependent; male versus female; child versus adult – and evokes as well a cosmological order that is also a trope for history.[5] In contemporary circumstances of reclaiming and reconstructing tradition, such memory acquires a particular urgency. It is in the context of this urgency that we can understand the significance of the fact that the intergenerational transfer of regalia and ritual lore has changed among the Tolowa. Traditionally such "wealth" was passed along kinship lines (Drucker, 1937). Now it is a matter of passing "tradition" along to those concerned with "preserving" it, whether close kin or not, and whether, as in the recent decades, they are involved in the cultural practice of dances or the linguistic practices of language documentation (Bommelyn, 1994; Collins, 1998b).

In a book concerned with the consequences of classical literate traditions, Havelock argued that writing was inscription "to assist the user in an act of recognition" (1982b, p. 54). It may seem, however, that the Tolowa practices of social memory involving dance, song, and display of regalia are simply too far afield from the textual preservation of memory. If so, it may be worthwhile to examine other, related cases involving the "mnemonic graphemes of American Indians." Let us consider, for example, Vizenor's (1998) discussion of *anishinaabe* (Chippewa) "picture writing." As we will see, it provides an intermediary between Tolowa lore, regalia, and song, and phonetic writing that "serves as a prod to memory."

The *anishinaabe*, of the northern Midwest (Minnesota, the Dakotas), were one among the many Native American societies that engaged in the practice of "picture writing." As Henry Schoolcraft, a nineteenth-century geologist, ethnologist, and Indian agent observed, the practice was longstanding and well known to earlier European and US explorers: "pictographic scrolls and devices, rudely cut or painted on wood, rocks, or the scarified trunks of trees, and even songs recorded by this method, are well known traits of our aboriginal tribes ... the practice of drawing pictures on skins, trees, and various other substances, has been noticed by travelers and writers from the earliest times" (Schoolcraft, 1860, pp. 333–334).

One such drawing is depicted in figure 7.1. It is taken from a collection recorded by Frances Densmore, an *anishinaabe* intellectual, at the turn of the century.[6] In Vizenor's discussion, he notes that the drawing is an *anishinaabe* picture of the "path of life," an account of life "from creation to old age" (p. 171) of the *midewiwin*, a traditional healing society. He summarizes Densmore's exegesis of the drawing as follows:

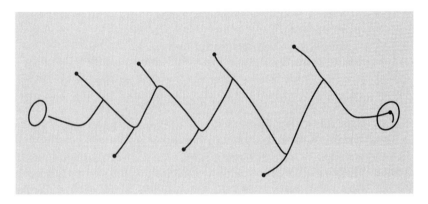

Figure 7.1   Anishinaabe *picture writing*

The tangent lines at the turn of each angle are representation of the seven temptations, a virtual cartography. Densmore pointed out that the sense of temptation in this connection "implies primarily a trial of strength and motive." The first and second tangent lines of temptation are resistance and the chance of life; the third, a spiritual initiation of the *midewiwin*; fourth, the temptation of middle age ... [and so forth].

(Vizenor, 1998, pp. 171–172)

Anticipating Havelock's later arguments about the mnemonic function of alphabetic writing, Densmore had the following to say about picture writing: "The purpose of 'picture writing' is to assist the memory and provide a means of record which is intelligible only to initiates of the [*midewiwin*] society" (cited in Vizenor, p. 172).

   Anishinaabe picture writing, song traditions, and ritual practices comprised what Vizenor calls a "virtual cartography," a system of inscription, memory, and ritual practice which recorded, reflected, and called forth a sense of being-in-place:

The *anishinaabe* song pictures ... are the cues of the virtual memories of music. The pictures animate the memories of the melody and the wavering voice of the native singer. The song pictures, incised on birch bark, are virtual cartography. These pictures are the creation of hundreds of distinctive songs and stories about dreams, love, war, animals, birds, motion, and ceremonial music of the *midewiwin*, the great society of healers, or the Grand Medicine Society.   (p. 170)

Like the Tolowa songs, regalia, and ritual dance, *anishinaabe* song pictures were elements in a system of everyday inhabitance and social memory which bear resemblances to what we call "writing." By considering *anishinaabe* pictures and Tolowa dance regalia as writing, we are led to recognize the uncertainty of the concepts with which we think. In the quest for, and the questioning of, "the origins of literacy," there are no final answers, but we may be reasonably sure that writing does not occur suddenly against a background of pure speech.

We learn to be wary of strict separations of writing from speech, to ask instead what purpose is served by one or the other term, when they are understood as dialectically related linguistic practices, social conditions, and visions of change.

These lessons notwithstanding, it is also undeniable that the virtual cartography of the *anishinaabe* was overwritten, so to speak, by "official cartography," that is, by the US Geological Surveys of the late nineteenth century and the system of fee-patent land registration the surveys underpinned. The great national surveys of the western United States were conducted as part of the General Allotment Acts of 1887; these Acts legalized the massive expropriation of Indian peoples during this period (Spicer, 1969). Concerning this process, Vizenor quotes novelist Louis Owens: "Mapping is, of course, an intensely political enterprise, an essential step toward appropriation and possession. Maps write the conqueror's stories over the stories of the conquered" (p. 170). The Tolowa experienced a similar process of physical, linguistic, and cartographic expropriation (Collins, 1998b).

It is with their dance songs and their stories of place that the Tolowa practice what Vizenor calls "survivance"; against appropriation they use dance regalia, songs, and stories to practice a "virtual cartography." As we have argued elsewhere, through traditional and contemporary stories, they create what de Certeau calls "spatial narratives," a memory, practice, and discourse of place. More pertinent to our current argument, Tolowa dance traditions, regalia, and stories of regalia allow them to organize and maintain counter-memories, to read against settler and academic histories of Del Norte County (Collins, 1998b, pp. 133–162; Slagle, 1987)

Vizenor marks the different historical outcomes of systems and practices of representation by distinguishing native virtual cartographies from the archives of *indians*. In Vizenor's account, which follows Derrida, archive denotes modes of inscription as well as repositories or collections. Contrasting "natives," who have a real if "fugitive" presence in history, with *indians*, the various, largely non-native representations about native peoples and places, Vizenor argues that "the *indian* is an archive; the simulations, discoveries, treaties, documents of ancestry, traditions in translation, museum remains, and the aesthetics of victimry. Culture and transethnic studies are common access to the *indian* archive, but not to a native presence, that unnameable sense of difference. The archive is institutive" (p. 50).

"The archive is institutive": this is a matter of institutions and military and economic power as well as modes of representation. It is certainly not a simple matter of "written" and "unwritten" traditions. The overarching historical outcome – the dominance of official mapping and representations in legal and intellectual arenas – should not distract us from the existence, indeed prevalence, of "alternative" inscriptions which organize alternative memories, "virtual cartographies" if not counter-archives to those of museums, research libraries, and land registration offices. Such virtual cartographies would include, among others, *anishinaabe* picture writing and story lore, Cumbal counter-reading and ritual practice, and Silas John's prayer skins and religious movement. As de Certeau reminds us, against the overarching power of national and colonial scriptural economies, we must not forget the practices of everyday life, which "poach" alternative or transgressive readings and organize memories through bodily practices.

"Picture writing" and civilization

At issue in the preceding discussion is the power of representation, ways of organizing representations, and ways of thinking about representations. In this context, we may ask anew what is gained, and what is lost, in the effort to draw sharp boundaries between language-writing and other modes of inscription? Many have argued that in identifying such writing we identify an arc of human history. A fundamental assumption of many attempts to separate "civilization" from other forms of human society is that civilization depends on language-writing.

In "The Alphabet and Absolute Representation," Derrida (1976b, pp. 295–313) argues that Rousseau, in his discourses on natural society, the social contract, and civilization, presumes an equation between kinds of inscription and stages of society. For Rousseau the scheme went like this:

"Savagery" (non-state societies) = "picture writing"
"Barbarism" (non-Western "ancient" or "asiatic" states) = "hieroglyphic writing"
"Civil Man" (Western states and empires) = "alphabetic writing"
(Derrida, 1976b, pp. 284, 295)

Such a schema is, of course, reminiscent of Goody's equation in *The Logic of Writing and the Organization of Society* between "Black Africa" and "oral society," the "Ancient Near East" and "restricted literacy," and "the West" and "full literacy." We draw this comparison not to poke fun at eighteenth-century prejudices in twentieth-century guise, but instead to highlight the durability of deeply problematic assumptions about human evolution and modes of language. The significance of such assumptions is that they influence how we think about our own society and epoch, as well as other societies and epochs. As Derrida argues, Rousseau was deeply preoccupied with the relations between writing and the state of civil society. His "discourses" on language and the social contract expressed a deep anxiety about the inadequacies of, and the relation between, linguistic and political representation: "Hence [for Rousseau] the third condition: civil man and alphabetic writing. It is here that, in the most conspicuous and grave manner, law supplements nature and writing speech." Moreover, "all Rousseau's thought is in one sense a critique of representation, as much in the linguistic as in the political sense" (pp. 295, 296).

Rousseau is famous for his critiques of government, civilization, and education; his positions, and Derrida's full analysis, are quite complex and cannot be done justice here. Suffice it for our purposes to note that the equation of reading and writing with "proper" political participation was common among other European, English, and American Enlightenment thinkers. As we have already noted in chapter 4, for the philosopher Kant the presumed inability of Africans to learn to read or write was a sign of their *inherent* irrationality – and their irrationality was a primary justification for their subhuman status as chattel (Gates, 1986). Moreover, such literate prejudice also circumscribed Kant's view of the role of reason in public life. In a perceptive discussion of Kant's major work on public debate and civil society, Asad notes that for Kant "using reason publically . . . is equivalent to addressing an argument, *in writing*, to a scholarly audience" (Asad, 1993, p. 202, emphasis in original).[7] As we discussed also, for Benjamin Franklin and other colonial and early US thinkers, concerns about the conditions of reading and writing ("publicity") were never far from discussions about political subjectivity and public discourse, that is, from discussion of how to shape, assess, and represent "the will of the people." Nor are anxieties about the relation between literacy conditions and political conditions only found in previous centuries. Instead, as we have previously discussed, drawing on analysts from situated or critical literacy perspectives, anxiety about literacy is usually the tip of the iceberg, a displacement or refiguration of other political, cultural, and economic contradictions (Edelsky, 1996; Gee, 1996; Graff, 1988; Rose, 1989).

The general lesson we should take is that literacy practices are suffused with power. This is not just the repressive power of a superior mode of documentation, registration, and overview, the classic power of bureaus, states, and empires. It is also the more intimate, conceptual–ethical or knowledge–power of modes and strategies for representing, understanding, and valuing self and others. The phenomena we have discussed in previous chapters are diverse: colonial and postcolonial legacies of the inscription, erasure, and rewriting of possible histories and identities; national legacies of schooled literacy versus a shifting domain of "illiteracy"; and personal legacies of conflicted self-understanding and self-making through practices of reading and writing. In all cases, however, we encounter myriad forms of the complementary categories written/spoken; many forms of what Derrida calls "logocentrism," the disposition to rank people by presence, absence, or kind of "writing"; and many instances of what Foucault described as "[t]he relationship between rationalization and excesses of political power" (1982, p. 210).

Ends, instrumentalities, and identities

If there are no sharp, sudden origins of writing, if there is no clear, strict separation of "oral society" from "literate tradition," then we may also be reasonably certain that the "ends" of literacy are neither singular nor certain. Holding this agnostic view, however, requires that we go against certain ingrained habits of mind. Along with the disposition to equate alphabetic writing with civilized man, a disposition shared by eighteenth- as well as twentieth-century thinkers, there is also the temptation to see our current era as somehow timeless, the capstone and completion. For after all, what could come after civilization? What we will see, in a reprise of arguments made elsewhere in this book, is that the visions of the end of literacy are closely connected to conceptions of literacy-as-technology and, further, that conceptions of ends and technologies implicate questions of identity.

End as death: questioning decline

For those holding the view that some level of literacy is a benchmark of civilized culture, any challenge to, or significant fluctuation in, the conditions of normative "full literacy" or "full democracy" is apt to be viewed as a sign of regression to "barbarism." Such a doomsday scenario is found in a range of books which see electronic media – radio, television, and, now, the internet – as eroding the literate capacities of today's citizens and, more particularly, today's children, for they are our current "primitives" in need of literacy's "progress." Sanders' (1994) *A is for Ox: the Collapse of Literacy and the Rise of Violence in an Electronic Age* is illustrative of such alarms. A proponent, along with Ivan Illich, of earlier arguments about the "alphabetic mind" (Illich and Sanders, 1988), Sanders rehearses arguments about literate consciousness and then develops his primary thesis: that standardized electronic media – radio, audio recordings, and television – erode the capacity both for literate inwardness and complex sense-making. The symptoms Sanders discusses are recognizable, and many of his analyses are stimulating. Few adults view television as a promoter of either complex knowledge or skeptical habits of mind, and Sanders' arguments about the relations between hearing unscripted human stories, reading well-wrought fiction, and handling complex arguments are suggestive. We must, however, be skeptical of global pronouncements about the death of literacy or the end of the book just because we are currently in an era of rapidly changing communications technology (Hobart and Schiffman, 1998; O'Donnell, 1998).

Although changes in communicative technology can substantially alter human societies over the long run, they must fit into existing communication practices; they supplement rather than replace existing modalities. This argument has recently been supported by two unlikely allies. As Goody has argued in his latest work, regarding the claim that television and the internet would eliminate book reading:

It is the same with the audiovisual mode, which some talk about as if it were *la fin du livre*. It is nothing of the sort. The number of books being published is forever increasing; the number of copies of newspapers sold is rising. In Britain the appearance of plays on television led to greater purchases of books associated with the broadcast. Parents still want their children to learn to speak, which they do in the home, and to read, which they do largely at school, and these activities will never be replaced, though they may be changed and even aided by audiovisual materials. (Goody, 2000, p. 155)

Although Derrida opened his immensely influential *Of Grammatology* with an essay "The End of the Book and the Beginning of Writing," it was less a prediction of the end of books and more a call to radically extend our thinking about both writing and reading. Recently, at a conference devoted to considering the fate of humanities in a era of the worldwide web and globalized "info-capitalism," Derrida has argued that the idea and project of "the book" remain very much alive, albeit in changing conditions of publication and distribution (see the web site www.albany.bookends.edu for Derrida's remarks and similar arguments by literary critics, historians of the book, and performance artists). What this means is that in considering prophecies of the death or decline of literacy, we must remember that literacy has never been a single thing. That granted, we must nonetheless acknowledge that there is often a link between thinking about literacy and thinking about technology.

Literacy as instrumentality: questioning technology

Visions of the death of the book or of some other valued form of literacy often stem from an "autonomous" conception of literacy. That is, they stem from viewing literacy as a technology which has a privileged, if not determining role, in desired social arrangements (say schooled literacy), from which privileged role it is superseded by some newer technology (say, electronic audiovisual media). As argued in prior chapters, such a conception contrasts sharply with a situated or sociocultural view of literacy-as-literacies, inherently plural practices, defined more by institutions, social relations, and social practices than by technical means.

The trope of literacy-as-technology is, of course, longstanding. It organized the many arguments about the "alphabetic mind," later discussed as the "literate" mind or consciousness. It was also central to Goody's (1977) characterization of literacy as a "technology of the intellect." Recently, in *The Power of the Written Tradition* (2000), he returns to that claim, arguing that by technology he means not just a form of inscription, but rather scripts, embodied dispositions, and socially organized textual collections:

when I speak of writing as a technology of the intellect, I refer not just to pen and paper, stylus and tablet, as complex as these instruments are, but to the training required, the acquisition of new motor skills, and the different uses of eyesight, as well as to the products themselves, the books that are stacked on library shelves, objects that one consults and from which one learns, and which one may also, in time, compose.
(p. 132)

There is a useful openness in such a definition of technology, referring, as it does, to training the body ("different uses of eyesight"), to processes of consulting ("objects which one consults"), to imaginative future acts "which one may also, in time, compose," as well as the more familiar "instruments." Additionally, in his latest work, Goody admits that earlier emphases on Greek alphabetic literacies were overdrawn: "it is important to realize that the shift to the alphabet is not so crucial to many kinds of social and intellectual development as was once thought" (p. 139). This reassessment of the "alphabetic mind" hypothesis is based on his awareness of greater historical complexity than originally thought: "much of what has been attributed to the Greeks existed embryonically in earlier written civilizations" (p. 139). It is based also on greater comparative awareness: "Earlier discussions [of alphabetic literacy] now seem very ethnocentric, Eurocentric, or Near East-centered, especially when we look at the current achievements not only of Japan, but also of Taiwan, Korea, and Hong Kong, committed as they are to the use of scripts of the logographic kind. Much of what has been attributed to Greece was possible with other writing systems" (p. 140).

Despite the broader vision of what a technology might consist of, and the recognition that earlier claims for the alphabetic script were flawed, Goody nonetheless falls back on old arguments. These arguments include that scripts allow greater durability of messages, an expansion of memory; that text-durability allows collecting, resulting in "immense quantities of books stored in libraries and archives" (p. 145); and that both inscription and storage enable different habits of mind to develop (making lists, forming tables, and "formalization in 'logic' " [p. 147] are his primary examples).

As we have noted elsewhere, much of the argument is plausible at a general level, but the reader is left wondering about the sociohistorical or sociopolitical framework within which to understand these general potentials of a technology. First, as Goody himself notes, we cannot ascribe that much to scripts *per se*: we have neither alphabetic "minds" nor (usefully) distinct alphabetic "traditions." Second, if we turn to the question of libraries and archives, then historical period, social purpose, and conception of writing enter into the picture. That was the thrust of our criticism of the historical periodization in *The Logic of Writing* in chapter 2, and it was also a theme in our earlier discussion in this chapter of kinds of writing and archives. Lastly, when we turn to the issue of "motor skills," "habits," and "cognitive procedures" (p. 146), we deal with claims that, where tested, have been found wanting. As various researchers have shown when examining claims about literacy's "cognitive consequences," either the effects of writing practices on cognition or consciousness were empirically discernible but due to institutional practices, such as schooling, rather than literacy *per se* (Cole and Scribner, 1981; Reder, 1994), or the effects were not distinctive, that is, they were found also in circumstances of "primarily oral" performance and practices (Bloch, 1998; Finnegan, 1988; Lloyd, 1990).

It is common to represent the technical infrastructure of society as driving all else forward, whether we are trying to capture the long arc of human history, as in the evolutionary schemes in which literacy has figured, or whether we are characterizing our current era. The recent global spread of audio-visual broadcast media (television) and, more recently, of interactive electronic media (the "web") has seized the attention of a host of actors concerned with education, literacy, and the economy. In addition to teachers, researchers, and parents, there is now a virtual cacophony of political, "nongovernmental," and private voices calling for "computer literacy" as well as "access to the internet" (Schement, 2000; Twist, 2000; Tyner, 1998; Warschauer, 1999; Wilhelm, 2000). Although the alarms concern plausible fears – in particular, that access or lack of access to new information technologies will parallel and exacerbate existing social inequalities[8] – we must repeat a now-familiar argument: historical contexts and social practices give essential shape and meaning to technological potentials.[9] Let us now indicate what we mean with regard to electronic literacies.

In our introduction to this book, we noted a call by Sherry Turkle, a leading student of information technology and consciousness, for a "critical simulation literacy" (1999, p. 82). That proposal was put forth during an interview about new identity practices and potentials offered by internet fora – e-mail, chat rooms, interactive games, and so forth. Turkle's argument was that such fora offer possibilities for people, especially adolescents, to "play around" with versions of the self – sexual selves, racial selves, older (or younger) selves – with relative anonymity and lack of commitment to the self presented. Electronic fora offer an arena for experimentation during a life phase (adolescence) when exploration of the self is a "hot button" issue. Turkle also observes that for an earlier generation of youth, going to college offered a period and space for such experimentation – away from home, not yet drawn into the work-world, a period of sexual rebellion. Due to familiar developments – skyrocketing tuition costs, increased living at home, generalized financial anxiety, an AIDS-era sexual caution, and so forth – the college years are now less likely to serve as a zone of relative freedom and experimentation. Instead, for contemporary youth, internet fora often do. In assessing the implications of this argument, we may note two things. First, there *is* an interesting identity potential offered by a media form which is simultaneously interactive (like speech) and yet not face-to-face (like writing). But, second, the media form is enabling and not determinative. Much of the identity play at issue was formerly done, as some doubtlessly still is, in actual rather than virtual interaction sites: in college dorm rooms, lecture halls, libraries, bars, and coffee shops.

In addition to discussing identity play, Turkle also calls for an *education* in "critical simulation literacy." She does this because familiarity with internet technologies, including games and simulations, does not in and of itself breed a habit of mind she values: a skeptical, inquiring disposition which questions the assumptions which underpin arguments and examines the perspective which frame representations. Access to the internet does not by itself foster any particular kind of literacy. It can be part of an expansive and judicious acquisition and synthesis of information, or consist of a browsing, without specific intent, what we term "surfing," and much else besides. "Electronic literacy" is like all other literacies: variable according to political and economic conditions, social institutions, and cultural values, all of which constrain, occasion, and give meaning to specific communicative practices.

This fluidity of potential can be understood in terms of power as well as identity. As one analyst has recently argued:

> Electronic literacies can be either empowering or stultifying; people will use the Internet for everything from creative construction of knowledge to passive reception of a multimedia glitz. Whether users fall on one end of this continuum or the other is likely to be highly influenced by class, race, gender, and country, but *highly influenced* does not mean *completely determined*. Literacy practices are influenced by day-to-day struggles of power (Street, 1993), as are uses of new technologies (Feenberg, 1991). Among the main sites of these struggles are schools (Giroux, 1993). To a large measure, it is in schools and colleges where people will become more or less knowledgeable users of electronic media, critical or less critical readers and writers in an electronic era. The nature of pedagogical practices and school reform will contribute to who becomes the *interacting* and who becomes the *interacted* in the network society.
>
> (Warschauer, 1999, p. 21, emphasis in original)

The concern expressed in this passage between members of society who are "interacting" versus "interacted" refers to an old dichotomy: between the productive, self-directing members of society and those who are somehow passively led, directed, or "acted upon." It raises the question of what literacies are to predominate in an era of postmodern global capitalism. Will it be literacies which maintain one aspect of the Enlightenment: hopes of knowledge, self-improvement, and social betterment through education, now improved and rendered fully democratic and multicultural? Or will it be literacies which further another modernist legacy: social regulation "from above," in which the poor and otherwise socially problematic are morally reconstructed in systems of surveillance, in institutions of caring, such as schooling, criminal justice, and health care?

Conclusion

This conundrum reflects an old contradiction in ideas about and practices of literacy. It was expressed early and clearly by the philosopher Plato in his Seventh Letter; it is found also in the work of critical literacy theorists such as Freire (1972), who was committed to using reading and writing for human emancipation and social transformation. The dilemma is simply this: once we allow that meaning is not in a text, but in an interpretation, how do we judge better or worse accounts? Or, in a more authoritarian vein, how do we ensure correct interpretations (Gee, 1996)? How we resolve this dilemma is clearly a matter of power as well as knowledge, but the attempted resolution also has implications for identity.

One current solution in the United States is to try to override the plurality of interpretations, the plurality of literacies, by imposing a unitary account. This is put forth by the pedagogical fundamentalists, often, interestingly, in league with religious fundamentalists, who argue that in essence reading and writing are matters of decoding and encoding language in a text (Lemann, 1997). Reflecting both a Protestant religious–cultural legacy (Olson, 1977) and a conservative view of "real science" (Coles, 2000), this approach to literacy is now ascendant in US Federal Government education policy (Allington and Woodside-Giron, 1999; Schemo, 2002). In this vision of literacy, reading or writing must begin with intensive drill in the sound-structure of spoken/written language. This is realized, for example, in the "phonics" programs for reading, which feature highly regulated instruction in phoneme–grapheme correspondences and in comprehension assessments (Adams, 1993). Such a vision of literacy is proposed for all school children but it is visited mostly on the disprivileged (Lemann, 1997). It is, in effect, another way of regulating the poor: through tightly scripting their literacy experiences, so that their earliest "lesson" is that literacy is about following orders and getting the correct answer. Let us not here go further in the long debate about whether and how such literacy experiences are oppressive or empowering. Instead, let us merely observe that there are undeniably forms of subjection/subjectivity, that is, of identity-formation, implied by pedagogies which give first priority to orchestrated drill and controlled textual encounters, which foreground carefully measured and quantitatively ranked progress as the only "valid assessment." The outcome, if not the conscious intention, of such pedagogies are what the sociologist Basil Bernstein (1996) analyzed as socially decentered, skill-based identities.

Another approach, often derided in the current reading debates as "whole language relativism," begins by building upon the plurality of interpretations, the plurality of literacies. It views literacy as a set of language practices, in which standard-issue reading and writing are prominent but not absolutely essential, and in which children's home-based discourses are essential building blocks in what are then, necessarily, a plurality of literacies (Edelsky, 1996). This vision of literacy accords with, having drawn upon as well as contributed to, situated accounts of literacy. This conception of plural literacies is clearly stated by Gee (1996), who argues for a sociocultural model of literacies, in which literacy is conceived as mastery of a discourse beyond that of the home, a "secondary" discourse, whether that of workplace, church, school, or other collective endeavor (such as birdwatching club, sports team, or a "youth gang"). Note the wide range of possible "literacies" licensed by Gee's definitions: "Therefore, literacy is always plural . . . If one wanted to be rather pedantic and literalistic, then we could define literacy as *mastery of a second Discourse involving print*... And one can substitute for 'print' various other sorts of texts and technologies: painting, literature, films, television, computers, telecommunications – 'props' in the Discourse..." (Gee, 1996, pp. 143, emphasis in original).

There are clear affinities between the view of literacy in this quote and the issues and cases discussed in this book. Note that like many others in the situated approach to literacy, discussed in chapter 3, Gee does not give first priority to print. Indeed, like those concerned with electronic literacies, he allows for a range of representational devices – "painting...films...computers" – on which literacies could draw. There are, however, complications which we must note, both to "whole language" pedagogies and Gee's expansive sociocultural approach. First, regarding "whole language" approaches, they, as well as phonics programs, are in the business of applying pedagogies and shaping identities. In terms of Bernstein's theory of pedagogy, social control, and identity, "whole language" presumes a "competence" model of knowledge and person, in the guise of a "self-regulating" learner. A self-regulating learner will be permitted a wider range of literacy practices within which to learn and demonstrate learning than under phonics "drill," but as Moore (2001) rightly argues, the learning will still be assessed – that is, judged and ranked – within nonlocal systems of power-knowledge. In the idiom earlier used, the problem of "correct interpretation" is not avoided, it is instead reconfigured (see also Luke [1993] for a similar argument). As a student of a situated or sociocultural approach to literacy, Gee has made a similar point, if not of "whole language" approaches *per se*, then of the dilemmas of schooling and literacy. Indeed Gee's (or Street's) concepts of literacy involving painting, films, and television instead of print is an expansion which some "whole language" adherents would feel gets too far from the school-based mission of ensuring "critical knowledge" (Hasan, 1999; Alverman, 2000).

It is not surprising that Gee's expansive view of literacy is coupled with an account of identity which emphasizes the fluid, changing nature of identity and the likelihood of identity-conflicts. This accords well with much discussed in our fifth chapter on literacy and self-fashioning: Rose's stark transformation, Gilyard's conflicts, working-class women's yearning for and stigmatization by schooled literacy. Gee does not give, however, the same emphasis as we have to constraint, to identities imposed, as well as chosen. This difference in emphasis points to an argument we have developed in this book: that the situated or sociocultural accounts, while a considerable advance over autonomous models and the literacy thesis, take insufficient account of the long-term historical pattern, of the place of literacy in "the great metaphysical, scientific, technical, and economic venture of the West."

As anthropologists as well as students of literacy on a global scale, we must understand that the histories of the West are implicated in, and appropriated by, the most far-flung "postcolonial" setting. In his discussion of discourses and identities, Gee has a thought-provoking discussion of "being a Real Indian" (1996, pp. 129–131), in which the point is correctly made that identity is negotiated with others. In this case, "being an Indian" requires talking and acting and being recognized by others. What is missing from such an account, however, is that identities are imposed as well as chosen, that for many "not being an Indian" may not be an option, that, for instance, near reservation areas, non-Indian prejudice and tribal anxiety assign and enforce identity based on looks, residence, and names, as well as mode of speaking and acting (Matthiessen, 1984). What is also missing is awareness that American Indians are probably the "ethnic group" most compelled to demonstrate "real" or "authentic" identity (Jaimes, 1992), and that such demonstrations, as collective projects over time, involve ongoing encounters with and appropriations of textual legacies: such as described in chapter 5; as surveyed by diverse indigenous scholars (Deloria and Lytle, 1983; Vizenor, 1998); and as analyzed in particular case studies (Collins, 1998b; Foley, 1995; Sider, 1993).

In our engagement with the ongoing debates about literacy and literacies, we have drawn upon practice theory, historical analysis, and ethnographic comparison to argue for a multifaceted view of power as enabling as well as regulative, identity as constructed as well as constrained, text as unstably and unavoidably attached to the binary writing:speaking. It remains for you, the readers, to judge whether the arguments hold, whether these particular historical and ethnographic explorations of text, power, and identity move us beyond the current terms of discussion. Whatever the outcome of that judgment, it should be clear that this book is closer in spirit to the sociocultural or situated understanding of literacy/ies than to an autonomous model. Such situated understandings are currently out of official favor: witness the ongoing attacks on "whole language" pedagogies by government think tanks as well as state legislatures (Allington and Woodside-Giron, 1999; Coles, 1998); and "relativist" is still a term of abuse directed at advocates of the sociocultural approach by those who would defend more foundational conceptions (Goody, 2000; MacCabe, 1998). The highly politicized state of the current educational field is not surprising, however, in terms of the perspective developed in this book: literacy remains hotly contested, as political program, domain of knowledge, and arena of social practice.

As we argued in the beginning of our book, literacy seems central to modern living, and yet it is easy to overestimate the significance of alphabetic script *per se*. As Diamond (1999) reminds us, although writing has importance in the "fates of human societies," it was never important on its own. The term "literacy" opens onto a wide range of kinds – school, vernacular, computer, and media literacy, to name a few – and yet "literacy" is also the focus of ongoing efforts to restrict its meaning to some essence, in which "reading" or "writing" will be defined only in accordance with officially approved diagnostics. Given the ongoing debates about the nature of text, the practice of power, and the dynamics of identity, that the meaning of literacy remains hotly contested should not surprise us. As forms of human engagement and meaning making that are intertwined in these debates, *literacies* remain puzzles, provocations, and invitations.

NOTES

2 The literacy thesis: vexed questions of rationality, development, and self

1. In addition to Tylor's *Anthropology*, L. H. Morgan's *Ancient Society* (1877) was another influential statement of the same evolutionary assumptions.

2. The very listing of terms – religion, economy, etc. – signifies an institutional autonomy that Weber held was characteristic of complex and especially modern social formations (Habermas, 1987). Goody seeks the precursor to institutional autonomy in ancient literate societies. In his account, writing allows an accumulation and differentiation of information that aids the specialization and growing organizational autonomy of sectors of society – an epochal transformation separating such societies from the structural–functional totality supposedly characterizing state-free social formations.

3. Goody's speculation provides an interesting elaboration of the equation of civilization with private property in nineteenth-century social thought, suggesting a third term: literacy–property–civilization. See Diamond's (1974b) essay on law versus custom for an excellent discussion of the private property/civilization nexus.

4. The complexity and arbitrariness of representation seems to have developed in this manner: first, tokens were differentiated by shape, and later by inscriptions, permitting further signal distinctions (say "sheep" and "goat" and "ox" versus generic "livestock"); second, collections of tokens were later enclosed in clay envelopes – termed *bullae* – with the contents inscribed on the surface of the envelopes; and, finally, the surface inscriptions, minus the actual tokens, were used to record an account, an early bill-of-lading (Schmandt-Besserat, 1978). Thus we have representations-of-representations, as inscriptions in clay refer to clay tokens that, in turn, refer to collections and classes of objects.

5. Halverson (1991), reviewing earlier work by Olson, provides an extended argument that it was an experimentalist and quantificationist orientation toward the natural world, and – contrary to the arguments in "Utterance" – skepticism about received textual traditions, including essayist traditions, that characterized the emerging modern scientific worldview, from the seventeenth century onwards. In his newer account, Olson seems to have responded to this argument, although Halverson is not cited.

6. See also Derrida (1976a) for a sustained and influential philosophical argument about the untenability of the contrast.

7. Note that print and electronic media coverage of national governments can devote great attention to questions of the form "What did the President (Prime Minister, cabinet official, etc.) mean when s/he said '...'?"

8. In a civilization haunted by "the death of God," that is, the loss of a source of authentic or certain meaning, it is not only the voice of God that becomes problematic. The relation of writers to their existence is frequently if not typically conflictual, expressed

in numerous modern narratives of literacy, education, and alienation (e.g. Rousseau [1998], Williams [1979], and the studies discussed in chapter 5). Also ambivalent and conflictual is the relation of the "ordinary voice" to those legions of inspectors, novelists, folklorists, anthropologists, case workers, and documentary film makers who would somehow inscribe and thus capture the "real world" in its "own words" (Bauman, 1986; Clifford, 1988; Silverstein and Urban, 1996).

3 Situated approaches to the literacy debate

1. De Certeau (1984) has a chapter on reading which depicts reading as "poaching," a furtive yet pervasive "taking" from texts, in unsanctioned ways, for diverse purposes and pleasures, including the simple ones of hiding and idling. He argues that reading is not "information processing," as in standard psychological models (Gibson and Levin, 1975), nor is it a simple reciprocal reader–text engagement, as posited in "reader-response" theories (Rosenblatt, 1978).

2. That dialogue has been taken up in some recent work (Foley, 1997a; Gee, 1996).

3. Heath does not begin with a given text, but proceeds from a description of the physical and social environment within which the events occur. A *literacy event* is then deemed "any occasion upon which an individual alone or in interaction attempts to comprehend or produce graphic signs" (Anderson, Teale, and Estrada, 1980, p. 59).

4. Heath found other patterned differences. For example, that where teachers had requested their preschoolers to "name objects or list discrete features of objects or events," Trackton adults' questions asked "for analogical comparisons" (1982b, p. 117). Young children in Trackton were adept at recognizing similarities and differences among situations, objects, and people's personalities, but Trackton adults did not ask them to list similar attributes. Naming objects and listing features of objects or events is a common activity in early school activities.

5. As noted, such silence was culturally prescribed, but also open to misinterpretation. Lack of response to a question could be judged as evidence of lack of knowledge or of noncompliance. That silence is a culturally variable communicative response has been well documented (Basso, 1990b; Philips, 1993).

6. Roadville was "a white working-class community of families steeped for four generations in the life of the textile mill" (1982c, p. 57).

7. These included instrumental, social interactional (e.g. greeting cards), news related, memory-supportive, substitutes for oral messages (e.g. notes from parents to teachers), provision of permanent record (e.g. birth certificates), and confirmation (e.g. directions for assembling items) (Heath, 1986, p. 21).

8. This section draws heavily upon "Speech, language and non-literacy: the Limba" found as chapter 3 of *Literacy and Orality*.

9. Finnegan's work is not unique in demonstrating the abilities of tribal peoples to philosophize in ways distinctive, yet analogous to Western philosophy. The works of many other anthropologists offer examples, notably Paul Radin's *Primitive Man as Philosopher* (1957) and *The World of Primitive Man* (1953), Claude Lévi-Strauss' *The Savage Mind* (1966), Stanley Diamond's *In Search of the Primitive* (1974a), and Gary Witherspoon's *Language and Art in the Navajo Universe* (1977).

10. A comparison with music may be useful here. During the Baroque era (1600–1750), it was common practice for a composer to write out a melodic line for a soloist and provide a basis for harmony in the accompaniment by means of what is referred to as a figured bass. The figured bass, numbers which indicated the pitches to be played above the bass note, could be realized in different ways, as long as they did

not overwhelm the melody. Further, the soloist, especially in the slow movements, was expected to ornament the melody through such devices as trills, turns, and such. The point here is that the fundamental harmonic structure of the piece, its skeleton, remained the same from performance to performance, but its various manifestations accounted for variability in performance.

4 Literacies and power in modern nation states

1. See also Marvin (1988) for a discussion of seventeenth-century Protestant Sweden and the first national literacy tests.
2. Briefly, Eisenstein argues that various aspects of the emergence and development of printing in Europe enabled new forms of thinking and individuality. The widespread and rapid dissemination of books that market-driven printing allowed gave individuals greatly increased access to a wide variety of publications, enabling a more synthetic, systematizing, intertextual style of thinking and scholarship. The regularized formatting of books, with tables of contents, footnotes, and indexes, and the standardization of visual guides (maps, charts, diagrams) and systems of notation both expressed and enabled systematic, methodical thinking. The "preservative powers of print" led to the fixing of literary vernaculars, which was an impetus to nationalist consciousness, the fragmenting of Western Christendom into print vernaculars, and the development, due to print-based ideas of authorship and creation, of a "new kind of individualism" (1968, p. 22).
3. See also Eisenstein (1968; 1980), whose account depends on an historical system that she mentions without ever analyzing. From the large-scale and widespread dissemination of book-commodities that are stipulated at the outset of her analysis, to the evolution of authors' and inventors' claims on intellectual property, to the savvy, competitiveness of the Dutch printer/publishers who enabled the international exchange of ideas underpinning the sixteenth- and seventeenth-century "scientific revolution," Eisenstein's argument assumes markets and capital as well as technology: print capitalism.
4. Eisenstein has reified the distinction between texts produced (a) by manual impression (manuscripts) and (b) mechanical impression (print), and this is revealed when she argues for the "preservative powers of print." Here it appears that print itself – as a semiotic means without sociological grounding – becomes the repository of secure meaning in politics, religion, law, and science. Manuscripts, it seems, are fatally ephemeral: "lines that prior generations had repeatedly traced, erased, retraced" (1968, p. 21). At this point it is useful to recall that such ephemeral meaning is also attributed to orality – the shifting senses of context-bound utterance and oral custom in Goody, Olson, or Ong – while fixity and security of meaning is attributed to *manuscripts* in the Ancient Near East (Goody, 1986), Classical Greece (Goody, 1977b; Olson, 1977), medieval Europe (Olson, 1994; Ong, 1967), or seventeenth-century England (Love, 1993). It is of course the contrast, the asymmetrical binary of written/oral and print/nonprint that is fixed in our thinking about these matters and not any given textual form.
5. There were of course exceptions, such as the prodigy Jane Turell, who read at age two, composed original hymns before age twelve, and read her clergyman father's entire library by age eighteen, or the intelligent, lucky, and persistent daughters of the well-to-do, such as Mary Otis Warren, who was permitted to sit in on her brother's lessons, and turned her skills to poetry, playwriting, political pamphleteering, and finally to writing a three-volume history of the revolutionary era – albeit facing male disapproval (Cremin, 1976, pp. 26–28).

6. As Cremin (1976) has summarized, colonial era education continued an English pattern in which family, church, and (private) school served as the basic educational triad and relatively high levels of literacy emerged from diverse educational provision for a mobile, religiously conflicted, socially ambitious population. It is clear that colonial and early national America emphasized schooling and literacy. At the beginning of the eighteenth century there were over a thousand schools and forty presses in the colonies; by mid-century, over half of all whites had undergone some form of systematic instruction in church or school. By mid-nineteenth century, universal schooling was provided for with thousands more local primary schools.

7. Equally pertinent, they were not all going to be able to gain the careers in business or the professions that had been the expected outcome of an elite (private) high school education.

8. In fact, the vocational track was intended for all daughters: "domestic science" and "home economics" defined girls' normative education.

9. Legacies of slavery do not, of course, have uniform effects regarding education. Postcolonial Barbados, a former slave colony, has quite high literacy rates for a country in the "developing world." Despite this, however, there is considerable and complex prejudice surrounding Bajan, the creole-based vernacular used by the majority of the country's Afro-Caribbean speakers. See Fenigsen (2000) for an informative discussion.

10. Lest it appear that such exclusion only occurred early in this century, let us add a personal footnote. One of the authors, Collins, lived several years as a boy in the small Alabama town of Clayton. One pleasure he remembers was the public library. It was small but well-stocked, cool on hot summer days, and the librarian was quick to forgive his overdue fines. In the mid-1960s Clayton had a sizable African-American population, but in those years schools, restaurants, and other public facilities were still segregated. Thinking back, he realizes he never saw an African-American person in that public library.

11. The thirty years since the 1960s have shown how deeply intertwined are class and race in America, in which nonwhite usually means working-class or poor, and in which the literacy struggles of minority youth continue to be a focus of fears, debates, and analysis (Delpit and Perry, 1998; Gadsden and Wagner, 1995).

12. The *Saturday Evening Post* was established in 1897, also quickly reached a readership of over a million, and was targeted at men, their more public spheres of concern, and their areas of consumption.

13. Completion of the tenth grade or equivalent was used to define adult functional literacy in the 1990s, although the use of grade levels is now being questioned in the US and internationally (Sum, 1999; UNESCO, 1992).

5 Literacies and identity formation: American cases

1. Discussing the role of examinations in disciplinary power, Foucault argues as follows:

> The examination leaves behind it a whole meticulous archive constituted in terms of bodies and days. The examination that places individuals in a field of surveillance also situates them in a network of writing; it engages them in a whole mass of documents that capture and fix them. The procedures of examination were accompanied at the same time by a system of intense registration and of documentary accumulation. A "power of writing" was constituted as an essential part in the mechanisms of discipline. (1975, p. 189)

2. "The mastery of language guarantees and isolates a new power, a 'bourgeois' power, that of making history and fabricating languages. This power, which is essentially scriptural, challenges not only the privilege of 'birth,' that is, of the aristocracy, but also defines the code governing socioeconomic promotion and dominates, regulates, or selects according to its norms all those who do not possess this mastery of language. Writing becomes a principle of social hierarchization that formerly privileged the middle class and now privileges the technocrat" (de Certeau, 1984, p. 139).

3. His account recalls as well Radway's (1984) descriptions of women reading romance novels in order to simultaneously escape, confront, and pleasurably transfigure the conditions of patriarchy. Compare also de Certeau "The creativity of the reader grows as the institution that controlled it declines" (p. 172); "to read is to be elsewhere, where *they* are not, in another world; it is to constitute a secret scene, a place one can enter and leave when one wishes" (p. 173).

4. The strains, resistance, and ambivalence of Gilyard's experience frequently express what we may think of as discursive-social positions, typically occupied by disprivileged working-class and minority students, who, unlike Gilyard, do not succeed in school (Bigler, 1996; Luttrell, 1997; Weis, 1990).

5. Racist attitudes and actions among Gilyard and his peers are quite sharply drawn in the later chapters: with apparent casualness "Whites" are fought, mugged, and stolen from.

6. "Country" is code in the American South for "rural and working-class or poor," whether of Euro-American or African-American affiliation.

7. See Labov (1972) for an early sociolinguistic statement about gender and "correct speech."

8. Mothers are often remembered as uninvolved, whether due to work commitments, "country ways," or lack of education: "I suppose the fact that my problem in school was because my mother just wasn't involved. She really had no time so I don't blame her. But I remember thinking how come my mother doesn't go to meetings like other kids' mothers" (Pam, Philadelphia woman) (p. 93).

9. Rockhill (1993) presents a theoretically innovative study of contradictions between official discourses of literacy, the lives of immigrant Mexicanas, and the conflicts they face between family responsibilities and educational aspirations.

10. Like Ella, a consistent theme of Jennie's life in relation to school, literacy and identity is shame about her "country," Appalachian way of speaking. Of early efforts at phonemic decoding she says: "That's why it was a little hard for me startin' to like . . . sound out my words . . . 'cause like I talk different . . . 'cause I'm you know . . . countrified. And my words don't come out the way they're supposed to" (p. 100).

11. A "somehow made" that Foucault (1975) would attribute to the micro-politics practiced through institutions of family, school, and workplace, by means of which bodies and subjects are adjusted to subordinate fates despite formal equalities. Luttrell (1997) provides a suggestive psychoanalytic analysis of class-and-gender exclusion, an interaction of identity, social position, and institutional experience, which, for reasons of space, we cannot address here.

6 Colonial legacies and indigenous transformations

1. There are, as always, exceptions. When a conquered people's literate legacy is valued by the conqueror, as in ancient Rome's domination of the Hellenic Greek world, it may be adopted for purposes of education of the elite from the conquerors' world. Thus, Roman administrators used Latin in administering the colonies, but had Greek

slaves teach their children the Greek language and its cultural legacy (Hadas, 1954; Marrou, 1956). But we are discussing the period of European colonialism, in which this rarely occurred.

2. Greenblatt, in *Marvelous Possessions*, underscores the juridical nature of writing to Columbus' taking possession:

> And because Columbus's culture does not entirely trust verbal testimony, because its judicial procedures require written proofs, he makes certain to perform his speech acts in the presence of the fleet's recorder (for a fleet which had no priest had a recorder), hence ensuring that everything would be written down and consequently have a greater authority. The papers are carefully sealed, preserved, carried back across thousands of leagues of ocean to officials who in turn countersign and process them according to the procedural rules; the notarized documents are a token of the truth of the encounter and hence of the legality of the claim. Or rather they help to produce "truth" and "legality," ensuring that the words Columbus speaks do not disappear as soon as their sound fades, ensuring that the memory of the encounter is fixed, ensuring that there are not competing versions of what happened on the beach on October 12th. A priest may be said to facilitate a transaction with eternity, but an *escrivano* facilitates a transaction with a more immediately useful form of temporality, the institutional form secured by writing . . . Ceremonies take the place of cultural contacts; rituals of possession stand in for negotiated contracts. *Columbus acts entirely within what Michel de Certeau calls "the scriptural operation" of his own culture, an operation that leads him not simply to pronounce certain words or alternatively to write them down but rather to perform them orally in the presence of the fleet's named and officially sanctioned recorder.* Writing here fixes a set of public linguistic acts, gives them official standing, makes them "historical" events.
>
> (Greenblatt, 1991, pp. 57, 58, emphasis added)

3. That the conjoining of religion and political authority in these "rituals of possession" was directed at other European powers may be clearly seen in an example Seed (1993, p. 118) provides: "The Dutch carved the name of their religion *in Spanish* on a board in Mauritius, clearly warning Spaniards to stay away" (emphasis in original).

4. The text of the sermon has been described by Stoudemire (1970, pp. 23–24) drawing upon Las Casas:

> After a few introductory remarks on the meaning of Advent, Montesinos plunged into a violent attack upon the Spaniards for the blindness in which they lived. He said that he had been sent to the island by Christ, that he was the voice of God crying in the wilderness. He insisted that the Spaniards were living in mortal sin, and that they would die in sin and go to hell as punishment for the cruelties and tyranny they had demonstrated toward the Indians. He pointed out that the Indians were required to work in the mines until they were unable to stand, that they did not receive proper food, that their illnesses went unnoticed, and that they were forced to work until they died. Montesinos insisted that the Spaniards were interested only in the amount of gold each Indian could dig out of the soil each day. The preacher went on to ask the Spaniards if they did not think the Indians were men and rational beings, and if the Spaniards were not obligated to love them as they loved each other. He asked them if they understood what he was saying, and if they were sorry for their behavior.

5. The *Laws of Burgos* offered little protection to the Indians who were to

> be taught the Ave Maria, Pater Noster, Creed, Salve Regina, and other prayers; they should learn to name the seven deadly sins, the Articles of Faith, and to know other basic Christian ritual. The Indians should be permitted to continue their traditional song-dance that they called *areito* throughout the islands, and they should always be well fed, have individual hammocks, and,

after a certain time, wear clothes. The only actual protection in the first thirty-two laws (1512) was the general enjoiner that Indians were not to be used as beasts of burden, nor were they to be beaten. (Stoudemire, 1970, p. 41)

6. The historian Lewis Hanke provides brief descriptions of the ways in which the mandate to read the Requirement was in fact carried out:

    it was read to trees and empty huts... Captains muttered its theological phrases into their beards on the edge of sleeping Indian settlements, or even a league away before starting the formal attack... Ship captains would sometimes have the document read from the deck as they approached an island, and at night would send out enslaving expeditions whose leaders would shout the traditional Castilian war cry "Santiago" rather than read the Requirement before the attack. (cited in Seed 1990, p. 13)

7. Some of the natives, in Pané's eyes, proved willing to accept the true faith, shown by their learning of the Apostle's Creed, the Our Father, and other testaments of faith, and engaging in those ritual practices sanctioned by the Christian faith. Others, resisting evangelical suasion, persisted in their native practices. These would be purged of the devil's influence and Christianized by force. López Maguiña cites Pané: "With others force and ingenuity are needed, because we are not all of the same nature. Just as [the catechumens] had a good beginning and a better end, there will be others who will begin well and laugh later at what has been taught to them; force and punishment is needed to deal with them" (1992, p. 293).

8. What follows relies heavily on Arrom (1992) and López Maguiña (1992).

9. Three mendicant orders responded to the order of Charles V establishing missions in New Spain, the Franciscans arriving in 1524, Dominicans in 1526, and Augustinians in 1533.

10. The use of "higher evolutionary plateau" might seem the imposition of a nineteenth-century schema onto a sixteenth-century context. Burkhart (personal communication) reminds us that while the Jesuit José de Acosta, in his *Historia natural y moral de las indias* (1590), viewed Mesoamerican writing as rudimentary as compared to Chinese and Japanese, his was not an evolutionary explanation. Nonetheless, and important to our argument here, Mignolo, in his discussion of Bishop Landa's attempt to translate Mayan hieroglyphs into alphabetic writing makes the following observation:

    The very act of looking for correspondences between signs representing ideas and signs standing for classes of sounds seems to indicate not only a conception of writing which is *clearly evolutionary* but also the assumption that the best form of writing is to represent speech in letter form. The problem, however, is not with Landa's perspective but rather with the tenacity of those beliefs, which are often expressed today in the explicit assumption that any system of graphic signs which could be used as an alternative to oral discourse could be considered true writing. (1992, p. 313, emphasis added)

    For an eighteenth-century evolutionary schema pairing scripts with people see the discussion of Rousseau in our chapter 7.

11. Temple schools also existed for girls, although apparently not for scribal education (Louise Burkhart, personal communication).

12. For fuller treatments of the appropriation of alphabetic literacy by Mesoamerican peoples see Burkhart (1996, 2000); Hill (1991); Karttunen (1982); Lockhart (1992); Mignolo (1995).

13. What follows relies heavily on Adorno (1989a; 1989b).
14. As did the Nahuas, the Mayas also used alphabetic writing (in Mayan) for civil purposes (wills, petitions, and other records) quite extensively, though fewer texts survive than for the Nahuas.
15. Rockwell, in support of her example, cites Tedlock's Introduction to his translation of the Popol Vuh, a sacred text from what is now Guatemala. Rockwell surmises that if the postconquest books of Chiapas were similar they may have contained, as Tedlock (1998, p. 30) states for the Popol Vuh, "what readers of the ancient book would say when they gave long performances, telling the full story that lay behind the charts, pictures and plot outlines of the ancient book."
16. Digges and Rappaport (1993, p. 145) cite Lockhart's (1982, p. 371) detailing of the composition of a title in the Spanish colonial world:

> The notion of "title" in the colonial Spanish world went beyond the concept of a simple deed. Full title – whether to land, territory, or jurisdiction – involved not only an original grant or sale, but also an investigation on the spot to consult third parties and see if the situation was as described, and finally formal acts of giving and taking possession. Only then did the grant or sale, until that point merely virtual or hypothetical, enter into force. A Spanish notary would keep a running record of the whole proceeding, repeatedly signed by officials and witnesses; this record, appended to the original grant, order, or the like, constituted the title.

17. As Pulis is careful to point out, "the Rastafarian Brethren are not a unitary movement and deployment of the terms brethren and movement has tended to mask a diversity of ideas, beliefs, and practices" (1999, p. 359).
18. Pulis notes that the Bible itself provides the evidence in support of the Rastafari's contention that the Bible is an incomplete testament:

> When I pushed Bongo he pointed out that there were citations to books that were omitted from his Bible. In 2 Esdras 14: 37–48, for example, some 90 books are recounted of which only 24 were "made public." Similarly, diffused throughout Isaiah, Jeremiah, and Ezekiel were references to Ethiopia, Zion, and blackness which were cited [sighted] as confirmations that the Bible was the oral history of African peoples "locked off" in print. Bongo's use of the term "Maccabbee Bible" was a reference to the pseudographical and deutrocanonical texts excluded from the standard King James. The book of Maccabbee was of especial importance because it was read as a test of faith and an expression of "knowledge" as revealed to the seventh generation of Africans exiled in Jamaica. Such texts were considered subversive literature and were banned in Jamaica until 1976.   (pp. 384–85)

19. De Certeau contrasts readers and writers:

> readers are travellers; they move across lands belonging to someone else, like nomads poaching their way across fields they did not write, despoiling the wealth of Egypt to enjoy it themselves. Writing accumulates, stocks up, resists time by the establishment of a place and multiplies its production through the expansion of reproduction. *Reading takes no measures against the erosion of time (one forgets oneself and also forgets), it does not keep what it acquires, or it does so poorly, and each of the places through which it passes is a repetition of the lost paradise.*   (1984, p. 174, emphasis added)

20. Acknowledging the constraints of colonial power relations, but emphasizing the agency of Nahua translators, Burkhart argues that "native mutations," that is, changes in received Christian texts, "amounted to a destabilizing critique of one of colonialism's dominant discourses" (2000, p. 78); that "at least some of these translators found it possible to construct meaningful cultural critiques under the guise of translating Old World Christian texts" (p. 87).

21. According to Basso's account, assistants in the new religion were pressed to follow the prayer texts exactly, to keep "it just like it was when [Silas John] heard it from God" (Basso, 1990, p. 31).

7 Conclusion: literacy lessons – beginnings, ends, and implications

1. Because of technological conditions, in particular, the lack of paper or paper-like materials, but also because of the ravages of time, the earliest writings we know of are those on the most durable materials: hardened clay for the tokens of the Ancient Near East, cut stone for the Maya and other monumental writing (Justeson and Mathews, 1990). Early writing on less durable materials is rarely preserved in the archeological record.
2. Hundreds of Tolowa and Oregon Athabaskans had been relocated to Siletz, Oregon, the site of a reservation, after military defeats in the 1850s and 1860s.
3. In his essay "The Violence of the Letter" Derrida critically examines Lévi-Strauss' (1964) account of the introduction of writing to the Amazonian Nambikwara. He challenges Lévi-Strauss' representation of the Nambikwara as preliterates "without writing," showing evidence (elsewhere in Lévi-Strauss' publications) of Nambikwara symbolic inscriptions ("designs on calabashes"), preoccupation with inscribing genealogy, and their name for "writing." Derrida prefers a broad conception of "writing," encompassing a wide range of signifying practices on a variety of materials, rather than a narrower conception restricted to language-writing.
4. Quite often when people are termed "illiterates" it is shortcomings in the latter competence, decoding representations of spoken language, that are at issue, not a general ability to make sense, to decipher the signs of the world in which they live.
5. A major ceremony, in precontact and current time, is the "World Renewal Ceremony," in which a story is told of the rebirth of the world. The theme of this story – cataclysm, death, and renewal – strongly informs Tolowa accounts of their history since conquest by Euro-Americans (Slagle, 1987).
6. Gerald Vizenor is himself *anishinaabe* as well as being a professor of Native American Literature at the University of California at Berkeley.
7. Kant also uses the term *die Leserwelt*, "the reading public," when alluding to the public realm. He meant by this the discriminating public that participated in political, religious, and cultural conversation and critique, that is, the readers of various popular and scholarly journals and writers (p.c. William Clohesy).
8. A key resource for arguments about the information-basis of much of the new economy is Castells (1996). An education policy proponent, building upon arguments about the new economy, put the danger of social inequalities in this fashion: "The basic paradigm shift is from an educational emphasis on people as recipients of information and knowledge to an emphasis on people as participants in the creation of information and knowledge. In a knowledge-based society and economy, intellectual capital is the means of production; its distribution is in large part a function of how we are educated. The overarching choice we will face nationally and globally is to decide what proportion of people will experience a level and kind of education that will enable them to participate as producers of knowledge as well as its consumers" (Hunt, cited in Tyner, 1998 p. 85).
9. Perhaps Goody's most useful formulation on "technology" is that it involves an interaction: "When one regards the processes of writing and reading as interactive – me, within, interacting with what is without, either your words or my words on a piece of paper – then the boundaries between the internal and the external, the material and the immaterial, dissolve or need to be reformulated" (2000, p. 148). But such interactions, such dissolving of boundaries between internal and external,

between material and immaterial, leave one rather close to situated or sociocultural views of literacy. And these lead to the following from Gee (1996, p. 42), who is arguing against an autonomous or technicist view of literacy: "literacy in and of itself, abstracted from historical conditions and social practices, has no effects, or at least no predictable effects."

REFERENCES

Achebe, C. (1975). Language and the Destiny of Man, *Morning Yet on Creation Day* (pp. 39–49). Garden City, NY: Anchor Books.

Adams, M. (1993). *Beginning to Read: Thinking and Learning about Print*. Cambridge, MA: MIT Press.

Adorno, R. (1985). The Rhetoric of Resistance: the "Talking" Book of Felipe Guaman Poma. *History of European Ideas, 6*, 447–464.

Adorno, R. (1989a). Arms, Letters and the Native Historian in Early Colonial Mexico. In R. Jara and N. Spadaccini (eds.), *1492/1992: Re/Discovering Colonial Writing* (pp. 201–224). Minneapolis: The Prisma Institute.

Adorno, R. (1989b). The Warrior and the War Community: Constructions of the Civil Order in Mexican Conquest History. *Dispositio* (36–38), 225–246.

Allington, R., and Woodside-Giron, H. (1999). The Politics of Literacy Research: How "Research" Shaped Educational Policy. *Educational Researcher, 28*, 4–13.

Alverman, D. (2001). Reading Adolescents' Reading Identities: Looking Back to See Ahead. *Journal of Adolescent and Adult Literacy, 44*, 676–691.

Anderson, A., Teale, W., and Estrada, E. (1980). Low-Income Children's Preschool Literacy Experiences: Some Naturalistic Observations. *The Quarterly Newsletter of the Laboratory of Comparative Human Cognition, 2*, 59–65.

Anderson, B. (1991). *Imagined Communities: Reflections on the Origin and Spread of Nationalism*, 2nd edition. London: Verso.

Anderson, R., and Pearson, P. D. (1984). A Schema-Theoretic View of Basic Processes in Reading Comprehension. In P. D. Pearson (ed.), *Handbook of Reading Research* (vol. 1, pp. 255–291). New York: Longman.

Apple, M. (1987). *Teachers and Texts: a Political Economy of Gender and Class Relations in Education*. New York: Routledge and Kegan Paul.

Apple, M. (1996). *Cultural Politics and Education*. New York: Teachers College Press.

Arnove, R. (1980). The Nicaraguan National Literacy Crusade of 1980. *Phi Delta Kappan, 62*, 702–706.

Aronowitz, S., and Giroux, H. (1985). *Education Under Siege: the Conservative, Liberal and Radical Debate Over Schooling*. South Hadley, MA: Bergin and Garvey.

Arrom, J. J. (1992). Fray Ramón Pané, Discoverer of the Taino People. In R. Jara and N. Spadaccini (eds.), *Amerindian Images and the Legacy of Columbus* (pp. 266–290). Minneapolis: University of Minnesota Press.

Asad, T. (1990). Multiculturalism and British Identity in the Wake of the Rushdie Affair. *Politics and Society, 18*(4), 455–480.

Asad, T. (1992). Conscripts of Western Civilization. In C. Gailey (ed.), *Dialectical Anthropology: Essays in Honor of Stanley Diamond*, vol. 1: *Civilization in Crisis:*

Anthropological Perspectives (pp. 333–351). Gainesville, FL: University Press of Florida.

Asad, T. (1993). *Genealogies of Religion*. Baltimore, MD: Johns Hopkins University Press.

Babb, V. (1993). Liberation and Literacy: Literacy and Empowerment. In S. Miller and B. McCaskill (eds.), *Multicultural Literature and Literacies* (pp. 37–54). Albany: State University of New York Press.

Baines, J. (1988). Literacy, Social Organization, and the Archaelogical Record: the Case of Early Egypt. In J. Gledhill, B. Bender, and M. T. Larsen (eds.), *State and Society: the Emergence and Development of Social Hierarchy and Political Centralization* (pp. 192–214). London: Unwin and Hyman.

Baker, H. (1984). *Blues, Ideology, and Afro-American Literature: a Vernacular Theory*. Chicago: University of Chicago Press.

Baker, H. (1988). *Afro-American Poetics: Revisions of Harlem and the Black Aesthetic*. Madison: University of Wisconsin Press.

Bakhtin, M. (1981). *The Dialogic Imagination*. Austin: University of Texas Press.

Barker-Benfield, G. (1993). *The Culture of Sensibility*. Chicago: University of Chicago Press.

Barton, D., and Ivanič, R. (eds.) (1991). *Writing in the Community*. Newbury Park, CA: Sage.

Bassard, J. (1992). Gender and Genre: Black Women's Autobiography and the Ideology of Literacy. *African American Review, 26*, 119–129.

Basso, K. (1990a). A Western Apache Writing System: the Symbols of Silas John, *Western Apache Language and Culture* (pp. 25–52). Tucson: University of Arizona Press.

Basso, K. H. (1990b). *Western Apache Language and Culture*. Tucson: University of Arizona Press.

Baugh, J. (1999). *Out of the Mouths of Slaves: African American Language and Educational Malpractice*. Austin, TX: University of Texas Press.

Bauman, R. (1986). *Story, Performance, and Event: Contextual Studies of Oral Narrative*. New York: Cambridge University Press.

Bauman, R. (1996). Transformations of the Word in the Production of Mexican Festival Drama. In M. Silverstein and G. Urban (eds.), *Natural Histories of Discourse* (pp. 301–328). Chicago: University of Chicago Press.

Bauman, R., and Briggs, C. L. (1990). Poetics and Performance as Critical Perspectives on Language and Social Life. *Annual Review of Anthropology, 19*, 59–88.

Bauman, Z. (1992). *Intimations of Postmodernity*. New York: Routledge.

Bauman, Z. (1997). *Postmodernity and Its Discontents*. New York: Routledge.

Bennett, W. (1996). *The Book of Virtues*. New York: Simon and Schuster.

Bernstein, B. (1996). *Pedagogy, Symbolic Control and Identity*. London: Taylor and Francis.

Besnier, N. (1995). *Literacy, Emotion, and Authority: Reading and Writing on a Polynesian Atoll*. New York: Cambridge University Press.

Bialostok, S. (1999). *Discourses of Literacy: Cultural Models of White, Urban, Middle-Class Parents of Kindergarten Children*. University of Arizona, Tucson, AZ.

Biber, D. (1988). *Variation Across Speech and Writing*. New York: Cambridge University Press.

Biber, D. (1995). *Dimensions of Register Variation: a Cross-Linguistic Comparison*. New York: Cambridge University Press.

Bigler, E. (1996). Telling Stories: On Ethnicity, Exclusion, and Education in Upstate New York. *Anthropology and Education Quarterly, 27*(2), 186–203.

Bledsoe, C., and Robey, K. (1993). Arabic Literacy and Secrecy Among the Mende of Sierra Leone. In B. Street (ed.), *Crosscultural Approaches to Literacy* (pp. 110–134). Cambridge: Cambridge University Press.

Bloch, M. (1961). *Feudal Society*. Chicago: University of Chicago Press.

Bloch, M. (1975). *Political Language and Oratory in Traditional Society*. New York: Academic Press.

Bloch, M. (1989). Literacy and Enlightenment. In K. Schousboe and M. T. Larsen (eds.), *Literacy and Society* (pp. 15–38). Copenhagen: Akademisk Forlag.

Bloch, M. (1993). The Uses of Schooling and Literacy in a Zafimaniry Village. In B. V. Street (ed.), *Crosscultural approaches to literacy* (pp. 87–109). Cambridge: Cambridge University Press.

Bloch, M. (1998). *How We Think They Think*. Boulder, CO: Westview.

Blommaert, J. (1999). *State Ideology and Language in Tanzania*. Cologne: Rudiger Koppe Verlag.

Boas, F. (1911). *The Mind of Primitive Man*. New York: Free Press.

Bommelyn, L. (1994). Tolowa. In M. Davis (ed.), *Native Americans in the Twentieth Century: an Encyclopedia* (pp. 639–640). New York: Garland Press.

Bommelyn, L., and Humphrey, B. (1984). *The Tolowa Language*. Arcata, CA: Center for Community Development, Humboldt State University.

Bommelyn, L., and Humphrey, B. (1989). *Xus We-Yo': Tolowa Language*, 2nd edition. Crescent City, CA: Tolowa Language Committee.

Bourdieu, P. (1977). *Outline of a Theory of Practice*. Cambridge: Cambridge University Press.

Bourdieu, P. (1984). *Distinction: a Social Critique of the Judgement of Taste*. Cambridge, MA: Harvard University Press.

Bourdieu, P. (1991). *Language and Symbolic Power* (John Thompson, trans.). Cambridge, MA: Harvard University Press.

Bourdieu, P., Boltanski, L., Passeron, J.-C., and Martin, M. S. (1993). *Academic Discourse*. New York: Columbia University Press.

Bourdieu, P., and Passeron, J.-C. (1977). *Reproduction in Education, Society, and Culture*. Beverly Hills: Sage.

Bowles, S., and Gintis, H. (1976). *Schooling in Capitalist America*. New York: Basic Books.

Boyarin, D. (1993). Placing Reading: Ancient Israel and Medieval Europe. In J. Boyarin (ed.), *The Ethnography of Reading* (pp. 10–37). Berkeley: University of California Press.

Boyarin, J. (ed.). (1993a). *The Ethnography of Reading*. Berkeley: University of California Press.

Boyarin, J. (1993b). Voices Around the Text: the Ethnography of Reading at Mesivta Tifereth Jerusalem. In J. Boyarin (ed.), *The Ethnography of Reading* (pp. 212–237). Berkeley: University of California Press.

Brandau, D., and Collins, J. (1994). Texts, Social Relations, and Work-Based Skepticism about Schooling: an Ethnographic Analysis. *Anthropology and Education Quarterly, 25*(2), 118–137.

Brenneis, D., and Myers, F. (eds.). (1986). *Dangerous Words: Language and Politics in the Pacific*. Prospect Heights, IL: Waveland Press.

Briggs, C. (1993). Generic Versus Metapragmatic Dimensions of Warao Narratives: Who Regiments Performance. In J. A. Lucy (ed.), *Reflexive Language: Reported Speech and Metapragmatics* (pp. 179–212). Cambridge: Cambridge University Press.

Briggs, C. (1998). "You're a Liar – Just Like a Woman!": Constructing Dominant Ideologies of Language in Warao Men's Gossip. In B. Schieffelin, K. Woolard, and

P. Kroskrity (eds.), *Language Ideologies* (pp. 229–255). Oxford: Oxford University Press.

Bright, J. (1964). The Phonology of Smith River Athapaskan (Tolowa). *International Journal of American Linguistics, 30*(2), 101–108.

Brody, J. (1996). The New Literacy. *Journal of Linguistic Anthropology, 6*, 96–105.

Burke, P. (1988). The Uses of Literacy in Early Modern Italy. In P. Burke and R. Porter (eds.), *The Social History of Language* (pp. 21–42). Cambridge: Cambridge University Press.

Burkhart, L. (1996). *Holy Wednesday: a Nahua Drama from Early Colonial Mexico.* Philadelphia: University of Pennsylvania Press.

Burkhart, L. (2000). The Native Translator as Critic: a Nahua Playwright's Interpretive Practice. In R. St. George (ed.), *Possible Pasts: Becoming Colonial in Early America* (pp. 73–87). Ithaca, NY: Cornell University Press.

Burroughs, E. R. (1963). *Tarzan of the Apes.* New York: Ballantine.

Camitta, M. (1993). Vernacular Writing: Varieties of Literacy Among Philadelphia High School Students. In B. Street (ed.), *Cross-Cultural Approaches to Literacy* (pp. 228–246). New York: Cambridge University Press.

Canada, O. S. (1996). *Literacy, Economy and Society.* Ottowa: OECD.

Carruthers, M. (1990). *The Book of Memory: a Study of Memory in Medieval Culture.* Evanston, IL: Northwestern University Press.

Castells, M. (1996). *The Rise of the Network Society.* Oxford: Blackwell.

Cazden, C. (1988). *Classroom Discourse.* Cambridge, MA: Harvard University Press.

Cazden, C., and Dickinson, D. (1981). Language in Education: Standardization versus Cultural Pluralism. In C. Ferguson and S. Heath (eds.), *Language in the USA* (pp. 446–468). New York: Cambridge University Press.

Chartier, R. (1988). Figures of the "Other": Peasant Reading in the Age of Enlightenment. In R. Chartier (ed.), *Cultural History* (pp. 151–171). Ithaca, NY: Cornell University Press.

Chartier, R. (1989a). The Practical Impact of Writing. In R. Chartier (ed.), *A History of Private Life*, vol. 3: *Passions of the Renaissance* (pp. 111–159). Cambridge, MA: Harvard University Press.

Chartier, R. (1989b). Leisure and Sociability: Reading Aloud in Early Modern Europe. In S. Zimmerman and R. Weissman (eds.), *Urban Life in the Renaissance* (pp. 103–120). Newark, DE: University of Delaware Press.

Chartier, R. (1989c). *Text, Printing, Readings.* In L. Hunt (ed.), *The New Cultural History* (pp. 154–175). Berkeley: University of California Press.

Chartier, R. (1995). *Forms and Meanings: Texts, Performances, and Audiences from Codex to Computer.* Philadelphia: University of Pennsylvania Press.

Chiseri-Strater, E. (1991). *Academic Literacies: the Public and Private Discourse of University Students.* Portsmouth, NH: Boynton Cook.

Chomsky, N. (1988). *Language and Problems of Knowledge.* Cambridge, MA: MIT Press.

Cipolla, C. (1969). *Literacy and Development in the West.* Harmondsworth, Middlesex: Penguin.

Clanchy, M. (1979). *From Memory to Written Record: England, 1066–1307.* Cambridge, MA: Harvard University Press.

Clifford, J. (1988). *The Predicament of Culture: Twentieth-Century Ethnography, Literature, and Art.* Cambridge, MA: Harvard University Press.

Cmiel, K. (1990). *Democratic Eloquence: the Fight Over Popular Speech in Nineteenth-Century America.* New York: William Morrow & Company.

Cochran-Smith, M. (1984). *The Making of a Reader.* Norwood, NJ: Ablex.

Cochran-Smith, M. (1986). Reading to Children: A Model for Understanding Texts. In B. Schieffelin and P. Gilmore (eds.), *The Acquisition of Literacy: Ethnographic Perspectives* (pp. 35–54). Norwood, NJ: Ablex Publishing Corporation.

Colby, G. (1995). *Thy Will Be Done: the Conquest of the Amazon: Nelson Rockefeller and Evangelism in the Age of Oil*. New York: HarperCollins.

Cole, M., and Scribner, S. (1981). *The Psychology of Literacy*. Cambridge, MA: Harvard University Press.

Coleman, J. (1996). *Public Reading and the Reading Public in Late Medieval England and France*. New York: Cambridge University Press.

Coles, G. (1998). *Reading Lessons: the Debate Over Literacy*. New York: Hill and Wang.

Coles, G. (2000). *Misreading Reading: the Bad Science that Hurts Children*. Portsmouth, NH: Heinemann.

Collins, J. (1986). Differential Instruction in Reading Groups. In J. Cook-Gumperz (ed.), *The Social Construction of Literacy* (pp. 117–137). New York: Cambridge University Press.

Collins, J. (1988). Language and Class in Minority Education. *Anthropology and Education Quarterly, 19*(4), 299–326.

Collins, J. (1989). Hegemonic Practice: Literacy and Standard Language in Public Education. *Journal of Education, 171*(2), 9–35.

Collins, J. (1996). Socialization to Text: Structure and Contradiction in Schooled Literacy. In M. Silverstein and G. Urban (eds.), *Natural Histories of Discourse* (pp. 203–228). Chicago: University of Chicago Press.

Collins, J. (1998a). Our Ideologies and Theirs. In B. Schieffelin, K. Woolard, and P. Kroskrity (eds.), *Language Ideologies* (pp. 156–170). New York: Oxford University Press.

Collins, J. (1998b). *Understanding Tolowa Histories: Western Hegemonies and Native American Responses*. New York: Routledge.

Collins, J. (1999). The Ebonics Controversy in Context: Literacies, Subjectivities, and Language Ideologies in the United States. In J. Blommaert (ed.), *Language Ideological Debates* (pp. 201–234). New York: Mouton de Gruyter.

Comaroff, J., and Comaroff, J. (1992). *Ethnography and the Historical Imagination*. Boulder, CO: Westview Press.

Cook-Gumperz, J. (1986). Literacy and Schooling: an Unchanging Equation? In J. Cook-Gumperz (ed.), *The Social Construction of Literacy* (pp. 16–44). New York: Cambridge University Press.

Coontz, S. (1992). *The Way We Never Were*. New York: Basic Books.

Cott, N. (ed.). (2000). *No Small Courage: a History of Women in the United States*. Oxford: Oxford University Press.

Crappanzano, V. (1996). "Self"-Centering Narratives. In M. Silverstein and G. Urban (eds.), *Natural Histories of Discourse* (pp. 106–131). Chicago and London: University of Chicago.

Cremin, L. (1976). *Traditions of American Education*. New York: Basic Books.

Crosby, A. (1997). *The Measure of Reality*. New York: Cambridge University Press.

Damon-Moore, H., and Kaestle, C. (1991). Gender, Advertising, and Mass-Circulation Magazines. In C. Kaestle (ed.), *Literacy in the United States: Readers and Reading Since 1880* (pp. 245–271). New Haven: Yale.

Danziger, K. (1990). *Constructing the Subject: Historical Origins of Psychological Research*. New York: Cambridge University Press.

Davis, N. (1975). *Society and Culture in Early Modern France: Eight Essays*. Stanford, CA: Stanford University Press.

de Castell, S., and Luke, A. (1983). Defining "Literacy" in North American Schools. *Journal of Curriculum Studies, 15*, 373–389.

de Castell, S., and Walker, T. (1991). Identity, Metamorphosis and Ethnographic Research: What Kind of Story Is "Ways with Words"? *Anthropology and Education Quarterly, 22*, 3–20.

de Certeau, M. (1984). *The Practice of Everyday Life*. Berkeley: University of California.

de Tocqueville, A. (1969). *Democracy in America*. Garden City, NY: Anchor Books.

Deloria, V., and Lytle, C. (1983). *American Indian, American Justice*. Austin: University of Texas Press.

Delpit, L., and Perry, T. (eds.). (1998). *The Real Ebonics Debate: Power, Language, and the Education of African-American Children*. New York: Beacon.

Derrida, J. (1976a). *Of Grammatology*. Baltimore: Johns Hopkins University Press.

Derrida, J. (1976b). Of the Supplement to the Source: the Theory of Writing, *Of Grammatology* (pp. 269–316). Baltimore: Johns Hopkins University Press.

Derrida, J. (1976c). The Violence of the Letter: from Levi-Strauss to Rousseau, *Of Grammatology* (pp. 101–140). Baltimore: Johns Hopkins University Press.

Derrida, J. (1976d). *Writing and Difference*. Chicago: University of Chicago.

Derrida, J. (1996). *Archive Fever*. Chicago: University of Chicago Press.

Diamond, J. (1999). *Guns, Germs, and Steel: the Fates of Human Societies*. New York: W. W. Norton.

Diamond, S. (1974a). *In Search of the Primitive: a Critique of Civilization*. New Brunswick, NJ: Transaction Books.

Diamond, S. (1974b). The Rule of Law versus the Order of Custom, *In Search of the Primitive: a Critique of Civilization* (pp. 255–280). New Brunswick, NJ: Transaction Books.

Díaz del Castillo, B. (1956). *The Discovery and Conquest of Mexico, 1517–1527*. New York: Farrar, Straus and Cydahy.

Digges, D., and Rappaport, J. (1993). Literacy, Orality, and Ritual Practice in Highland Colombia. In J. Boyarin (ed.), *The Ethnography of Reading* (pp. 139–155). Berkeley: University of California Press.

Donald, J. (1983). How Illiteracy Became a Problem (and Literacy Stopped Being One). *Journal of Education, 165*(1), 35–52.

Dorsey, J. O. (1889). Indians of Siletz Reservation, Oregon. n.s. *American Anthropologist, 2*, 55–60.

Douglass, F. (1995). *The Education of Frederick Douglass*. New York: Penguin.

Drucker, P. (1937). The Tolowa and their Southwest Oregon Kin. *University of California Publications in American Archeology and Ethnology, 36*, 221–300.

Dunn, O., and Kelley, J. (1989). *The Diario of Christopher Columbus' First Voyage to America, 1492–1493*. Norman, OK: University of Oklahoma Press.

Duranti, A., and Ochs, E. (1986). Literacy Instruction in a Samoan Village. In B. Schieffelin and P. Gilmore (eds.), *The Acquisition of Literacy: Ethnographic Perspectives* (pp. 213–232). Norwood, NJ: Ablex.

Durkheim, E. (1960). *The Division of Labor in Society*. Glencoe, IL: Free Press.

Edelsky, C. (1996). *With Literacy and Justice For All: Rethinking the Social in Language and Education*. London: Taylor and Francis.

Eder, D. (1986). Organizational Constraints on Reading Group Mobility. In J. Cook-Gumperz (ed.), *The Social Construction of Literacy*. New York: Cambridge University Press.

Edmondson, J. (2000). *America Reads: a Critical Policy Analysis*. Newark, DE: International Reading Association.

Eisenstein, E. (1968). Some Conjectures about the Impact of Printing on Western Society and Thought: a Preliminary Report. *Journal of Modern History, 40*, 1–57.

Eisenstein, E. (1980). *The Printing Press as an Agent of Change: Communications and Cultural Transformations in Early-Modern Europe*. Cambridge: Cambridge University Press.

Ellis, C. (1996). *To Change Them Forever: Indian Education at the Rainy Mountain Boarding School, 1893–1920*. Norman, OK: University of Oklahoma Press.

Erickson, F. (1984). Rhetoric, Anecdote, and Rhapsody: Coherence Strategies in a Conversation Among Black Adolescents. In D. Tannen (ed.), *Coherence in Spoken and Written Discourse* (pp. 81–154). Norwood, NJ: Ablex Publishing Corporation.

Erikson, E. H. (1959). *Identity and the Life Cycle*. New York: International Universities Press.

Fabian, J. (1991). *Language and Colonial Power: the Appropriation of Swahili in the Former Belgian Congo 1880–1938*. Berkeley: University of California Press.

Fabian, J. (1993). Keep Listening: Ethnography and Reading. In J. Boyarin (ed.), *The Ethnography of Reading* (pp. 80–97). Berkeley: University of California Press.

Fairclough, N. (1992). *Discourse and Social Change*. Cambridge: Polity Press.

Farkas, G. (1996). *Human Capital or Cultural Capital? Ethnicity and Poverty Groups in an Urban School District*. New York: Mouton de Gruyter.

Fenigsen, J. (2000). Regimes of Inequality: Linguistic Ideologies and Practices in Barbados. Unpublished Dissertation, Brandeis University, Waltham, MA.

Fingaret, A. (1983). Social Network: a New Perspective on Independence and Illiterate Adults. *Adult Education Quarterly, 33*(3), 133–4.

Finnegan, R. (1976). What is Oral Literature Anyway? Comments in the Light of Some African and Other Comparative Material. In B. Stolz and R. Shannon (eds.), *Oral Literature and the Formula* (pp. 127–176). Ann Arbor, MI: Center for the Coordination of Ancient and Modern Studies.

Finnegan, R. (ed.) (1978). *A World Treasury of Oral Poetry*. Bloomington: Indiana University Press.

Finnegan, R. (1988). *Literacy and Orality*. Oxford and New York: Basil Blackwell.

Fischer, C. (1996). *Inequality by Design: Cracking the Bell Curve Myth*. Princeton, NJ: Princeton University Press.

Foley, D. (1990). *Learning Capitalist Culture: Deep in the Heart of Tejas*. Philadelphia: University of Pennsylvania Press.

Foley, D. (1995). *The Heartland Chronicles*. Philadelphia: University of Pennsylvania Press.

Foley, W. (1997a). Literacy, *Anthropological Linguistics* (pp. 417–434). Oxford: Blackwell.

Foley, W. (1997b). Politeness, Face, and the Linguistic Construction of Personhood, *Anthropological Linguistics* (pp. 249–259). Oxford: Blackwell.

Foley, W. (1997c). Standard Languages and Linguistic Engineering, *Anthropological Linguistics* (pp. 398–416). Oxford: Blackwell.

Foucault, M. (1975). *Discipline and Punish*. New York: Random House.

Foucault, M. (1978). *The History of Sexuality: an Introduction*. New York: Vintage Books.

Foucault, M. (1982). Afterword: Subject and Power. In H. Dreyfus and P. Rabinow (eds.), *Michel Foucault: Beyond Structuralism and Hermeneutics* (pp. 208–226). New York: The Harvester Press.

Fox, M., and Baker, C. (1990). Adult Illiteracy in the United States: Rhetoric, Recipes and Reality. In J.-P. Hautecoeur (ed.), *ALPHA 90: Current Research in Literacy* (pp. 81–112). Hamburg: UNESCO Institute for Education.

Frake, C. (1985). Cognitive Maps of Time and Tide among Medieval Seafarers. *Man*, n.s. *20*, 254–271.

Franklin, B. (1964). *The Autobiography of Benjamin Franklin*. New Haven, CT: Yale University Press.

Fraser, N. (1989). *Unruly Practices: Power, Discourse, and Gender in Contemporary Social Theory*. Minneapolis, MN: University of Minnesota Press.

Freebody, P., and Welch, A. (eds.) (1993). *Knowledge, Culture and Power: International Perspectives on Literacy as Policy and Practice*. Philadelphia: Falmer Press.

Freire, P. (1972). *The Pedagogy of the Oppressed*. London: Penguin.

Friedman, J. (1994). *Cultural Identities and Global Process*. Thousand Oaks, CA: Sage Publications.

Friedmann, F. (1960). *The Hoe and the Book: an Italian Experiment in Community Development*. Ithaca, NY: Cornell University Press.

Gadsden, V., and Wagner, D. (eds.) (1995). *Literacy and African American Youth*. Cresskill, NJ: Hampton Press.

Gates, H. L. (ed.) (1986). *Race, Writing, and Difference*. Chicago: University of Chicago Press.

Gates, H. L. (ed.) (1990). *Reading Black, Reading Feminist: a Critical Anthology*. New York: Meridian.

Gee, J. (1996). *Social Linguistics and Literacies*, 2nd edition. London: Taylor and Maxwell.

Gelb, I. J. (1963). *A Study of Writing*, 2nd edition. Chicago: University of Chicago.

Gellner, E. (1983). *Nations and Nationalism*. Ithaca, NY: Cornell University Press.

Gibson, E., and Levin, H. (1975). *The Psychology of Reading*. Cambridge, MA: MIT Press.

Giddens, A. (1984). *The Constitution of Society*. Berkeley: University of California Press.

Giddens, A. (1991). *Modernity and Self-identity: Self and Society in the Late Modern Age*. Cambridge: Polity Press.

Gilmore, P. (1986). Sub-rosa Literacy: Peers, Play, and Ownership in Literacy Acquisition. In B. Schieffelin and P. Gilmore (eds.), *The Acquisition of Literacy: Ethnographic Perspectives* (pp. 155–168). Norwood, NJ: Ablex.

Gilroy, P. (1987). *There Ain't No Black in the Union Jack*. London: Hutchison.

Gilyard, J. (1991). *Voices of the Self*. Detroit: Wayne State University Press.

Ginzburg, C. (1982). *The Cheese and the Worms: the Cosmos of a Sixteenth-Century Miller*. New York: Penguin Books.

Goddard, I. (1996). The Description of the Native Languages of North America before Boas. In I. Goddard (ed.), *Handbook of North American Indians 17: Language* (pp. 17–42). Washington: Smithsonian Institution.

Goddard, P. (1909–11a). Unpublished field notebooks on Tolowa lexicon and grammar. Library of the American Philosophical Society. Philadelphia, PA.

Goddard, P. (1909–11b). Unpublished typescripts of Tolowa stories. Archives of the Bancroft Library, University of California at Berkeley.

Goelman, H., Oberg, A., and Smith, F. (eds.) (1984). *Awakening to Literacy*. Portsmouth, NH: Heinemann Educational Books.

Goldman, E. (1970). *Living My Life*. New York: Da Capo Press.

Goody, E. (1977). Towards a Theory of Questions. In E. Goody (ed.), *Questions and Politeness: Strategies in Social Interaction* (pp. 17–43). Cambridge: Cambridge University Press.

Goody, J. (1968). Restricted Literacy in Northern Ghana. In J. Goody (ed.), *Literacy in Traditional Society* (pp. 198–264). Cambridge: Cambridge University Press.

Goody, J. (1977). *The Domestication of the Savage Mind*. Cambridge: Cambridge University Press.

Goody, J. (1982). Alternative Paths to Knowledge in Oral and Literate Cultures. In D. Tannen (ed.), *Spoken and Written Language: Exploring Orality and Literacy* (pp. 201–215). Norwood, NJ: Ablex.

Goody, J. (1986). *The Logic of Writing and the Organization of Society.* Cambridge: Cambridge University Press.

Goody, J. (1987). *The Interface Between the Written and the Oral.* New York: Cambridge University Press.

Goody, J. (2000). *The Power of the Written Tradition.* Washington, DC: Smithsonian Institution.

Goody, J., and Watt, I. (1963). The Consequences of Literacy. *Comparative Studies in Society and History, 5*(3), 304–345.

Gough, K. (1968). Implications of Literacy in Traditional China and India. In J. Goody (ed.), *Literacy in Traditional Societies* (pp. 70–84). New York: Cambridge University Press.

Gould, R. (1978). Tolowa. In R. F. Heizer (ed.), *Handbook of North American Indians,* vol. 8: *California* (pp. 128–136). Washington, DC: Smithsonian Institution.

Gould, S. (1981). *The Mismeasure of Man.* New York: W. W. Norton.

Graff, H. (ed.). (1981a). *Literacy and Social Development in the West: a Reader.* Cambridge: Cambridge University Press.

Graff, H. (1981b). Literacy, Jobs, and Industrialization: the Nineteenth Century. In H. Graff (ed.), *Literacy and Social Development in the West: A Reader.* Cambridge: Cambridge University Press.

Graff, H. (1988). The Legacies of Literacy. In E. Kintgen, B. Knoll, and M. Rose (eds.), *Perspectives on Literacy* (pp. 82–94). Carbondale, IL: Southern Illinois University Press.

Graff, H. J. (1979). *The Literacy Myth.* New York: Academic Press.

Green, J. C. (1994). Misperspectives on Literacy: a Critique of an Anglocentric Bias in Histories of American Literacy. *Written Communication, 11*(2), 251–269.

Greenblatt, S. (1980). *Renaissance Self-Fashioning: from More to Shakespeare.* Chicago: University of Chicago Press.

Greenblatt, S. (1991). *Marvelous Possessions: the Wonder of the New World.* Chicago: University of Chicago Press.

Greenfield, P. (1972). Oral or Written Language: the Consequences for Cognitive Development in Africa, the United States, and England. *Language and Speech, 15,* 169–178.

Grenoble, L., and Whaley, L. (eds.) (1998). *Endangered Languages: Current Issues and Future Prospects.* Cambridge: Cambridge University Press.

Grinevald, C. (1998). Language Endangerment in South America: a Programmatic Approach. In L. Grenoble and L. Whaley (eds.), *Endangered Languages: Current Issues and Future Prospects* (pp. 124–159). Cambridge: Cambridge University Press.

Guillory, J. (1993). *Cultural Capital: the Problem of Literary Canon Formation.* Chicago and London: University of Chicago Press.

Gumperz, J. (1982). *Discourse Strategies.* New York: Cambridge University Press.

Gumperz, J., and Cook-Gumperz, J. (eds.) (1982). *Language and Social Identity.* New York: Cambridge University Press.

Guss, D. (1986). Keeping It Oral: Yekuana Ethnology. *American Ethnologist, 13,* 413–429.

Habermas, J. (1987). *Lifeworld and System: a Critique of Functionalist Reason. The Theory of Communicative Action,* vol. 2. Boston, MA: Beacon Press.

Habermas, J. (1989). *The Structural Transformation of the Public Sphere*. Cambridge, MA: MIT Press.

Hadas, M. (1954). *Ancilla to Classical Reading*. New York: Columbia University Press.

Hall, D. (1993). Readers and Reading in America: Historical and Critical Perspectives. *American Antiquarian Society, 103*, 337–357.

Hall, D. (1996). *Cultures of Print: Essays in the History of the Book*. Amherst, MA: University of Massachusetts Press.

Halverson, J. (1991). Olson on Literacy. *Language in Society, 20*, 619–640.

Halverson, J. (1992). Goody and the Implosion of the Literacy Thesis. *Man, 27*, 301–317.

Hanks, W. (1996a). Exorcism and the Description of Participant Roles. In M. Silverstein and G. Urban (eds.), *Natural Histories of Discourse* (pp. 160–200). Chicago: University of Chicago Press.

Hanks, W. F. (1996b). *Language and Communicative Practices*. Boulder, CO: Westview Press.

Harbsmeier, M. (1988). Inventions of Writing. In J. Gledhill, B. Bender, and M. T. Larsen (eds.), *State and Society: the Emergence and Development of Social Hierarchy and Political Centralization* (pp. 253–276). London: Unwin Hyman.

Hasan, R. (1998). The Disempowerment Game: Bourdieu and Language in Literacy. *Linguistics and Education, 10*, 25–80.

Havelock, E. (1963). *Preface to Plato*. Cambridge, MA: Harvard University Press.

Havelock, E. (1982a). *The Literate Revolution in Greece and Its Cultural Consequences*. Princeton, NJ: Princeton University Press.

Havelock, E. (1982b). Spoken Sound and Inscribed Sign, *The Literate Revolution in Greece and Its Cultural Consequences* (pp. 39–59). Princeton, NJ: Princeton University Press.

Havelock, E. (1986). *The Muse Learns to Write: Reflections on Orality and Literacy from Antiquity to the Present*. New Haven, CT: Yale University Press.

Heath, S. B. (1972). *Telling Tongues: Language Policy in Mexico, Colony to Nation*. New York: Teachers College Press.

Heath, S. B. (1981). English in Our Language Heritage. In C. Ferguson and S. Heath (eds.), *Language in the U.S.A.* (pp. 6–20). Cambridge: Cambridge University Press.

Heath, S. B. (1982a). Protean Shapes in Literacy Events: Ever Shifting Oral and Literate Traditions. In D. Tannen (ed.), *Spoken and Written Language: Exploring Literacy and Orality* (pp. 91–118). Norwood, NJ: Ablex.

Heath, S. B. (1982b). Questioning at Home and at School: a Comparative Study. In G. Spindler (ed.), *Doing the Ethnography of Schooling: Educational Anthropology in Action* (pp. 102–131). New York: Holt, Rinehart and Winston.

Heath, S. B. (1982c). What No Bedtime Story Means: Narrative Skills at Home and at School. *Language in Society, 11*(2), 49–76.

Heath, S. B. (1983). *Ways with Words: Language, Life, and Work in Communities and Classrooms*. New York: Cambridge University Press.

Heath, S. B. (1986). The Functions and Uses of Literacy. In S. de Castell, A. Luke, and K. Egan (eds.), *Literacy, Society, and Schooling* (pp. 15–26). New York: Cambridge University Press.

Heller, M. (ed.) (1988). *Codeswitching*. Berlin: Mouton de Gruyter.

Herrnstein, R., and Murray, C. (1994). *The Bell Curve: Intelligence and Class Structure in American Life*. New York: Free Press.

Herzfeld, M. (1996). National Spirit or Breath of Nature? The Expropriation of Folk Positivism in the Discourse of Greek Nationalism. In M. Silverstein and G. Urban (eds.), *Natural Histories of Discourse* (pp. 277–300). Chicago: University of Chicago Press.

Hill, J. (2000). "Read My Article": Ideological Complexity and the Overdetermination of Promising in American Presidential Politics. In P. Kroskrity (ed.), *Regimes of Language: Ideologies, Polities, and Identities* (pp. 259–292). Santa Fe, NM: School of American Research Press.

Hill, R. (1991). The Social Uses of Writing among the Colonial Cakchiquel Maya: Nativism, Resistance, and Innovation. In D. Thomas (ed.), *Columbian Consequences*, vol. 3: *The Spanish Borderlands in Pan-American Perspective* (pp. 283–299). Washington, DC: Smithsonian Institution Press.

Hirsch, E. (1987). *Cultural Literacy: What Every American Needs to Know*. Boston: Houghton Mifflin.

Hirschfield, L., and Gelman, S. (eds.). (1994). *Mapping the Mind: Domain Specificity in Cognition and Culture*. Cambridge: Cambridge University Press.

Hobart, M., and Schiffman, Z. (1998). *Information Ages: Literacy, Numeracy, and the Computer Revolution*. Baltimore, MD: Johns Hopkins University Press.

Hobsbawm, E. (1996). *The Age of Extremes*. New York: Vintage.

Hoggart, R. (1957). *The Uses of Literacy*. London: Chatto and Windus.

Holdaway, D. (1979). *The Foundations of Literacy*. New York: Ashton Scholastic.

Hornberger, N. (ed.) (1997). *Indigenous Literacies in the Americas: Language Planning from the Bottom Up*. Berlin: Mouton De Gruyter.

Howard, U. (1991). Self, Education, and Writing in Nineteenth-Century English Communities. In D. Barton and R. Ivanič (eds.), *Writing in the Community* (pp. 78–108). Newbury Park, CA: Sage.

Howard-Malverde, R. (ed.) (1997). *Creating Contexts in Andean Cultures*. New York: Oxford University Press.

Howe, N. (1993). The Cultural Construction of Reading in Anglo-Saxon England. In J. Boyarin (ed.), *The Ethnography of Reading* (pp. 58–79). Berkeley: University of California Press.

Hymes, D. (1972). Models of the Interaction of Language and Social Life. In J. Gumperz and D. Hymes (eds.), *Directions in Sociolinguistics: the Ethnography of Communication* (pp. 35–71). New York: Holt, Rinehart, Winston.

Illich, I., and Sanders, B. (1988). *The Alphabetization of the Popular Mind*. San Francisco: North Point Press.

Irvine, J. (1996). Shadow Conversations: the Indeterminacy of Participant Roles. In M. Silverstein and G. Urban (eds.), *Natural Histories of Discourse* (pp. 131–159). Chicago: University of Chicago Press.

Jaimes, M. A. (1992). Federal Indian Identification Policy: A Usurpation of Indigenous Sovereignty in North America. In M. A. Jaimes (ed.), *The State of Native America* (pp. 123–138). Boston: South End Press.

Jencks, C. (1972). *Inequality: a Reassessment of the Effect of Family and Schooling in America*. New York: Basic Books.

Jenkins, R. (1996). *Social Identity*. London: Routledge.

Johnston, P. (1997). *Knowing Literacy: Constructive Literacy Assessment*. York, ME: Stenhouse Publishers.

Jones, L. (1963). *Blues People: Negro Music in White America*. New York: Wm Morrow.

Jordan, J. (1988). Ain't Nobody Mean More to Me than You: or the Future Life of Willie Jordan. *Harvard Education Review, 58*, 363–374.

Justeson, J. (1989). The Representational Conventions of Mayan Hieroglyphic Writing. In W. Hanks and D. Rice (eds.), *Word and Image in Maya Culture: Explorations in Language, Writing, and Representation* (pp. 25–38). Salt Lake City: University of Utah Press.

Justeson, J., and Mathews, P. (1990). Evolutionary Trends in Mesoamerican Hiero-
    glyphic Writing. *Visible Language, 24*(1), 88–129.
Kaestle, C. (1991). Studying the History of Literacy. In C. Kaestle (ed.), *Literacy in the
    United States: Readers and Reading Since 1880* (pp. 3–32). New Haven, CT: Yale
    University Press.
Kaestle, C., Stedman, L., Tinsley, K., and Trollinger, W. (1991). *Literacy in the United
    States: Readers and Reading since 1880.* New Haven: Yale University Press.
Karttunen, F. (1982). Nahuatl Literacy. In G. Collier, R. Rosaldo, and J. Wirth (eds.),
    The Inca and Aztec States, 1400–1800: Anthropology and History (pp. 395–417).
    New York: Academic Press.
Katz, M. (1969). *The Irony of Early School Reform.* Cambridge, MA: Harvard University
    Press.
Kay, D. (1998). *Literacy Shutdown.* Newark, DE: International Reading Association.
King, L. (1994). *Roots of Identity: Language and Literacy in Mexico.* Stanford, CA:
    Stanford University Press.
Kintgen, E., Kroll, B., and Rose, M. (eds.) (1988). *Perspectives on Literacy.* Carbondale,
    IL: Southern Illnois University Press.
Kirsch, I., and Jungeblut, A. (1986). *Literacy: Profiles of America's Young Adults: Final
    Report.* Princeton, NJ: National Assessment of Educational Progress, Educational
    Testing Service.
Kontopoulos, K. (1993). *The Logics of Social Structure.* New York: Cambridge Univer-
    sity Press.
Kozol, J. (1978). A New Look at the Literacy Campaign in Cuba. *Harvard Educational
    Review, 48*, 341–377.
Kristeva, J. (1993). *Nations without Nationalism* (Leon Roudiez, trans.). New York:
    Columbia University Press.
Kroskrity, P. (1999). Identity. *Journal of Linguistic Anthropology, 9*(1), 111–114.
Kulick, D., and Stroud, C. (1993). Conceptions and Uses of Literacy in a Papua
    New Guinean Village. In B. Street (ed.), *Crosscultural Approaches to Literacy*
    (pp. 30–61). New York: Cambridge University Press.
Kuper, A. (1999). *Culture: the Anthropologists' Account.* Cambridge, MA: Harvard
    University Press.
Labov, W. (1972). *Sociolinguistic Patterns.* Philadelphia: University of Pennsylvania.
Labov, W. (1995). Can Reading Failure Be Reversed? In V. Gadsden and D. Wagner
    (eds.), *Literacy Among African-American Youth* (pp. 39–68). Cresskill, NJ:
    Hampton Press.
LaClau, E., and Mouffe, C. (1985). *Hegemony and Socialist Strategy.* London: Verso.
Lamont, M. (1998). *The Dignity of Work: Morality and the Boundaries of Race, Class
    and Immigration.* Cambridge, MA: Harvard.
Larsen, M. (1988). Introduction: Literacy and Social Complexity. In J. Gledhill,
    B. Bender, and M. T. Larsen (eds.), *State and Society: the Emergence and Devel-
    opment of Social Hierarchy and Political Centralization* (pp. 173–191). London:
    Unwin Hyman.
Lasch, C. (1991). *The True and Only Heaven.* New York: W. W. Norton.
Lasch, C. (1996). *The Revolt of the Elites and the Decline of American Democracy.* New
    York: W. W. Norton.
Lederman, R. (1986). Who Speaks Here? Gender and Power Among the Mende of Papua
    New Guinea. In D. Brenneis and F. Myers (eds.), *Dangerous Words: Language and
    Politics in the Pacific* (pp. 85–107). Prospect Heights, IL: Waveland.
Lee, D. (1976). What Price Literacy?, *Valuing the Self* (pp. 42–49). Englewood Cliffs,
    NJ: Prentice-Hall.

Lemann, N. (1997). The Reading Wars. *The Atlantic Monthly, 282* (November), 128–134.

Lepore, J. (1998). *The Name of the War: King Philip's War and the Origins of American Identity.* New York: Knopf.

Lévi-Bruhl, L. (1926). *How Natives Think.* Princeton, NJ: Princeton University Press.

Lévi-Strauss, C. (1964). *Tristes Tropiques.* New York: Atheneum.

Lévi-Strauss, C. (1966). *The Savage Mind.* Chicago: University of Chicago Press.

Lewontin, R. C. (2000). *It Ain't Necessarily So: the Dream of the Human Genome and Other Illusions.* New York: New York Review of Books.

Lightfoot, L. (1998). Schools Told How to Teach Reading. *The Daily Telegraph*, March 20, pp. 1, 2.

Lloyd, G. E. R. (1990). *Demystifying Mentalities.* Cambridge: Cambridge University Press.

Lockhart, J. (1982). Views of Corporate Self and History in Some Valley of Mexico Towns: Late 17th and 18th Centuries. In G. Collier, R. Rosaldo, and J. Wirth (eds.), *The Inca and Aztec States, 1400–1800: Anthropology and History* (pp. 367–393). New York: Academic Press.

Lockhart, J. (1992). *The Nahuas After the Conquest: a Social and Cultural History of the Indians of Central Mexico, Sixteenth through Eighteenth Centuries.* Stanford, CA: Stanford University Press.

Lofty, J. (1992). *Time to Write: the Influence of Time and Culture on Learning to Write.* Albany, NY: SUNY Press.

Long, E. (1993). Textual Interpretation as Collective Action. In J. Boyarin (ed.), *The Ethnography of Reading* (pp. 180–211). Berkeley: University of California Press.

Long, M. (2003). Ebonics, Language and Power. In R. Blot (ed.), *Language and Social Identity.* Westport CT: Bergin and Garvey.

López Maguiña, S. (1992). Colonial Writing and Indigenous Discourse in Ramón Pané's *Relación acerca de las antigüedades de los indios.* In R. Jara and N. Spadaccini (eds.), *Amerindian Images and the Legacy of Columbus* (pp. 291–311). Minneapolis: University of Minnesota Press.

Lounsbury, F. (1989). The Ancient Writing of Middle America. In W. Senner (ed.), *The Origins of Writing* (pp. 203–237). Lincoln: University of Nebraska Press.

Love, H. (1993). *Scribal Publication in Seventeenth-Century England.* New York: Oxford University Press.

Lowi, T. (1969). *The End of Liberalism: Ideology, Policy, and the Crisis of Public Authority.* New York: Norton.

Lucy, J. (ed.). (1993). *Reflexive Language: Reported Speech and Metapragmatics.* New York: Cambridge University Press.

Luke, A. (1993). The Body Literate. *Linguistics and Education, 4,* 107–129.

Luke, C. (1989). *Pedagogy, Printing, and Protestantism: the Discourse on Childhood.* Albany, NY: State University of New York Press.

Luttrell, W. (1996). Taking Care of Literacy: One Feminist's Critique. *Educational Policy, 3*(3), 342–365.

Luttrell, W. (1997). *Schoolsmart and Motherwise: Working-Class Women's Identity and Schooling.* New York: Routledge.

MacCabe, C. (1998). A Response to Brian Street. *English in Education, 32,* 26–28.

MacLeod, D. (1998). A Healthy Sense of Urgency. *Guardian Education*, February 24, pp. 4.

Macpherson, C. B. (1962). *The Political Theory of Possessive Individualism: Hobbes to Locke.* New York: Oxford University Press.

Marable, M. (1984). *Race, Reform, and Rebellion.* Jackson: University Press of Mississippi.

Marrou, H. I. (1956). *A History of Education in Antiquity* (George Lamb, trans.). New York: Sheed and Ward.

Marvin, C. (1984). Constructed and Reconstructed Discourse: Inscription and Talk in the History of Literacy. *Communications Research, 11*, 563–594.

Marvin, C. (1988). Attributes of Authority: Literacy Tests and the Logic of Strategic Conduct. *Communication, 11*, 63–82.

Matthiessen, P. (1984). *Indian Country*. New York: Viking Penguin.

McKenzie, D. (1987). The Sociology of a Text: Oral Culture, Literacy, and Print in Early New Zealand. In P. Burke and R. Porter (eds.), *The Social History of Language* (pp. 161–197). New York: Cambridge University Press.

Mehan, H. (1979). *Learning Lessons*. Cambridge, MA: Harvard University Press.

Menchú, R. (1984). *I, Rigoberta Menchú: an Indian Woman in Guatemala*. London: Verso.

Mertz, E. (1996). Recontextualization as Socialization: Texts and Pragmatics in the Law School Classroom. In M. Silverstein and G. Urban (eds.), *Natural Histories of Discourse* (pp. 229–250). Chicago: University of Chicago Press.

Mickelson, R. (1990). The Attitude-Achievement Paradox Among Black Adolescents. *Sociology of Education, 63*(1), 44–61.

Mickelson, R. (1992). Why Does Jane Read and Write So Well? The Anomaly of Women's Achievement. In J. Wrigley (ed.), *Education and Gender Equality* (pp. 149–171). Washington, DC: Falmer.

Mignolo, W. (1989). Literacy and Colonization: the New World Experience. In R. Jara and N. Spadaccini (eds.), *1492/1992: Re/Discovering Colonial Writing* (pp. 51–95). Minneapolis: The Prisma Institute.

Mignolo, W. (1992). On the Colonization of Amerindian Languages and Memories: Renaissance Theories of Writing and the Discontinuity of the Classical Tradition. *Comparative Studies in Society and History, 34*, 301–330.

Mignolo, W. (1995). *The Darker Side of the Renaissance: Literacy, Territoriality, and Colonization*. Ann Arbor, MI: University of Michigan Press.

Miller, P., Nemoianu, A., and DeJong, J. (1986). Early Reading at Home: Its Practice and Meanings in a Working Class Community. In B. Schieffelin and P. Gilmore (eds.), *The Acquisition of Literacy: Ethnographic Perspectives* (pp. 3–15). Norwood, NJ: Ablex.

Miller, W. (1997). *Richard Wright and the Library Card*. New York: Scholastic, Inc.

Mitchell-Kernan, C. (1970). On the Status of Black English for Native Speakers: an Assessment of Attitudes and Values. In C. Cazden, V. John, and D. Hymes (eds.), *Functions of Language in the Classroom* (pp. 195–210). New York: Teachers College Press.

Mitchell-Kernan, C. (1972). Signifying and Marking: Two Afro-American Speech Acts. In J. Gumperz and D. Hymes (eds.), *Directions in Sociolinguistics* (pp. 161–179). New York: Holt, Rinehart and Winston.

MOE. (1998). *National Literacy Strategy*. London: Ministry of Education.

Moghadam, V. M. (ed.) (1993). *Identity Politics and Women: Cultural Reassertions and Feminisms in International Perspective*. Boulder, CO: Westview Press.

Monaghan, J. (1989). Literacy Instruction and Gender in Colonial New England. In C. Davidson (ed.), *Reading in America: Literature and Social History* (pp. 53–80). Baltimore: Johns Hopkins University Press.

Monaghan, J. (1990). "She Loved to Read in Good Books": Literacy and the Indians of Martha's Vineyard, 1643–1725. *History of Education Quarterly, 30*, 493–521.

Moore, H. (2001). Telling What Is Real: Competing Views in Assessing ESL Development in Australia. In M. Heller and M. Martin-Jones (eds.), *Voices of Authority: Education and Linguistic Difference* (pp. 335–379). Westport, CT: Ablex.

Morgan, L. H. (1877). *Ancient Society*. Chicago: Charles H. Kerr & Co.

Morgan, M. (1994). The African-American Speech Community: Reality and Sociolinguistics. In M. Morgan (ed.), *Language and the Social Construction of Identity in Creole Situations* (pp. 121–148). Los Angeles: Center for Afro-American Studies, UCLA.

Morgan, M. (1998). More than a Mood or an Attitude: Discourse and Verbal Genre in African-American Culture. In S. Mufwene, J. Rickford, G. Bailey, and J. Baugh (eds.), *African-American English: Structure, History, and Use* (pp. 251–281). New York: Routledge.

Myers, M. (1996). *Changing Our Minds: Negotiating English and Literacy*. Urbana, IL: National Council of Teachers of English.

Nasaw, D. (1979). *Schooled to Order: A Social History of Public Schooling in the United States*. New York: Oxford University Press.

NCEE. (1983). *A Nation at Risk*. Washington, DC: The National Commission on Excellence in Education.

Nettle, D., and Romaine, S. (2000). *Vanishing Voices: the Extinction of the World's Languages*. New York: Oxford University Press.

Ngũgĩ wa Thiong'o (1986). *Decolonizing the Mind: the Politics of Language in African Literature*. Portsmouth, NH: Heinemann.

Nicholson, L. (1986). *Gender and History*. New York: Columbia University Press.

Oakes, J. (1985). *Keeping Track*. New Haven, CT: Yale University Press.

Ochs, E. (1986). From Feelings to Grammar: a Samoan Case Study. In B. B. Scheiffelin and E. Ochs (eds.), *Language Socialization Across Cultures* (pp. 251–272). Cambridge: Cambridge University Press.

O'Donnell, J. (1998). *Avatars of the Word: From Papyrus to Cyberspace*. Cambridge, MA: Harvard University Press.

Ogbu, J. (1979). *Minority Education and Caste: the American System in Crosscultural Perspective*. New York: Academic Press.

Ogbu, J. (1988). Literacy and Schooling in Subordinate Cultures: the Case of Black America. In E. Kintgen, B. Kroll, and M. Rose (eds.), *Perspectives on Literacy* (pp. 227–243). Carbondale: Southern Illinois University Press.

Ohmann, R. (1987). Literacy, Technology, and Monopoly Capital, *Politics of Letters* (pp. 230–235). Middletown: Wesleyan University Press.

Ohmann, R. (1996). *Selling Culture: Magazines, Markets, and Class at the Turn of the Century*. New York: Verso.

Olson, D. (1977). From Utterance to Text: the Bias of Language in Speech and Writing. *Harvard Education Review, 47*, 257–81.

Olson, D. (1994). *The World on Paper*. New York: Cambridge University Press.

O'Neil, W. (1998). If Ebonics Isn't a Language, Then Tell Me, What Is? In L. Delpit and T. Perry (eds.), *The Real Ebonics Debate* (pp. 38–47). Boston: Beacon.

Ong, W. (1982). *Orality and Literacy: the Technologizing of the Word*. London and New York: Methuen.

Ong, W. J. (1967). *The Presence of the Word: Some Prolegomena for Cultural and Religious History*. New Haven: Yale University Press.

Palmer, R. (1969). *Hermeneutics*. Evanston: Northwestern University Press.

Pateman, C. (1988). *The Sexual Contract*. New York: Cambridge University Press.

Patterson, O. (1997). *The Ordeal of Integration: Progress and Resentment in America's "Racial" Crisis*. Washington, DC: Civitas.

Perry, T. (1998). "I'on Know Why They Be Trippin'": Reflections on the Ebonics Debate. In L. Delpit and T. Perry (eds.), *The Real Ebonics Debate* (pp. 3–16). Boston: Beacon.

Philips, H. M. (1979). *Literacy and Development*. Paris: UNESCO.

Philips, S. (1993). *The Invisible Culture: Communication in Classroom and Community on the Warm Springs Indian Reservation*. Prospect Heights, IL: Waveland Press.

Polanyi, K. (1957). *The Great Transformation*. Boston: Beacon.

Pollit, K. (1993). *Reasonable Creatures*. New York: Knopf.

Postgate, J. N. (1992). *Early Mesopotamia: Society and Economy at the Dawn of History*. London: Routledge.

Powers, S. (1976). *Tribes of California*. Berkeley: University of California.

Pratt, M. (1987). Linguistic Utopias. In N. Fabb (ed.), *The Linguistics of Writing*. Manchester: Manchester University Press.

Prinsloo, M., and Breier, M. (eds.) (1996). *The Social Uses of Literacy: Theory and Practice in Contemporary South Africa*. Philadelphia: John Benjamins.

Probst, P. (1993). The Letter and the Spirit: Literacy and Religious Authority in the History of the Aladura Movement in Western Nigeria. In B. Street (ed.), *Cross-Cultural Approaches to Literacy* (pp. 198–220). New York: Cambridge University Press.

Puckett, A. (1992). "Let the Girls Do the Spelling and Dan Will Do the Shooting": Literacy, the Division of Labor, and Identity in a Rural Appalachian Community. *Anthropological Quarterly, 65*, 137–147.

Pulis, J. (1993). Up-full Sounds: Language, Identity, and the Worldview of Rastafari. *Ethnic Groups, 10*, 285–300.

Pulis, J. (1999). "Citing[Sighting]-Up": Words, Sounds, and Reading Scripture in Jamaica. In J. Pulis (ed.), *Religion, Diaspora, and Cultural Identity: a Reader in the Anglophone Caribbean* (pp. 357–401). Newark, NJ: Gordon and Breach.

Pulis, J. (forthcoming). *Gates to Zion: Voice, Text and Narrative in Jamaica*. London: Gordon and Breach.

Purcell-Gates, V. (1995). *Other People's Words*. Cambridge, MA: Harvard University Press.

Rabasa, J. (1993). Writing and Evangelization in Sixteenth-Century Mexico. In J. Williams and R. Lewis (eds.), *Early Images of the Americas: Transfer and Innovation* (pp. 65–92). Tucson: University of Arizona Press.

Rabinow, P. (1986). Representations are Social Facts: Modernity and Post-Modernity in Anthropology. In J. Clifford and G. Marcus (eds.), *Writing Culture: the Poetics and Politics of Ethnography* (pp. 194–233). Berkeley: University of California Press.

Radin, P. (1953). *The World of Primitive Man*. New York: H. Schuman.

Radin, P. (1957). *Primitive Man as Philosopher*. New York: Dover.

Radway, J. A. (1984). *Reading the Romance: Women, Patriarchy, and Popular Literature*. Chapel Hill, NC: University of North Carolina Press.

Rampton, B. (1995). *Crossing: Language and Ethnicity Among Adolescents*. London: Longman.

Rappaport, J. (1994). Object and Alphabet: Andean Indians and Documents in the Colonial Period. In E. H. Boone and W. Mignolo (eds.), *Writing without Words: Alternative Literacies in Mesoamerica and the Andes* (pp. 271–292). Durham, NC: Duke University Press.

Rappaport, J. (1998). *The Politics of Memory: Native Historical Interpretation in the Colombian Andes*. Durham, NC: Duke University Press.

Rappaport, J., and Cummins, T. (1997). Literacy and Power in Colonial Latin America. In G. Bond and A. Gilliam (eds.), *Social Construction of the Past: Representation as Power* (pp. 89–109). London: Routledge.

Reder, S. (1993). Literacy Development and Ethnicity: an Alaskan Example. In B. Street (ed.), *Cross-Cultural Perspectives on Literacy*. (pp. 176–197). Cambridge: Cambridge University Press.

Reder, S. (1994). Practice-Engagement Theory: a Sociocultural Approach to Literacy Across Languages and Cultures. In B. Ferdman, R.-M. Weber, and A. Ramirez (eds.), *Literacy across Languages and Cultures* (pp. 33–74). Albany, NY: State University of New York Press.

Redman, C. (1978). *The Rise of Civilization: from Early Farmers to Urban Society in the Ancient Near East*. San Francisco, CA: W. H. Freeman & Co.

Resnick, L., and Resnick, D. (1988). The Nature of Literacy. In E. Kintgen, B. Kroll, and M. Rose (eds.), *Perspectives on Literacy* (pp. 190–202). Carbondale, IL: Southern Illinois Press.

Rhodes, J. (1998). *Mary Ann Shadd Cary: the Black Press and Protest in the Nineteenth Century*. Bloomington: Indiana University Press.

Rockhill, K. (1993). Gender, Language and the Politics of Literacy. In B. Street (ed.), *Cross-Cultural Approaches to Literacy* (pp. 156–175). New York: Cambridge University Press.

Rockwell, E. (forthcoming). Indigenous Accounts of Dealing with Writing. In T. McCarty (ed.), *Language, Literacy and Power in Education*. Albany, NY: State University of New York Press.

Rogers, R. (2000). Discourse and Literate Identities: a Critical and Ethnographic Study of Family Literacy in an Urban Community. Unpublished dissertation, University at Albany/SUNY, Albany.

Romaine, S. (1994). *Language in Society*. Oxford: Oxford University Press.

Rosaldo, M. (1986). Words That Are Moving: the Social Meanings of Ilongot Verbal Art. In D. Brenneis and F. R. Myers (eds.), *Dangerous Words: Language and Politics in the Pacific* (pp. 131–160). Prospect Heights, IL: Waveland Press.

Rosaldo, M., and Lamphere, L. (eds.) (1974). *Woman, Culture, and Society*. Stanford: Stanford University Press.

Rose, M. (1985). The Language of Exclusion: Writing Instruction at the University. *College English, 47*, 341–359.

Rose, M. (1989). *Lives on the Boundary*. New York: Penguin.

Rosen, H. (1985). The Voices of Communities and Languages in the Classroom. *Harvard Education Review, 55*, 448–456.

Rosenbaum, J. (1980). The Social Implications of Educational Grouping. In D. Berliner (ed.), *Review of Research in Education, 8*, 361–401. Washington, DC: American Educational Research Association.

Rosenblatt, L. (1978). *The Reader, the Text, the Poem: the Transactional Theory of the Literary Work*. Carbondale, IL: Southern Illinois University Press.

Rousseau, J.-J. (1998). *Discourse on the Origins of Inequality*. Hanover, NH: University Press of New England.

Ryan, M. (1981). *The Cradle of the Middle Class: the Family in Oneida County, 1790–1865*. New York: Cambridge University Press.

Sahlins, M. (1972). *Stone Age Economics*. Chicago: Aldine Publishing Company.

Salvino, D. (1989). The Word in Black and White: Ideologies of Literacy in Antebellum America. In C. Davidson (ed.), *Reading in America: Literature and Social History* (pp. 140–153). Baltimore: Johns Hopkins University Press.

Sanders, B. (1994). *A is for Ox: Violence, Electronic Media, and the Silencing of the Written Word*. New York: Pantheon Books.

Sapir, E. (1949). *Selected Writings*. Berkeley: University of California Press.

Sarris, G. (1993). Keeping Slug Woman Alive: the Challenge of Reading in a Reservation Classroom. In J. Boyarin (ed.), *The Ethnography of Reading* (pp. 238–269). Berkeley: University of California Press.

Schement, J. (2000). *Thorough Americans: Minorities and the New Media*. Available: http://www.benton.org/Policy/Schement/Minorities.

Schemo, D. (2002). Education Bill Urges New Emphasis on Phonics. *The New York Times*, January 9, p. A16.

Schieffelin, B. (1995). Invited Comments on David Olson's "The World on Paper". Paper presented at the American Education Research Association, San Francisco, April 20.

Schieffelin, B. (2000). Introducing Kaluli Literacy: a Chronology of Influences. In P. Kroskrity (ed.), *Regimes of Language: Ideologies, Polities, and Identities* (pp. 293–328). Santa Fe, NM: School of American Research Press.

Schieffelin, B., and Doucet, R. (1998). The "Real" Haitian Creole: Ideology, Metalinguistics, and Orthographic Choice. In B. Schieffelin, K. Woolard, and P. Kroskrity (eds.), *Language Ideologies* (pp. 285–316). Oxford: Oxford University Press.

Schieffelin, B., and Gilmore, P. (eds.). (1986). *The Acquisition of Literacy: Ethnographic Perspectives*. Norwood, NJ: Ablex.

Schieffelin, B., and Ochs, E. (eds.). (1986). *Language Socialization Across Cultures*. Cambridge: Cambridge University Press.

Schmandt-Besserat, D. (1978). The Earliest Precursor of Writing. *Scientific American*, *238*(6), 50–59.

Schmandt-Besserat, D. (1989). Two Precursors of Writing: Plain and Complex Tokens. In W. Senner (ed.), *The Origins of Writing* (pp. 27–41). Lincoln, NE: University of Nebraska Press.

Schmandt-Besserat, D. (1992). *Before Writing*, vol. 1: *From Counting to Cuneiform*. Austin, TX: University of Texas Press.

Schoolcraft, H. (1860). *Archives of Aboriginal Knowledge*. Philadelphia: J. B. Lippincott.

Scott, J. (1990). *Domination and the Arts of Resistance*. New Haven, CT: Yale University Press.

Scott, J. (1998). *Seeing Like a State: How Certain Schemes to Improve the Human Condition Have Failed*. New Haven, CT: Yale University Press.

Seed, P. (1990). "Failing to Marvel": Atahualpa's Encounter with the Word. *Latin American Research Review, 26*, 7–32.

Seed, P. (1993). Taking Possession and Reading Texts: Establishing the Authority of Overseas Empires. In J. Williams and R. Lewis (eds.), *Early Images of the Americas: Transfer and Innovation* (pp. 111–147). Tucson: University of Arizona Press.

Sennett, R. (1998). *The Corrosion of Character: the Personal Consequences of Work in the New Capitalism*. New York: W. W. Norton & Company.

Sennett, R., and Cobb, J. (1972). *The Hidden Injuries of Class*. London: Faber.

Shopen, T., and Williams, J. (eds.). (1982). *Standards and Dialects in English*. Cambridge, MA: Winthrop.

Sicherman, B. (1989). Sense and Sensibility: a Case Study of Women's Reading in Late-Victorian America. In C. Davidson (ed.), *Reading in America: Literature and Social History* (pp. 201–225). Baltimore, MD: Johns Hopkins University Press.

Sider, G. (1993). *Lumbee Indian Histories*. New York: Cambridge University Press.

Silverstein, M. (1996). The Secret Life of Texts. In M. Silverstein and G. Urban (eds.), *Natural Histories of Discourse* (pp. 81–105). Chicago: University of Chicago Press.

Silverstein, M. (2000). Whorfianism and the Linguistic Imagination of Nationality. In P. Kroskrity (ed.), *Regimes of Language: Ideologies, Polities, and Identities* (pp. 35–84). Santa Fe, NM: School of American Research Press.

Silverstein, M., and Urban, G. (eds.). (1996). *Natural Histories of Discourse*. Chicago: University of Chicago.

Singer, D. (1999). *Whose Millennium?* New York: Monthly Review Press.

Slagle, A. (1987). The Native American Tradition and Legal Status: Tolowa Tales and Tolowa Places. *Cultural Critique, 7*, 103–118.

Sledd, J. (1973). Doublespeak: Dialectology in the Service of Big Brother. In R. Bentley and S. Crawford (eds.), *Black Language Reader* (pp. 191–214). Glenview, IL: Scott Foresman.

Soltow, L., and Stevens, E. (1981). *The Rise of Literacy and the Common School in the United States: a Socioeconomic Analysis to 1870*. Chicago: University of Chicago Press.

Spear-Swerling, L., and Sternberg, R. (1996). *Off Track: When Poor Readers Become "Learning Disabled"*. Boulder, CO: Westview Press.

Sperber, D. (1996). *Explaining Culture*. Cambridge, MA: Blackwell.

Spicer, E. (1969). *A Short History of the Indians of the United States*. New York: D. Van Nostrand.

Spring, J. (1972). *Education and the Rise of the Corporate State*. Beacon: Vintage Press.

Steedman, C. (1987). *Landscape for a Good Woman*: Virago Press.

Steiner, C. (1997). *Achieving Emotional Literacy*: New York: Simon and Shuster.

Stocking, G. (1968). *Race, Culture, and Evolution: Essays in the History of Anthropology*. New York: Free Press.

Stoudemire, S. (1970). Introduction. In S. Stoudemire (ed.), *Pedro de Córdoba, Christian Doctrine for the Instruction and Information of the Indians*. Coral Gables, FL: University of Miami Press.

Street, B. (1984). *Literacy in Theory and Practice*. New York: Cambridge University Press.

Street, B. (1993). *Cross-Cultural Approaches to Literacy*. New York: Cambridge University Press.

Sum, A. (1999). *Literacy in the Labor Force: Results from the National Adult Literacy Survey*. Washington, DC: US Department of Education. National Center for Educational Statistics.

Swearingen, J. (1988). Oral Hermeneutics During the Transition to Literacy: the Contemporary Debate. *Cultural Anthropology, 1*(2), 138–156.

Szwed, J. (1981). The Ethnography of Literacy. In M. Whiteman (ed.), *Writing: the Nature, Development, and Teaching of Written Communication*, vol. 1: *Variation in Writing: Functional and Linguistic-Cultural Differences* (pp. 13–23). Hillsdale, NJ: Lawrence Erlbaum.

Tannen, D. (ed.) (1982). *Spoken and Written Language: Exploring Literacy and Orality*. Norwood, NJ: Ablex.

Taylor, C. (1992). *Multiculturalism and the Politics of Recognition: an Essay*. Princeton, NJ: Princeton University Press.

Taylor, D. (1983). *Family Literacy: Young Children Learning to Read and Write*. Exeter, NH: Heinemann Educational Books.

Thompson, E. P. (1963). *The Making of the English Working Class*. New York: Vintage Books.

Tinsley, K., and Kaestle, C. (1991). Autobiographies and the History of Reading: the Meaning of Literacy in Individual Lives. In C. Kaestle (ed.), *Literacy in the United States: Readers and Reading Since 1880* (pp. 225–244). New Haven: Yale University Press.

Todorov, T. (1984). *The Conquest of America* (Richard Howard, trans.). New York: Harper and Row.

Trudgill, P. (1974). *Sociolinguistics*. New York: Penguin.

Tuchman, B. (1984). The Renaissance Priests, *The March of Folly*. New York: Ballantine Books.

Turkle, S. (1999). An Interview with Sherry Turkle. *Hedgehog Review, 1*, 71–85.
Twist, K. (2000). *Four Directions to Making the Internet Indian*. Available: http://www.benton.org/Library/Native/.
Tylor, E. B. (1898). *Anthropology: an Introduction to the Study of Man and Civilization*. New York: D. Appleton and Company.
Tyner, K. (1998). *Literacy in a Digital World: Teaching and Learning in the Age of Information*. Hillsdale, NJ: Lawrence Erlbaum.
UNESCO. (1957). *World Illiteracy at Mid-Century*. Paris: UNESCO.
UNESCO. (1992). *The Future of Literacy and the Literacy of the Future: Report of the Seminar on Adult Literacy in Industrialized Countries*. Hambourg: UNESCO Institute for Education.
Urban, G. (1996). Entextualization, Replication, and Power. In M. Silverstein and G. Urban (eds.), *Natural Histories of Discourse* (pp. 21–44). Chicago: University of Chicago Press.
Urciuoli, B. (1996). *Exposing Prejudice: Puerto Rican Experiences of Language, Race, and Class*. Boulder, CO: Westview.
Vizenor, G. (1998). *Fugitive Poses: Native American Scenes of Absence and Presence*. Lincoln, NE: University of Nebraska Press.
Voloshinov, V. N. (1973). *Marxism and the Philosophy of Language*. New York: Academic Press.
Wagner, D. (ed.). (1987). *The Future of Literacy in a Changing World*. New York: Pergamon.
Walker, W. (1981). Native American Writing Systems. In C. Ferguson and S. Heath (eds.), *Language in the USA* (pp. 145–174). Cambridge: Cambridge University Press.
Wallerstein, I. (1995). *After Liberalism*. New York: The New Press.
Wallis, E. (1964). *Two Thousand Tongues to Go: the Story of the Wycliffe Bible Translators*. New York: Harper and Row.
Warner, M. (1990). *The Letters of the Republic: Publication and the Public Sphere in Eighteenth-Century America*. Cambridge, MA: Harvard University Press.
Warschauer, M. (1999). *Electronic Literacies: Language, Culture, and Power in Online Education*. Hillsdale, NJ: Lawrence Erlbaum.
Webb, R. K. (1950). Working Class Readers in Early Victorian England. *English Historical Review, 65*, 333–351.
Weis, L. (1990). *Working Class without Work: High School Students in a De-Industrialized Economy*. New York: Routledge.
White, H. (1987). *The Content of the Form: Narrative Discourse and Historical Representation*. Baltimore: Johns Hopkins University Press.
Whiteman, M. (ed.). (1981). *Writing: the Nature, Development, and Teaching of Written Communication*, vol. 1: *Variation in Writing: Functional and Linguistic-Cultural Differences*. Hillsdale, NJ: Lawrence Erlbaum Associates.
Wilhelm, T. (2000). *In-Depth Summary of Tony Wilhelm's Democracy in the Digital Age*. Available: http://www.benton.org/Home/Bibliographies/Democracy in the Digital Age.doc/.
Williams, R. (1979). *Politics and Letters: Interviews with the New Left Review*. London: Verso.
Williams, R. (1983). Notes on English Prose 1780–1950, *Writing in Society*. London: Verso.
Williams, R. (1990). *The American Indian in Western Legal Thought: the Discourses of Conquest*. New York: Oxford University Press.

Willis, P. (1981). *Learning to Labor: How Working Class Kids Get Working Class Jobs.* New York: Teachers College Press.

Witherspoon, G. (1977). *Language and Art in the Navajo Universe.* Ann Arbor: University of Michigan Press.

Wright, E. (1981). "School English" and Public Policy. *College English, 42,* 327–42.

Wrigley, J. (ed.). (1992). *Education and Gender Equality.* Washington, DC: Falmer Press.

Zboray, R. (1993). *A Fictive People: Antebellum Economic Development and the American Reading Public.* New York: Oxford University Press.

Zinn, H. (1980). *A People's History of the United States.* New York: Harper and Row.

Zinsser, C. (1986). The Bible Tells Me So: Teaching Children in a Fundamentalist Church. In B. Schieffelin and P. Gilmore (eds.), *The Acquisition of Literacy: Ethnographic Persepctives* (pp. 55–71). Norwood, NJ: Ablex.

INDEX

Studies in the Social and Cultural Foundations of Language

Editors
JUDITH T. IRVINE
BAMBI SCHIEFFELIN